ARIZONA
REAL ESTATE
SALES EXAM

ARIZONA REAL ESTATE SALES EXAM

LEARNINGEXPRESS®

NEW YORK

Library of Congress Cataloging-in-Publication Data

Arizona real estate sales exam / LearningExpress.
    p. cm.
  ISBN 978-1-57685-585-0 (pbk. : alk. paper)
  1. Real estate agents—Licenses—Arizona—Examinations, questions, etc.
2. Real estate business—Licenses— Arizona—Examinations, questions, etc.
I. LearningExpress (Organization)
HD278.A75 2007
333.33076—dc22

                                                            2007017911

Printed in the United States of America

9 8 7 6 5 4 3 2 1

ISBN: 978-1-57685-585-0

For more information or to place an order, contact LearningExpress at:
    55 Broadway
    8th Floor
    New York, NY 10006

Or visit us at:
    www.learnatest.com

About the Contributors

Carlton C. Casler is a practicing Arizona attorney, an Arizona real estate broker, owner of the Casler School of Real Estate, and the author of the *Arizona Landlord's Deskbook* and the *Tenant's Survival Guide.*

Dean Wegner, president of teamdean.com, has held an Arizona real estate license for more than 12 years. He is currently a mortgage originator for Lions Gate Mortgage and a national sales coach for the Core Training Inc. Dean regularly discusses various real estate topics on several television stations and is a certified teacher with the state of Arizona for real estate renewal hours. He is an active member of more than 22 real estate organizations and is a board member for the International Mortgage Lenders Association (IMLA).

Nov-Dec 2007
Reviewed & Scored
88% on 1400
Questions

Contents ▶

Q & A's   700
+
AZ Principles   700
Book   _____
Total   1400

1 ▶ The Arizona Real Estate Sales Exam

CHAPTER SUMMARY

A career in real estate sales can be challenging, rewarding, and profitable. Arizona has a broad range of properties. You can sell anything from commercial real estate in Phoenix, to condominiums in Flagstaff, to horse properties in Prescott. Licensed, knowledgeable, and qualified salespeople are in demand. This is great news for you, because you have already decided that you want to get your real estate sales license.

N OW YOU NEED to pass the exam. But, becoming a licensed salesperson in Arizona requires more than simply passing the exam. There are many other steps you must complete (either before and/or after the exam) in order to arrive at your ultimate goal—receiving your real estate sales license. This chapter will guide you through these steps, including the requirements, the exam application process, the exam content and format, and the sales license application process.

This chapter also serves as a guide for using this book effectively. LearningExpress wants you to succeed, so use this book to maximize your preparation for your upcoming exam.

▶ Who Needs to Take the Arizona Real Estate Sales Exam?

Anyone wishing to make official, licensed real estate transactions in Arizona must have a valid Arizona real estate sales license and be employed by a broker licensed by the state of Arizona. In order to receive your license, you must first pass the exam.

Arizona requires 90 hours of real estate education to obtain a real estate salesperson or broker license. The state of Arizona does NOT have reciprocity with any other state. Arizona may, however, waive the national portion (i.e., Arizona may waive 63 hours of the required 90 hours) of the education and testing requirements if you already have a real estate license in another state and the other state has a real estate examination that is substantially similar to Arizona's real estate examination. If you qualify, then you will need to take only 27 hours of Arizona-specific education and the Arizona-specific part of the state examination.

To receive a copy of the *Candidate Information Bulletin*, which includes information and a waiver application form for the national portion of the education and testing requirements, go online to www.prometric.com/Arizona/RealEstate.

You may obtain additional information by calling the Arizona Department of Real Estate (ADRE) at 602-468-1414 or by visiting their website at www.AZRE.gov.

Note: You may not legally perform any type of real estate activity until you have been hired by a broker and have activated your license with the ADRE.

▶ Eligibility Requirements

Arizona law requires that all licensees meet the following minimum requirements:

- **Age**—You must be at least 18 years old.
- **Moral Character**—You must have a reputation for honesty and fair dealing. Conviction of a criminal offence (i.e., repeated DUI or domestic violence) may be cause for denial of your application.
- **Education**—You must take 90 hours of classroom instruction and pass a state examination, which consists of two portions: a national portion and an Arizona-specific portion.

Important Contact Information

If you have Internet access, consult the ADRE website for more information at www.AZRE.gov.

If you do not have Internet access, or if you are unable to get your question(s) answered on the website, please contact the ADRE for all examination and licensing questions at:

Arizona Department of Real Estate
2910 North 44th Street, Suite 140
Phoenix, AZ 85018
Phone: 602-468-1414

Education Requirement

All applicants must satisfy the education requirement by taking classroom instruction or by receiving a waiver from the ADRE or both (i.e., a waiver for part of the education requirement). To satisfy the education requirement, applicants must either apply for a waiver (discussed previously) or successfully complete an ADRE-approved pre-licensing course. The course for a real estate salesperson's license is 90 hours of classroom instruction, which must follow an outline of topics prescribed by the ADRE. The course for a broker's license is also 90 hours of classroom instruction and is similar to the outline of topics for salespersons, but also includes additional topics applicable only to brokers. Although the ADRE permits distance learning (i.e., online courses, CD courses, etc.), for renewal courses, the ADRE does not permit any portion of any pre-licensing course to be accomplished via distance learning.

You must submit evidence of successfully completing the education requirement at the time you appear at the state-approved testing site to take the state real estate examination (for salesperson or broker).

All pre-licensing classroom instruction must be provided by a real estate school that has been approved by the ADRE to teach pre-licensing courses. Local community colleges and state universities may also offer real estate courses that satisfy the education requirement and are approved by the ADRE.

Attorney Exemption

Arizona does not have an exemption for attorneys. An attorney may engage in a real estate transaction if it is related to a matter the attorney is handling (e.g., settling an estate, conducting a foreclosure sale), but an Arizona attorney who regularly engages in real estate activities, as defined by the state statutes, must apply for and obtain a real estate license. Attorneys may apply for a waiver for all or part of the education requirements.

Examination Fees

The Arizona real estate sales exam is administered by Thomson Prometric. You may obtain additional information about Thomson Prometric by visiting their website at www.prometric.com.

Thomson Prometric
Attn: Arizona Real Estate Exam Registration
1260 Energy Lane
St. Paul, MN 55108
1-800-899-4091

Fees change from time to time, but currently, the examination fee is $90 for the salesperson exam and $115 for the broker exam. You may confirm the current exam fees by visiting Thomson Prometric's website at www.prometric.com/Arizona/RealEstate.

Within Arizona, the Arizona real estate sales exam is given at testing sites located in:

- Casa Grande
- Flagstaff

- Goodyear
- Phoenix
- Tempe
- Tucson

Applicants may be able to take the state exam by visiting a Thomson Prometric testing site located in another state. Applicants should contact the specific testing site or visit Thomson Prometric's website to see if testing in another state is available.

▶ Applying for the Exam

After you pass the school exam, you will receive the education certification form from the school where you attended the approved course. You have ten years after the date on your education certification form to pass the state exam AND submit your application for a real estate license to the ADRE, or you must repeat the education requirement.

You must preregister with Thomson Prometric to take the Arizona real estate sales exam. Walk-in exams are not available. You must present the education certification form and proper identification when you appear to take the exam. After you have passed the state exam, the state-approved testing site will provide a real estate application form to the prospective licensee.

You must submit your completed application and a fingerprint card (for a criminal background check) to the ADRE in sufficient time for the ADRE to process your application. You must activate your license (i.e., a salesperson must be hired by a broker and the salesperson's license must be activated) by paying a fee to the ADRE within one year after you pass the state exam or you must repeat the state exam.

What to Bring
- Two forms of signature identification, one of which must be a picture ID (you will not be admitted without proper identification)
- Correct exam fees (unless prepaid)
- Completed (front and back) education certification form
- Confirmation number provided to you at the time of the reservation
- A calculator. Only a silent, handheld, solar- or battery-operated, non-programmable calculator (without paper tape–printing capabilities or alphabetic keypads) may be used. Calculators are available at the test center.

There are two parts to the exam: the general portion and the state portion. If you pass one portion of the exam, but fail the other, you need to retake only the failed portion. However, you must wait 24 hours to schedule a reexamination. You must pass the other portion of the state exam within one year of passing the first portion or you will need to retake both portions.

The exam fee for the state exam for a real estate salesperson, membership camping salesperson, or cemetery salesperson is $90. The exam fee for the state exam for a real estate broker, membership camping broker, or cemetery broker is $115.

▶ Exam Content

You will have three and a half hours to complete your Arizona real estate sales exam: two hours for the 80-question national portion, and one and a half hours for the 60-question Arizona-specific portion.

The law requires that you demonstrate adequate reading skills in the English language and the ability to perform basic real estate math computations. Furthermore, you must have proficient knowledge of real estate principles and practices, real estate law, and real estate mathematics.

The following are the major sections that will be tested on the exam. This list of items covered in the Arizona real estate sales exam is from the *Candidate Information Bulletin* and can be found online at www.prometric.com.

The 80 questions on the national portion of the state exam for a **salesperson's license** will be broken down as follows. The percentage next to the main topic reflects the relative weight assigned to each section of the examination. For example, if a section has 10% assigned, then 8 of the 80 questions will be drawn from that section.

Business Practice and Ethics—21%
Professional Ethics
Federal Requirements for Real Estate
Risk Reduction
Trust Accounts

Agency—15%
Principles of Agency
Listing Procedures
Listing Agreement
Buyer Representation

Property—17%
Characteristics of Property
Ownership and Estates in Land
Government Restrictions
Private Restrictions

Property Valuation and the Appraisal Process—6%
Principles of Valuation
Determining Value
Appraisal

Real Estate Sales Contracts—17%

Purpose, Scope, and Elements of Real Estate
    Sales Contracts

Offers and Counteroffers

Earnest Money

Completion, Termination, and Breach

Financing—9%

Essentials of Financing

Lender Qualification Process

Types of Financing

Foreclosure and Alternatives

Pertinent Laws and Regulations

Closing/Settlement and Transferring Title—5%

Settlement Statement and Other Critical
    Documents

Closing/Settlement

Transferring Title

Title Insurance

Property Management—5%

Leases

Property Manager and Owner Relationships

Income Property Concepts

Trust Accounts

The 80 questions on the national portion of the state exam for a **broker's license** will be broken down as follows. The percentage next to the main topic reflects the relative weight assigned to each section of the examination. For example, if a section has 10% assigned, then 8 of the 80 questions will be drawn from that section.

Business Practice and Ethics—23%

Professional Ethics

Federal Requirements for Real Estate

Risk Reduction

Trust Accounts

Agency—13%

Principles of Agency

Listing Procedures

Listing Agreement

Buyer Representation

Property—17%

Characteristics of Property

Ownership and Estates in Land

Government Restrictions

Private Restrictions

**Property Valuation and the Appraisal
    Process—6%**

Principles of Valuation

Determining Value

Appraisal

Real Estate Sales Contracts—17%

Purpose, Scope, and Elements of Real Estate
    Sales Contracts

Offers and Counteroffers

Earnest Money

Completion, Termination, and Breach

Financing—9%

Essentials of Financing

Lender Qualification Process

Types of Financing

Foreclosure and Alternatives

Pertinent Laws and Regulations

Closing/Settlement and Transferring Title—10%

Settlement Statement and Other Critical Documents

Closing/Settlement

Transferring Title

Title Insurance

Property Management—5%

Leases

Property Manager and Owner Relationships

Income Property Concepts

Trust Accounts

The 60 questions on the Arizona-specific portion of the state exam for a **salesperson's** or **broker's license** will be broken down as follows. The percentage next to the main topic reflects the relative weight assigned to each section of the exam. For example, if a section has 10% assigned, then 6 of the 60 questions will be drawn from that section.

Ownership/Transfer—30%

Legal Descriptions

Deeds

Liens and Judgments

Title/Recordation

Community Property

Homestead Exemptions

Subdivided and Un-Subdivided Lands

Common Interest Ownerships

Water Rights

Environmental Hazards and Regulations

Licensing—10%

Activities Requiring a License

Issuance, Renewal, Revocation, and Suspension Procedures

General Licensing Requirements and Recovery Fund

Powers and Duties of the Real Estate Commissioner

Activities of Licensees—35%

Employment Contracts

Advertising

Offers

Purchase Contracts

Disclosures

Handling of Funds

Record Keeping and Documentation

Agencies

License Violations and Penalties

Broker-Salesperson Relationships

Compensation/Commissions

Finance/Settlement—20%

Instruments

Settlement Procedures

Property Taxation

Foreclosure and Forfeiture

Leasing and Property Management—5%

Arizona Residential Landlord and Tenant Act

Property Management

Passing the Exam

You will have three and a half hours to complete your Arizona real estate sales exam: two hours for the 80-question national portion, and one and a half hours for the 60-question Arizona-specific portion. To pass, you must score 75% or better on both portions, which means you must get 60 or more of the 80 national questions correct AND 45 or more of the 60 Arizona-specific questions correct. If you pass one portion, but fail the other, you need to retake only the portion that you did not pass.

Calculators

Only a silent, handheld, solar- or battery-operated, non-programmable calculator (without paper tape–printing capabilities or alphabetic keypads) may be used. Calculators are available at the test center.

It is a good idea to bring a calculator that you are already familiar with using and make sure you have extra batteries. Calculators in PDAs or cell phones are not permitted to be used at the exam site.

If you do not pass, the testing center will provide you with a statistical printout regarding your exam, showing you the areas that you need to study in order to pass the exam. If you pass, you will know only that you "passed"; your exact score will not be released to you.

Real Estate Math

If you are worried about the math that will be covered on the exam—relax. The math problems on the exam will not be awfully complex, and they will all relate to real estate, so you may have already tackled problems like these in your real estate courses. Plus, LearningExpress understands that math can intimidate many people, especially on exams, so there is an entire chapter in this book devoted to reviewing real estate math to help you brush up on those skills.

Also, you will not be expected to figure out these problems entirely in your head. You will be provided with scratch paper at the exam, and you are allowed to bring a calculator with you. Remember to take each problem step by step, reading it carefully and using your scratch paper to set up the problem before you start punching in numbers.

► Exam Day

Try to get a good night's sleep the night before the exam, and allow plenty of time in the morning to get to your exam location, especially if you are unfamiliar with the area. You should report to the exam center 30–45 minutes before your exam in order to sign in, present your identification, and get yourself settled.

Receiving Your Arizona Salesperson License

All examinees must score 75 or above on both portions of the exam (i.e., the national and Arizona-specific portions) to pass the exam. Within one year after passing the state exam, you must activate your license with the ADRE. To activate your license with the ADRE, you must submit an application for a real estate salesperson license (provided by the testing center after you pass the exam), a fingerprint card, and a licensing fee to the ADRE. The ADRE will process your application and may issue a license the same day or, depending on information revealed in your application, may take additional time before issuing you a license, or may deny your request for a license.

License Application Fees

The license fee for salespersons is $119. The license fee for brokers is $174.

▶ How to Prepare for the Exam

You have made it this far—you have completed the required real estate course and have made the decision to read this book—so you have already shown that you have the commitment it will take to prepare for the exam. This book is designed to be a valuable tool in preparing you for the big day.

Test-Taking Techniques

Chapter 2, "The LearningExpress Test Preparation System," does exactly as the title suggests—it teaches you how to prepare for the test effectively. In this chapter, you will learn to:

- set up a realistic study plan
- use your study time and exam time efficiently
- overcome test anxiety

The best approach for effective studying is to be disciplined, stay on your study schedule, and not procrastinate.

Study Materials

Utilize all of your study materials. By reviewing information from a variety of sources, you are more likely to cover all of the material that might be included on the exam. This book is a great source of information and can be used as a foundation for your study plan. In addition, use your study materials, notes, exams, and texts from your real estate course.

Using This Book

In addition to this chapter and the LearningExpress Test Preparation System, this book contains three content and review chapters and four practice exams. We suggest that you take the first practice exam (Chapter 3) before moving on to the content and review material. This way, you will be able to better assess your personal strengths and weaknesses, allowing you to direct your time where you need it the most.

Chapter 4, "Real Estate Refresher Course," is an overview of real estate concepts and criteria that will be covered on the exam.

Chapter 5 is dedicated to real estate math review. This chapter reviews the types of problems and computations you will face on the exam, allowing you to practice and polish your math skills.

Chapter 6 is a real estate glossary, providing an excellent list of real estate terminology needed for the exam and your career.

Although you should focus most of your efforts on the areas in which you need the most improvement, you should read all of the chapters in this book to ensure that you do not miss out on valuable information. You will find that some of the information and terminology in Chapters 4 through 6 is repeated, but this will only help reinforce your knowledge.

Use the other three practice tests in the book (Chapters 7, 8, and 9) to gauge your progress as you go along, so you can continue to focus your concentration where needed. Based on the exam content and time allotted for the actual 140-question multiple-choice exam, the practice tests in this book each have 140 questions.

Do not forget about the bonus CD-ROM included with this book. It includes practice questions, so you can practice on a computer if you wish. The CD-ROM is designed to be user-friendly; however, please consult the "How to Use the CD-ROM" section, located in the back of the book, should you have any questions.

► Important Note

This book covers the most commonly used key terms and concepts that are likely to be covered on the exam. However, it would be impossible to include everything; thus, we suggest that you utilize a variety of study materials. Please note that real estate laws and regulations change from time to time, so it is important that you be aware of the most up-to-date information (consult the *Candidate Information Bulletin* for topics covered). Our book is intended to be just one of the many study tools you will use and is designed to reinforce and round out your knowledge of real estate sales. In addition, information about application processes, fees, and practices may change. For the most accurate information, visit the ADRE website at www.AZRE.gov.

► The Path to Success

Each person has his or her own personal goals and individual path to take to achieve those goals. Desire, dedication, and know-how are essential, no matter what path you take. You have already shown that you have the desire and dedication, just by reading this chapter. You are well on your way to a new career in real estate! You have shown that you are serious; now let this book help give you the know-how you need to pass your exam.

2 ▶ The LearningExpress Test Preparation System

CHAPTER SUMMARY

Taking the Arizona real estate sales exam can be tough. It demands a lot of preparation if you want to achieve a top score. Your career depends on your passing the exam. The LearningExpress Test Preparation System, developed exclusively for LearningExpress by leading test experts, gives you the discipline and attitude you need to be a winner.

FACT: TAKING THE real estate licensing exam is not easy, and neither is getting ready for it. Your future career as a real estate salesperson depends on your getting a passing score, but there are all sorts of pitfalls that can keep you from doing your best on this exam. Here are some of the obstacles that can stand in the way of your success:

- being unfamiliar with the format of the exam
- being paralyzed by test anxiety
- leaving your preparation to the last minute
- not preparing at all!
- not knowing vital test-taking skills: how to pace yourself through the exam, how to use the process of elimination, and when to guess
- not being in tip-top mental and physical shape
- arriving late at the test site, having to work on an empty stomach, or being uncomfortable through the exam because the room is too cold or hot

What's the common denominator in all these test-taking pitfalls? One word: control. Who's in control, you or the exam?

Here's some good news: The LearningExpress Test Preparation System puts you in control. In nine easy-to-follow steps, you will learn everything you need to know to make sure that you are in charge of your preparation and your performance on the exam. Other test takers may let the test get the better of them; other test takers may be unprepared or out of shape, but not you. You will have taken all the steps you need to take to get a high score on the real estate licensing exam.

Here's how the LearningExpress Test Preparation System works: Nine easy steps lead you through everything you need to know and do to get ready to master your exam. Each step discussed in this chapter includes both reading about the step and one or more activities. It's important that you do the activities along with the reading, or you won't be getting the full benefit of the system. Each step tells you approximately how much time that step will take you to complete.

Step 1: Get Information	50 minutes
Step 2: Conquer Test Anxiety	20 minutes
Step 3: Make a Plan	30 minutes
Step 4: Learn to Manage Your Time	10 minutes
Step 5: Learn to Use the Process of Elimination	20 minutes
Step 6: Know When to Guess	20 minutes
Step 7: Reach Your Peak Performance Zone	10 minutes
Step 8: Get Your Act Together	10 minutes
Step 9: Do It!	10 minutes
Total	**3 hours**

We estimate that working through the entire system will take you approximately three hours, although it's perfectly okay if you work faster or slower. If you take an afternoon or evening, you can work through the whole LearningExpress Test Preparation System in one sitting. Otherwise, you can break it up, and do just one or two steps a day for the next several days. It's up to you—remember, you are in control.

▶ Step 1: Get Information

Time to complete: 50 minutes
Activity: Read Chapter 1, "The Arizona Real Estate Sales Exam"

Knowledge is power. The first step in the LearningExpress Test Preparation System is finding out everything you can about the Arizona real estate sales exam. Once you have your information, the other steps in the Learning-Express Test Preparation System will show you what to do with it.

Part A: Straight Talk about the Arizona Real Estate Sales Exam

Why do you have to take this exam, anyway? You have already been through your pre-license course; why should you have to go through a rigorous exam? It's simply an attempt on the part of your state to be sure you have the knowledge and skills necessary for a licensed real estate agent. Every profession that requires practitioners to exercise financial and fiduciary responsibility to clients also requires practitioners to be licensed—and licensure requires an exam. Real estate is no exception.

It's important for you to remember that your score on the Arizona real estate sales exam does not determine how smart you are, or even whether you will make a good real estate agent. There are all kinds of things an exam like this can't test: whether you have the drive and determination to be a top salesperson, whether you will faithfully exercise your responsibilities to your clients, or whether you can be trusted with confidential information about people's finances. Those kinds of things are hard to evaluate, while a computer-based test is easy to evaluate.

This is not to say that the exam is not important! The knowledge tested on the exam is knowledge you will need to do your job. And your ability to enter the profession you've trained for depends on your passing this exam. And that's why you are here—using the LearningExpress Test Preparation System to achieve control over the exam.

Part B: What's on the Test

If you haven't already done so, stop here and read Chapter 1 of this book, which gives you an overview of the Arizona real estate sales exam.

▶ Step 2: Conquer Test Anxiety

Time to complete: 20 minutes
Activity: Take the Test Stress Quiz

Having complete information about the exam is the first step in getting control of the exam. Next, you have to overcome one of the biggest obstacles to test success: test anxiety. Test anxiety not only impairs your performance on the exam itself, but also keeps you from preparing! In Step 2, you will learn stress management techniques that will help you succeed on your exam. Learn these strategies now, and practice them as you work through the exams in this book, so they will be second nature to you by exam day.

Test Stress Quiz

You need to worry about test anxiety only if it is extreme enough to impair your performance. The following questionnaire will provide a diagnosis of your level of test anxiety. In the blank before each statement, write the number that most accurately describes your experience.

0 = Never   1 = Once or twice   2 = Sometimes   3 = Often

___ I have gotten so nervous before an exam that I simply put down the books and didn't study for it.

___ I have experienced disabling physical symptoms such as vomiting and severe headaches because I was nervous about an exam.

___ I did not show up for an exam because I was scared to take it.

___ I have experienced dizziness and disorientation while taking an exam.

___ I have had trouble filling in the little circles because my hands were shaking too hard.

___ I have failed an exam because I was too nervous to complete it.

___ **Total: Add up the numbers in the blanks above.**

Your Test Stress Score

Here are the steps you should take, depending on your score. If you scored:

0–2: Your level of test anxiety is nothing to worry about; it's probably just enough to give you that little extra edge.

3–6: Your test anxiety may be enough to impair your performance, and you should practice the stress management techniques listed in this section to try to bring your test anxiety down to manageable levels.

7+: Your level of test anxiety is a serious concern. In addition to practicing the stress management techniques listed in this section, you may want to seek additional help.

Combating Test Anxiety

The first thing you need to know is that a little test anxiety is a good thing. Everyone gets nervous before a big exam—and if that nervousness motivates you to prepare thoroughly, so much the better. It's said that Sir Laurence Olivier, one of the foremost British actors of the twentieth century, felt ill before every performance. His stage fright didn't impair his performance; in fact, it probably gave him a little extra edge—just the kind of edge you need to do well, whether on a stage or in an examination room.

Above is the Test Stress Quiz. Stop and answer the questions to find out whether your level of test anxiety is something you should worry about.

Stress Management before the Test

If you feel your level of anxiety getting the best of you in the weeks before the test, here is what you need to do to bring the level down again:

- **Get prepared.** There's nothing like knowing what to expect and being prepared for it to put you in control of test anxiety. That's why you are reading this book. Use it faithfully, and remind yourself that you are better prepared than most of the people taking the test.
- **Practice self-confidence.** A positive attitude is a great way to combat test anxiety. This is no time to be humble or shy. Stand in front of the mirror and say to your reflection, "I am prepared. I am full of self-confidence. I am going to ace this test. I know I can do it." Say it into a tape recorder and play it back once a day. If you hear it often enough, you will believe it.
- **Fight negative messages.** Every time someone starts telling you how hard the exam is or how it's almost impossible to get a high score, start saying your self-confidence messages. Don't listen to the negative messages. Turn on your tape recorder and listen to your self-confidence messages.
- **Visualize.** Imagine yourself reporting for duty on your first day as a real estate salesperson. Think of yourself talking with clients, showing homes, and best of all, making your first sale. Visualizing success can help make it happen—and it reminds you of why you are going through all this work in preparing for the exam.
- **Exercise.** Physical activity helps calm your body down and focus your mind. Besides, being in good physical shape can actually help you do well on the exam. Go for a run, lift weights, go swimming—and do it regularly.

Stress Management on Test Day

There are several ways you can bring down your level of test anxiety on test day. They will work best if you practice them in the weeks before the test, so you know which ones work best for you.

- **Deep breathing.** Take a deep breath while you count to five. Hold it for a count of one, then let it out on a count of five. Repeat several times.
- **Move your body.** Try rolling your head in a circle. Rotate your shoulders. Shake your hands from the wrist. Many people find these movements very relaxing.
- **Visualize again.** Think of the place where you are most relaxed: lying on the beach in the sun, walking through the park, or whatever. Now close your eyes and imagine you are actually there. If you practice in advance, you will find that you need only a few seconds of this exercise to experience a significant increase in your sense of well-being.

When anxiety threatens to overwhelm you right there during the exam, there are still things you can do to manage the stress level:

- **Repeat your self-confidence messages.** You should have them memorized by now. Say them silently to yourself, and believe them!
- **Visualize one more time.** This time, visualize yourself moving smoothly and quickly through the test answering every question right and finishing just before time is up. Like most visualization techniques, this one works best if you have practiced it ahead of time.

- **Find an easy question.** Find an easy question, and answer it. Getting even one question finished gets you into the test-taking groove.
- **Take a mental break.** Everyone loses concentration once in a while during a long test. It's normal, so you shouldn't worry about it. Instead, accept what has happened. Say to yourself, "Hey, I lost it there for a minute. My brain is taking a break." Put down your pencil, close your eyes, and do some deep breathing for a few seconds. Then you will be ready to go back to work.

Try these techniques ahead of time, and see if they work for you!

▶ Step 3: Make a Plan

Time to complete: 30 minutes
Activity: Construct a study plan

Maybe the most important thing you can do to get control of yourself and your exam is to make a study plan. Too many people fail to prepare simply because they fail to plan. Spending hours on the day before the exam poring over sample test questions not only raises your level of test anxiety, but is simply no substitute for careful preparation and practice over time.

Don't fall into the cram trap. Take control of your preparation time by mapping out a study schedule. On the following pages are two sample schedules, based on the amount of time you have before you take the Arizona real estate sales exam. If you are the kind of person who needs deadlines and assignments to motivate you for a project, here they are. If you are the kind of person who doesn't like to follow other people's plans, you can use the suggested schedules here to construct your own.

Even more important than making a plan is making a commitment. You can't review everything you learned in your real estate courses in one night. You have to set aside some time every day for study and practice. Try for at least 20 minutes a day. Twenty minutes daily will do you much more good than two hours on Saturday.

Don't put off your study until the day before the exam. Start now. A few minutes a day, with half an hour or more on weekends, can make a big difference in your score.

Schedule A: The 30-Day Plan

If you have at least a month before you take the Arizona real estate sales exam, you have plenty of time to prepare—as long as you don't waste it! If you have less than a month, turn to Schedule B.

TIME	PREPARATION
Days 1–4	Skim over the written materials from your training program, particularly noting areas you expect to be emphasized on the exam and areas you don't remember well. On Day 4, concentrate on those areas.
Day 5	Take the first practice exam in Chapter 3.
Day 6	Score the first practice exam. Use "Exam 1 for Review" to see which topics you need to review most. Identify two areas that you will concentrate on before you take the second practice exam.
Days 7–10	Study the two areas you identified as your weak points. Don't forget, there is the Arizona real estate refresher course in Chapter 4, the real estate math review in Chapter 5, and the real estate glossary in Chapter 6. Use these chapters to improve your score on the next practice test.
Day 11	Take the second practice exam in Chapter 7.
Day 12	Score the second practice exam. Identify one area to concentrate on before you take the third practice exam.
Days 13–18	Study the one area you identified for review. Again, use the refresher course, math review, and glossary for help.
Day 19	Take the third practice exam in Chapter 8.
Day 20–21	Once again, identify one area to review, based on your score on the third practice exam. Study the one area you identified for review. Use the refresher course, math review, and glossary for help.
Days 22–25	Take an overview of all your training materials, consolidating your strengths and improving on your weaknesses.
Days 26–27	Review all the areas that have given you the most trouble in the three practice exams you have taken so far.
Day 28	Take the fourth practice exam in Chapter 9. Note how much you have improved!
Day 29	Review one or two weak areas by studying the refresher course, math review, and glossary.
Day before the exam	Relax. Do something unrelated to the exam and go to bed at a reasonable hour.

Schedule B: The Ten-Day Plan

If you have two weeks or less before you take the exam, use this ten-day schedule to help you make the most of your time.

TIME	PREPARATION
Day 1	Take the first practice exam in Chapter 3 and score it using the answer key at the end. Use "Exam 1 for Review" to see which topics you need to review most.
Day 2	Review one area that gave you trouble on the first practice exam. Use the Arizona real estate refresher course in Chapter 4, the real estate math review in Chapter 5, and the real estate glossary in Chapter 6 for extra practice in these areas.
Day 3	Review another area that gave you trouble on the first practice exam. Again, use the refresher course, math review, and glossary for extra practice.
Day 4	Take the second practice exam in Chapter 7 and score it.
Day 5	If your score on the second practice exam doesn't show improvement on the two areas you studied, review them. If you did improve in those areas, choose a new weak area to study today.
Day 6	Take the third practice exam in Chapter 8 and score it.
Day 7	Choose your weakest area from the third practice exam to review. Use the refresher course, math review, and glossary for extra practice.
Day 8	Review any areas that you have not yet reviewed in this schedule.
Day 9	Take the fourth practice exam in Chapter 9 and score it.
Day 10	Use your last study day to brush up on any areas that are still giving you trouble. Use the refresher course, math review, and glossary.
Day before the exam	Relax. Do something unrelated to the exam and go to bed at a reasonable hour.

▶ Step 4: Learn to Manage Your Time

Time to complete: 10 minutes to read, many hours of practice!
Activity: Practice these strategies as you take the sample tests in this book

Steps 4, 5, and 6 of the LearningExpress Test Preparation System put you in charge of your exam by showing you test-taking strategies that work. Practice these strategies as you take the sample tests in this book, and then you will be ready to use them on test day.

First, you will take control of your time on the exam. It's a terrible feeling to know there are only five minutes left when you are only three-quarters of the way through the test. Here are some tips to keep that from happening to *you*.

- **Follow directions.** Because the Arizona real estate sales exam is given on the computer, you should take your time reviewing the tutorial before the exam. Read the directions carefully and ask questions before the exam begins if there's anything you don't understand.
- **Pace yourself.** There is a timer on the screen as you take the exam. This will help you pace yourself. For example, when one-quarter of the time has elapsed, you should be a quarter of the way through the test, and so on. If you are falling behind, pick up the pace a bit.
- **Keep moving.** Don't waste time on one question. If you don't know the answer, skip the question and move on. You can always go back to it later.
- **Don't rush.** Although you should keep moving, rushing won't help. Try to keep calm and work methodically and quickly.

▶ Step 5: Learn to Use the Process of Elimination

Time to complete: 20 minutes
Activity: Complete worksheet on Using the Process of Elimination

After time management, your next most important tool for taking control of your exam is using the process of elimination wisely. It's standard test-taking wisdom that you should always read all the answer choices before choosing your answer. This helps you find the right answer by eliminating wrong answer choices. And, sure enough, that standard wisdom applies to your exam, too.

Let's say you are facing a question that goes like this:

Alicia died, leaving her residence in town and a separate parcel of undeveloped rural land to her brother Brian and her sister Carrie, with Brian owning one-quarter interest and Carrie owning three-quarters interest. How do Brian and Carrie hold title?

a. as tenants in survivorship
b. as tenants in common
c. as joint tenants
d. as tenants by the entirety

You should always use the process of elimination on a question like this, even if the right answer jumps out at you. Sometimes, the answer that jumps out isn't right after all. Let's assume, for the purpose of this exercise, that you are a little rusty on property ownership terminology, so you need to use a little intuition to make up for what you don't remember. Proceed through the answer choices in order.

So you start with choice **a**. This one is pretty easy to eliminate; this tenancy doesn't have to do with survivorship. Because the Arizona real estate sales exam is given on a computer, you won't be able to cross out answer choices; instead, make a mental note that choice **a** is incorrect.

Choice **b** seems reasonable; it's a kind of ownership that two people can share. Even if you don't remember much about tenancy in common, you could tell it's about having something "in common." Make a mental note, "Good answer, I might use this one."

Choice **c** is also a possibility. Joint tenants also share something in common. If you happen to remember that joint tenancy always involves equal ownership rights, you mentally eliminate this choice. If you don't, make a mental note, "Good answer" or "Well, maybe," depending on how attractive this answer looks to you.

Choice **d** strikes you as a little less likely. Tenancy by the entirety doesn't necessarily have to do with two people sharing ownership. This doesn't sound right, and you have already got a better answer picked out in choice **b**. If you are feeling sure of yourself, you can mentally eliminate this choice.

If you're pressed for time, you should choose choice **b**. If you have got the time to be extra careful, you could compare your answer choices again. Then, choose one and move on.

If you are taking a test on paper, like the practice exams in this book, it's good to have a system for marking good, bad, and maybe answers. We recommend this one:

X = bad
✓ = good
? = maybe

If you don't like these marks, devise your own system. Just make sure you do it long before test day—while you're working through the practice exams in this book—so you won't have to worry about it just before the exam.

Even when you think you are absolutely clueless about a question, you can often use process of elimination to get rid of one answer choice. If so, you are better prepared to make an educated guess, as you will see in Step 6. More often, the process of elimination allows you to get down to only two possibly right answers. Then you are in a strong position to guess. And sometimes, even though you don't know the right answer, you find it simply by getting rid of the wrong ones, as you did in the previous example.

Try using your powers of elimination on the questions in the worksheet Using the Process of Elimination. The questions aren't about real estate work; they're just designed to show you how the process of elimination works. The answer explanations for this worksheet show one possible way you might use the process to arrive at the right answer.

The process of elimination is your tool for the next step, which is knowing when to guess.

Using the Process of Elimination

Use the process of elimination to answer the following questions.

1. Ilsa is as old as Meghan will be in five years. The difference between Ed's age and Meghan's age is twice the difference between Ilsa's age and Meghan's age. Ed is 29. How old is Ilsa?
   a. 4
   b. 10
   c. 19
   d. 24

2. "All drivers of commercial vehicles must carry a valid commercial driver's license whenever operating a commercial vehicle." According to this sentence, which of the following people need NOT carry a commercial driver's license?
   a. a truck driver idling his engine while waiting to be directed to a loading dock
   b. a bus operator backing her bus out of the way of another bus in the bus lot
   c. a taxi driver driving his personal car to the grocery store
   d. a limousine driver taking the limousine to her home after dropping off her last passenger of the evening

3. Smoking tobacco has been linked to
   a. increased risk of stroke and heart attack.
   b. all forms of respiratory disease.
   c. increasing mortality rates over the past ten years.
   d. juvenile delinquency.

4. Which of the following words is spelled correctly?
   a. incorrigible
   b. outragous
   c. domestickated
   d. understandible

Answers

Here are the answers, as well as some suggestions as to how you might have used the process of elimination to find them.

1. d. You should have eliminated choice **a** right away. Ilsa can't be four years old if Meghan is going to be Ilsa's age in five years. The best way to eliminate other answer choices is to try plugging them in to the information given in the problem. For instance, for choice **b**, if Ilsa is 10, then Meghan must be 5. The difference in their ages is 5. The difference between Ed's age, 29, and Meghan's age, 5, is 24. Does 24 equal 2 times 5? No. Then choice **b** is wrong. You could eliminate answer **c** in the same way and be left with choice **d**.

2. c. Note the word *not* in the question, and go through the answers one by one. Is the truck driver in choice **a** "operating a commericial vehicle"? Yes, idling counts as "operating," so he needs to have a commercial driver's license. Likewise, the bus operator in choice **b** is operating a commercial vehicle; the question doesn't say the operator has to be on the street. The limo driver in choice **d** is operating a commercial vehicle, even if it doesn't have passenger in it. However, the cabbie in choice **c** is not operating a commercial vehicle, but his own private car.

3. a. You could eliminate choice **b** simply because of the presence of the word *all*. Such absolutes hardly ever appear in correct answer choices. Choice **c** looks attractive until you think a little about what you know—aren't fewer people smoking these days, rather than more? So how could smoking be responsible for a higher mortality rate? (If you didn't know that *mortality rate* means the rate at which people die, you might keep this choice as a possibility, but you would still be able to eliminate two answers and have only two to choose from.) And choice **d** is not logical, so you could eliminate that one, too. And you are left with the correct choice, **a**.

4. a. How you used the process of elimination here depends on which words you recognized as being spelled incorrectly. If you knew that the correct spellings were *outrageous*, *domesticated*, and *understandable*, then you were home free. You probably knew that at least one of those words was wrong!

▶ Step 6: Know When to Guess

Time to complete: 20 minutes
Activity: Complete worksheet on Your Guessing Ability

Armed with the process of elimination, you are ready to take control of one of the big questions in test taking: Should I guess? The first and main answer is *yes*. Some exams have what's called a "guessing penalty," in which a fraction of your wrong answers is subtracted from your right answers—but the Arizona real estate sales exam doesn't work like that. The number of questions you answer correctly yields your raw score. So you have nothing to lose and everything to gain by guessing.

The more complicated answer to the question "Should I guess?" depends on you—your personality and your "guessing intuition." There are two things you need to know about yourself before you go into the exam:

- Are you a risk taker?
- Are you a good guesser?

You will have to decide about your risk-taking quotient on your own. To find out if you are a good guesser, complete the worksheet Your Guessing Ability. Frankly, even if you are a play-it-safe person with lousy intuition, you're still safe in guessing every time. The best thing would be if you could overcome your anxieties and go ahead and mark an answer. But you may want to have a sense of how good your intuition is before you go into the exam.

Your Guessing Ability

The following are ten really hard questions. You are not supposed to know the answers. Rather, this is an assessment of your ability to guess when you don't have a clue. Read each question carefully, just as if you did expect to answer it. If you have any knowledge at all of the subject of the question, use that knowledge to help you eliminate wrong answer choices.

1. September 7 is Independence Day in
  a. India.
  b. Costa Rica.
  c. Brazil.
  d. Australia.

2. Which of the following is the formula for determining the momentum of an object?
  a. $p = mv$
  b. $F = ma$
  c. $P = IV$
  d. $E = mc^2$

3. Because of the expansion of the universe, the stars and other celestial bodies are all moving away from each other. This phenomenon is known as
  a. Newton's first law.
  b. the big bang.
  c. gravitational collapse.
  d. Hubble flow.

4. American author Gertrude Stein was born in
  a. 1713.
  b. 1830.
  c. 1874.
  d. 1901.

5. Which of the following is NOT one of the Five Classics attributed to Confucius?
  a. the *I Ching*
  b. the *Book of Holiness*
  c. the *Spring and Autumn Annals*
  d. the *Book of History*

6. The religious and philosophical doctrine that holds that the universe is constantly in a struggle between good and evil is known as
  a. Pelagianism.
  b. Manichaeanism.
  c. neo-Hegelianism.
  d. Epicureanism.

7. The third chief justice of the U.S. Supreme Court was
   a. John Blair.
   b. William Cushing.
   c. James Wilson.
   d. John Jay.

8. Which of the following is the poisonous portion of a daffodil?
   a. the bulb
   b. the leaves
   c. the stem
   d. the flowers

9. The winner of the Masters golf tournament in 1953 was
   a. Sam Snead.
   b. Cary Middlecoff.
   c. Arnold Palmer.
   d. Ben Hogan.

10. The state with the highest per capita personal income in 1980 was
   a. Alaska.
   b. Connecticut.
   c. New York.
   d. Massachusetts.

Answers

Check your answers against the correct answers below.
   1. c.
   2. a.
   3. d.
   4. c.
   5. b.
   6. b.
   7. b.
   8. a.
   9. d.
   10. a.

► How Did You Do?

You may have simply gotten lucky and actually known the answer to one or two questions. In addition, your guessing was more successful if you were able to use the process of elimination on any of the questions. Maybe you didn't know who the third chief justice was (question 7), but you knew that John Jay was the first. In that case, you would have eliminated choice **d** and, therefore, improved your odds of guessing right from one in four to one in three.

According to probability, you should get $2\frac{1}{2}$ answers correct, so getting either two or three right would be average. If you got four or more right, you may be a really terrific guesser. If you got one or none right, you may be a really bad guesser.

Keep in mind, though, that this is only a small sample. You should continue to keep track of your guessing ability as you work through the sample questions in this book. Circle the numbers of questions you guess on as you make your guesses; or, if you don't have time while you take the practice exams, go back afterward and try to remember which questions you guessed on. Remember, on an exam with four answer choices, your chances of getting a right answer is one in four. So keep a separate "guessing" score for each exam. How many questions did you guess on? How many did you get right? If the number you got right is at least one-fourth of the number of questions you guessed on, you are at least an average guesser, maybe better—and you should always go ahead and guess on the real exam. If the number you got right is significantly lower than one-fourth of the number you guessed on, you would, frankly, be safe in guessing anyway, but maybe you would feel more comfortable if you guessed only selectively, when you can eliminate a wrong answer or at least have a good feeling about one of the answer choices.

▶ Step 7: Reach Your Peak Performance Zone

Time to complete: 10 minutes to read, weeks to complete!
Activity: Complete the Physical Preparation Checklist

To get ready for a challenge like a big exam, you have to take control of your physical, as well as your mental, state. Exercise, proper diet, and rest will ensure that your body works with, rather than against, your mind on test day, as well as during your preparation.

Exercise

If you don't already have a regular exercise program going, the time during which you are preparing for an exam is actually an excellent time to start one. And if you are already keeping fit—or trying to get that way—don't let the pressure of preparing for an exam fool you into quitting now. Exercise helps reduce stress by pumping wonderful good-feeling hormones called endorphins into your system. It also increases the oxygen supply throughout your body, including your brain, so you will be at peak performance on test day.

A half hour of vigorous activity—enough to raise a sweat—every day should be your aim. If you are really pressed for time, every other day is okay. Choose an activity you like, and get out there and do it. Jogging with a friend always makes the time go faster, or take a radio.

But don't overdo it. You don't want to exhaust yourself. Moderation is the key.

Diet

First of all, cut out the junk. Go easy on caffeine and nicotine, and eliminate alcohol and any other drugs from your system at least two weeks before the exam. Promise yourself a reward the night after the exam, if need be.

What your body needs for peak performance is simply a balanced diet. Eat plenty of fruits and vegetables, along with protein and carbohydrates. Foods high in lecithin (an amino acid), such as fish and beans, are especially good "brain foods."

The night before the exam, you might "carbo-load" the way athletes do before a contest. Eat a big plate of spaghetti, rice and beans, or your favorite carbohydrate.

Rest

You probably know how much sleep you need every night to be at your best, even if you don't always get it. Make sure you do get that much sleep, though, for at least a week before the exam. Moderation is important here, too. Extra sleep will just make you groggy.

If you are not a morning person and your exam will be given in the morning, you should reset your internal clock so that your body doesn't think you are taking an exam at 3:00 A.M. You have to start this process well before the exam. The way it works is to get up half an hour earlier each morning, and then go to bed half an hour earlier that night. Don't try it the other way around; you will just toss and turn if you go to bed early without having gotten up early. The next morning, get up another half an hour earlier, and so on. How long you will have to do this depends on how late you are used to getting up. Use the Physical Preparation Checklist on the next page to make sure you are in tip-top form.

▶ Step 8: Get Your Act Together

Time to complete: 10 minutes to read, time to complete will vary
Activity: Complete Final Preparations worksheet

You are in control of your mind and body; you are in charge of test anxiety, your preparation, and your test-taking strategies. Now it's time to take charge of external factors, like the testing site and the materials you need to take the exam.

Find Out Where the Exam Is and Make a Trial Run

Do you know how to get to the testing site? Do you know how long it will take to get there? If not, make a trial run, preferably on the same day of the week at the same time of day. Make note on the Final Preparations worksheet of the amount of time it will take you to get to the exam site. Plan on arriving 30–45 minutes early so you can get the lay of the land, use the bathroom, and calm down. Then figure out how early you will have to get up that morning and make sure you get up that early every day for a week before the exam.

Gather Your Materials

The night before the exam, lay out the clothes you will wear and the materials you have to bring with you to the exam. Plan on dressing in layers; you won't have any control over the temperature of the examination room. Have a sweater or jacket you can take off if it's warm. Use the checklist on the Final Preparations worksheet to help you pull together what you will need.

Don't Skip Breakfast

Even if you don't usually eat breakfast, do so on exam morning. A cup of coffee doesn't count. Don't eat doughnuts or other sweet foods, either. A sugar high will leave you with a sugar low in the middle of the exam. A mix of protein and carbohydrates is best: Cereal with milk or eggs with toast will do your body a world of good.

▶ Step 9: Do It!

Time to complete: 10 minutes, plus test-taking time
Activity: Ace the Arizona real estate sales exam!

Physical Preparation Checklist

For the week before the exam, write down what physical exercise you engaged in and for how long and what you ate for each meal. Remember, you are trying for at least half an hour of exercise every other day (preferably every day) and a balanced diet that's light on junk food.

Exam minus 7 days
Exercise: _____ for _____ minutes
Breakfast: _____
Lunch: _____
Dinner: _____
Snacks: _____

Exam minus 6 days
Exercise: _____ for _____ minutes
Breakfast: _____
Lunch: _____
Dinner: _____
Snacks: _____

Exam minus 5 days
Exercise: _____ for _____ minutes
Breakfast: _____
Lunch: _____
Dinner: _____
Snacks: _____

Exam minus 4 days
Exercise: _____ for _____ minutes
Breakfast: _____
Lunch: _____
Dinner: _____
Snacks: _____

Exam minus 3 days
Exercise: _____ for _____ minutes
Breakfast: _____
Lunch: _____
Dinner: _____
Snacks: _____

Exam minus 2 days
Exercise: _____ for _____ minutes
Breakfast: _____
Lunch: _____
Dinner: _____
Snacks: _____

Exam minus 1 day
Exercise: _____ for _____ minutes
Breakfast: _____
Lunch: _____
Dinner: _____
Snacks: _____

Fast-forward to exam day. You are ready. You made a study plan and followed through. You practiced your test-taking strategies while working through this book. You are in control of your physical, mental, and emotional state. You know when and where to show up and what to bring with you. In other words, you are better prepared than most of the other people taking the Arizona real estate sales exam with you. You are psyched.

Just one more thing. When you are done with the exam, you will have earned a reward. Plan a celebration. Call up your friends and plan a party, or have a nice dinner for two—whatever your heart desires. Give yourself something to look forward to.

Final Preparations

Getting to the Exam Site

Location of exam: _____

Date: _____

Departure time: _____

Do I know how to get to the exam site? Yes _____ No _____
If no, make a trial run.

Time it will take to get to exam site: _____

Things to Lay Out the Night Before

Clothes I will wear   _____

Sweater/jacket   _____

Watch   _____

Photo ID   _____

No. 2 pencils   _____

Calculator   _____

_____   _____

_____   _____

And then do it. Go into the exam, full of confidence, armed with the test-taking strategies you have practiced until they're second nature. You are in control of yourself, your environment, and your performance on the exam. You are ready to succeed. So do it. Go in there and ace the exam. And look forward to your future career as a real estate salesperson!

3 ▶ Arizona Real Estate Sales Exam 1

CHAPTER SUMMARY

This is the first of the four practice tests in this book based on the Arizona real estate sales exam. Take this test to see how you would do if you took the exam today, and to get a handle on your strengths and weaknesses.

L IKE THE OTHER practice tests in this book, this test is based on the actual Arizona real estate sales exam. See Chapter 1 for a complete description of this exam. Take this exam in as relaxed a manner as you can, without worrying about timing. You can time yourself on the other three exams. You should, however, make sure that you have enough time to take the entire exam in one sitting. Find a quiet place where you can work without interruptions.

The answer sheet is on the following page, and is followed by the exam. After you have finished, use the answer key and explanations to learn your strengths and your weaknesses. Then use the scoring section at the end of this chapter to see how you did overall.

►Arizona Real Estate Sales Exam 1

1. The commissioner of real estate in Arizona is appointed by the
a. senator.
b. mayor.
c. designated broker.
d. governor.

2. A 12-mile square contains how many townships?
a. 24
b. four
c. 144
d. 36

3. Which of the following statements is true?
a. FHA guarantees the lender against borrower default.
b. FHA is a government-credit life insurance program protecting the lender.
c. A Section 203(b) FHA loan is for one- to four-family investment properties.
d. FHA insures the lender against borrower default.

4. The trustor is also known as
a. seller.
b. borrower.
c. listing agent.
d. assessor.

5. Once a licensee has a listing agreement, it would legally terminate if
a. the licensee does not sell the house in a month.
b. the licensee went insane.
c. the seller will not spend money on advertising.
d. a buyer does not offer the asking price.

6. The homestead exemption in Arizona goes up to what amount?
a. $150,000
b. $30,000
c. $90,000
d. $5,000

7. A buyer plans to give a 50% down payment on a house purchase. The house is being purchased for $1,250,000. What is the loan amount?
a. $625,000
b. $750,000
c. $450,000
d. $250,000

8. Real estate property taxes in Arizona are based on
a. article 4.
b. 10%.
c. assessed value.
d. riparian *pro rata* share.

9. Which lien will be paid first after a foreclosure?
a. property taxes
b. mortgage up to $250,000
c. IRS federal tax lien
d. deed of trust

10. If a borrower has private mortgage insurance on his or her loan and wants to eliminate it, the current loan balance would have to be less than what percent of the original loan balance?
a. 60%
b. 75%
c. 80%
d. 95%

11. An elderly couple hired a maid to assist them and then willed their property to the maid. Thirty years later, the maid died without leaving a will or having any known family heirs. The government could acquire the property through
 a. escheat.
 b. disclosure act.
 c. testate.
 d. tenancy.

12. A mortgage that is in second position to first mortgages and is subordinate to them is known as
 a. purchase money second.
 b. the secondary mortgage market.
 c. a VA mortgage.
 d. primary mortgage.

13. Tax lien sales in Arizona are held the third Monday of which month?
 a. March
 b. May
 c. October
 d. February

14. The only time when business days are used in Arizona real estate practice is
 a. listings.
 b. landlord tenant act.
 c. mechanics' liens.
 d. public report.

15. Which one of the following is NOT a deed?
 a. trust deed
 b. disclaimer deed
 c. general deed
 d. quitclaim deed

16. Once a buyer-broker agreement has terminated, the licensee can
 a. do nothing about it.
 b. reveal confidential information to the office.
 c. become a licensee of a seller with written consent of the original buyer.
 d. reveal material information if the party promises to keep the information confidential.

17. A tenant has a lease that begins on May 1 and terminates on the following April 30. What kind of lease is this?
 a. estate for years
 b. periodic estate
 c. estate at will
 d. estate of definition

18. The right of water use by a landowner next to a river is called
 a. *ad valorem.*
 b. owner occupied.
 c. riparian.
 d. defeasance clause.

19. The definition of a subdivision is
 a. six or more parcels fewer than 36 acres each.
 b. six or more parcels 36 to 160 acres each.
 c. 36 equal sections.
 d. a quadrant of 640 acres.

20. A buyer promises to pay the lender by signing a(n)
 a. note.
 b. mortgage.
 c. deed.
 d. affidavit of property value.

21. A *cloud on the title* has the ability to
   a. stop a transaction.
   b. add value to a property.
   c. make a licensee responsible.
   d. have a buyer lose his or her deposit.

22. A projected annual operating statement that shows anticipated income, expenses, and net income is a(n)
   a. balance sheet.
   b. closing statement.
   c. appraisal.
   d. *pro forma* statement.

23. A purchase and sales agreement would be an example of what type of contract?
   a. unconscionable
   b. executory
   c. executed
   d. all of the above

24. Mr. Rivera executed a deed to his nephew, citing the consideration as $1. The deed is
   a. voidable.
   b. incomplete.
   c. valid.
   d. void.

25. An appraiser is hired to estimate the value of a retail shopping center and will use the income approach to value. Which of the following items will NOT be used in his determination of value?
   a. debt service
   b. property taxes
   c. insurance payments
   d. maintenance expenses

26. If you have a name change due to a marriage, you must notify the real estate commissioner within how many days?
   a. five
   b. 30
   c. 180
   d. ten

27. If you want to put a sign in an owner's yard, you must have
   a. a sign that is visible from the road.
   b. written permission.
   c. your picture on it.
   d. a minimum of two feet above the ground.

28. A multiple-listing property sells for $319,000. The shared commission is 5%; 2.5% to the listing office and 2.5% to the buyer agent. The listing salesperson earns 40% of the commission. What does his broker principal of the listing office earn?
   a. $15,950
   b. $7,975
   c. $6,000
   d. $4,785

29. To obtain your salesperson's license, you must be _____ years old; to obtain your broker's license, you must be _____ years old.
   a. 18; 21
   b. 21; 21
   c. 18; 18
   d. 21; 18

30. When a deed of trust is paid, the trustee will send a
   a. thank-you letter.
   b. deed of reconveyance.
   c. quitclaim deed.
   d. beneficiary waiver.

31. A new tenant is leasing a store in Paradise Valley Mall and has to pay a fixed amount of rent for the space, plus a certain amount of the gross receipts. This would be called a
   a. gross lease.
   b. net lease.
   c. triple net lease.
   d. percentage lease.

32. Agent Evan is licensed in a state that requires a residential seller to provide a buyer with a statutory property disclosure statement, and Agent Robbins is licensed in a state that does not require such disclosures. In either case, what is the best way they can avoid misrepresentation of property condition to prospective buyers?
   a. Require buyers to sign a statement of understanding regarding *caveat emptor*.
   b. Recommend that all buyers purchase a home warranty.
   c. Recommend that all buyers discuss the property condition with the seller before closing.
   d. Strongly recommend that all buyers have the property inspected by a qualified inspector.

33. Delinquent taxes in Arizona become a lien on
   a. May 21.
   b. December 31.
   c. the first Monday in January.
   d. the last Thursday in October.

34. A buyer is describing a loan that does not have a schedule of principal reductions, and never goes up in balance. This loan would be known as
   a. negative amortization.
   b. two-one buydown.
   c. 15-year fixed rate.
   d. interest only.

35. A licensee is working at a real estate firm and the broker's license is terminated. The licensee must
   a. keep selling until all of his or her transactions close.
   b. wait until his or her license expires.
   c. find another broker.
   d. utilize the 60-day grace period.

36. A purchaser from a subdivider must have
   a. permanent access.
   b. closing incentives.
   c. an in-house mortgage company.
   d. a real estate license.

37. Property taxes in Arizona are paid
   a. in your PITI payment.
   b. twice per year.
   c. by your broker.
   d. on April 15.

38. The appraisal process became regulated and licensed by the U.S. government in 1989 after the failure of the savings and loan associations and the passing of what bill?
   a. Title IX
   b. FIRREA
   c. USP
   d. MAI

39. A material defect is a defect that can materially
   a. hurt the public health.
   b. impede on the sale of real estate.
   c. influence a buyer's decision to buy or not buy a particular property.
   d. hurt the value of real estate that the seller should not disclose.

40. The real estate commissioner can do all of the following EXCEPT
    a. travel to foreign countries.
    b. terminate a license.
    c. investigate complaints.
    d. hold a real estate license.

41. For real estate to be able to depreciate, it must first be
    a. free and clear.
    b. encumbered.
    c. assigned a parcel number.
    d. improved.

42. If you are redoing a bathroom floor that is 10' × 12' at a cost of $5 per square foot with 16-inch tiles, how many tiles will you need?
    a. 67.5
    b. 600
    c. 17,280
    d. 120

43. Every listing must have which of the following?
    a. signatures
    b. beginning and ending dates
    c. a sign in the yard
    d. both **a** and **b**

44. A father owns a house in Phoenix and decides to retire to Chino Valley. His son wants to buy the house, but has limited financial resources, so the father gives the son a very favorable price. This is an example of
    a. ratification.
    b. arm's-length transaction.
    c. non–arm's-length transaction.
    d. undue influence.

45. A change on a contract must be
    a. initialed or signed by all parties.
    b. verbally agreed upon.
    c. signed by the designated broker.
    d. reviewed by the seller only.

46. State regulations require that a broker keep all closed contracts for
    a. three years.
    b. five years.
    c. ten years.
    d. seven years.

47. Alex Rivera has an easement across Alice Dean's land to access his property since he has no other access to the property. Which of the following statements describes this arrangement?
    a. This is an easement in gross and Alex has a servient easement.
    b. Alex has a dominant easement with license to use Alice's land.
    c. Alex has a servient easement and Alice has a dominant easement.
    d. Alex has a dominant easement and Alice has the servient easement.

48. If you sublease, you would be
    a. terminating your lease.
    b. making way to another lien holder.
    c. giving up any future rights.
    d. turning the original lessee into a lessor.

49. If you were conveying personal property, you would use a(n)
    a. affidavit.
    b. bill of sale.
    c. agreement for sale.
    d. deed of trust.

50. The income approach would most likely be used to estimate value on
   a. a 36-acre parcel and up.
   b. a condo.
   c. homes with guesthouses.
   d. a commercial office building.

51. Which of the following is NOT a mortgage?
   a. 30-year fixed rate
   b. FHA loan
   c. lease with option to buy
   d. ARM loan

52. Foreclosure allows a lender to
   a. provide defeasance.
   b. terminate a borrower's interest in property.
   c. take immediate title to real estate.
   d. recapture the mortgage.

53. ABC Investments, Inc., the owner of an apartment building built in 1967, is required by federal law to furnish to all prospective tenants which of the following?
   a. disclosure of property condition
   b. environmental assessment report not more than one year old
   c. lead-based paint and lead-based paint hazards disclosure
   d. good faith estimate of rental and use charges

54. The three traditional approaches used by appraisers in valuation include
   a. sales, income, and cost approaches.
   b. comparables, residual, and highest/best use approaches.
   c. highest/best use, reconciliation, and fee approaches.
   d. contributory, adjustment, and valuation approaches.

55. The mortgagee is also the
   a. lender.
   b. bank.
   c. mortgage company.
   d. all of the above

56. Regulation Z requires that a lender inform the borrower of
   a. closing costs.
   b. three-day right of rescission.
   c. the appraised value.
   d. the true cost of obtaining credit.

57. Pete is a landlord and wants to see the unit that is occupied by his tenant, Jeff. How much notice does Pete have to give Jeff?
   a. one day
   b. none, because they are friends
   c. two days
   d. seven days after rent is received

58. A deposit is given with an offer because
   a. it is the only means to possibly bind an offer.
   b. a seller cannot accept offers without consideration.
   c. it indicates to a seller that the buyer is serious.
   d. it takes the property off the market.

59. An individual who chooses to hire a licensee to represent his or her best interests is called a
   a. buyer.
   b. subagent.
   c. principal.
   d. fiduciary.

60. As it relates to residential real estate, the Federal Fair Housing Act of 1968 makes it illegal to discriminate based on
  a. sex, religion, health, or age.
  b. race, color, age, or health.
  c. sex, race, color, or religion.
  d. race, color, religion, sex, or national origin.

61. A licensee was puffing at an open house for more than one hour. What was the licensee doing?
  a. falsifying documents
  b. overstating his or her personal opinion of the subject property
  c. promising to obtain an over-market appraisal of the home
  d. smoking cigars

62. A contract that is voidable is considered
  a. not valid.
  b. valid until the next business day.
  c. valid until an action is taken to move it to void.
  d. valid.

63. Taking a protected class to the same area is
  a. redlining.
  b. blockbusting.
  c. steering.
  d. all of the above

64. Which of the following terms has no relation to personal property?
  a. realty
  b. chattel
  c. chattel real
  d. none of the above

65. An appraisal report must be presented
  a. in writing.
  b. verbally.
  c. dependent on the client.
  d. in detail with all the supporting information.

66. The office policy for your office is to do a two-call listing presentation. When must disclosure of agency be given?
  a. at the first meeting
  b. at the signing of the listing agreement
  c. at the time of the offer
  d. at the time of the closing

67. A mortgage broker
  a. originates, funds, and services home mortgage loans.
  b. is the same as a mortgage banker.
  c. brings borrowers together with mortgage lenders.
  d. originates and services home mortgage loans.

68. When you take a listing in Arizona, it is customary to charge
  a. 3.5%.
  b. 6%.
  c. an amount set by the nature of the listing.
  d. what the seller agrees to.

69. A home loan is set for repayment over 240 months. How many years is this loan for?
  a. 20
  b. 30
  c. ten-year fixed, then adjusts to the index and margin
  d. two

70. Which of the following terms does NOT go along with the trustee?
a. beneficiary
b. bare legal title
c. power of sale
d. equitable title

71. Which act prohibits discrimination based on race, color, religion, national origin, sex, marital status, or age when granting credit?
a. ECOA
b. ADA
c. HUD
d. RESPA

72. The type of recorded judgment that is *Arizona Court v. an Arizona Citizen* is
a. foreign.
b. domestic.
c. small claims.
d. ARS 26.

73. A licensee listed a house and was told by the seller that it had a leaky roof. A prospective buyer asked about any physical defects. The licensee, to protect the seller, answered none that he or she was aware of; therefore, the buyer decided to make an offer. The licensee's comments are known as
a. misrepresentation.
b. fiduciary responsibility.
c. expression of opinion.
d. acting under duress.

74. A seller is closing on August 21 and will pay off the balance of a 6.75% mortgage loan of $187,523. Having made the August 1 payment, what will be the prorated amount of accrued interest due at closing? Use a banker's year.
a. $1,265.78
b. $728.26
c. $795.36
d. $738.37

75. Rupert Labinsky borrowed $18,000 at 8% interest and paid it back in full at the end of two months. How much did Rupert pay?
a. $1,440
b. $18,240
c. $19,440
d. $240

76. An office building has rents that total $25,456 per month. The annual operating expenses total $211,923. The annual debt service equals $23,444. What is the annual net operating income?
a. $305,472
b. $93,549
c. $70,105
d. $186,467

77. An affidavit of property value must be signed by
a. the listing agent and the selling agent.
b. the salesperson and the designated broker.
c. the buyer and the seller.
d. the plaintiff and the judge.

78. A tenant may do self-help for minor repairs as long as the tenant waits how many days after notifying the landlord?
　a. seven
　b. ten
　c. three
　d. Tenant can never make any type of repair.

79. Assured water supply is consistent with how many years of assured water?
　a. 30
　b. 50
　c. 100
　d. none of the above

80. A loan has just been accelerated. What happened?
　a. The loan was called all due and payable.
　b. The borrower paid off the loan.
　c. The trustee has the power of sale.
　d. The certificate of sale has been released.

81. The Telephone Consumer Protections Act (TCPA) states that calls cannot be made before _____ and after _____.
　a. 8:00 A.M.; 9:00 P.M.
　b. 9:00 A.M.; 8:00 P.M.
　c. 10:00 A.M.; 7:00 P.M.
　d. 9:30 A.M.; 8:30 P.M.

82. A sheriff deed is granted in what type of foreclosure?
　a. deed of trust
　b. mortgage
　c. quitclaim
　d. wraparound agreement for sale

83. Molly has a first loan for $190,000 and a second loan for $72,500. Her home is appraised for $375,000. What is her combined loan-to-value (CLTV)?
　a. 50.67%
　b. 19.33%
　c. 70%
　d. 19.70%

84. A prospective land developer wants to divide a 12-acre parcel of land into lots that are 100' × 100'. He must allow 22,720 square feet for streets and sidewalks. How many lots will he have when he is done?
　a. 50
　b. 52.27
　c. 82
　d. 36

85. What is the purpose of the closing?
　a. to show the title search
　b. to show the financial obligations of the buyer and seller
　c. to show the liability of the lessee
　d. none of the above

86. What type of agency relationship exists between the primary broker of a firm and a sponsored salesperson licensee?
　a. general agency
　b. special agency
　c. universal agency
　d. No agency exists because the salesperson is an independent contractor.

87. What is the balance on an amortized loan of $340,000 after the first payment if the interest rate is 6% with principal and interest payments of $2,028?
   a. $319,600
   b. $338,300
   c. $337,972
   d. $339,672

88. Broker Peter Eklund listed Byron Hindley's house for $395,000. Byron is very anxious to sell the property and must close within 60 days. Peter showed the property to a prospective buyer and told the buyer he could most likely get the property for $15,000 below the asking price. Which of the following statements best describes this situation?
   a. Peter has represented his client Byron well by encouraging an offer.
   b. Peter has followed his agency obligation to bring a ready, willing, and able buyer to the seller.
   c. Peter has violated his fiduciary duties.
   d. Peter has not violated any duty to his client, Byron.

89. Jesse Ruiz is selling a tract of land that is 175 feet by 338 feet. The county recently paved the road in front of the property and Mr. Ruiz will be charged special assessment tax at closing. How will this tax be computed?
   a. per square foot
   b. per acre
   c. per front foot
   d. per foot of perimeter

90. The appraisal principle that determines a value most likely to produce the highest price in the sale of a property is known as the principle of
   a. supply and demand.
   b. highest and best use.
   c. growth and decline.
   d. competition.

91. The relationship of a broker to a buyer in an exclusive buyer agency contract is that of a
   a. principal agent.
   b. single agent.
   c. facilitator.
   d. dual agent.

92. A mortgage company turned down a borrower because he is 87 years old and told him a 30-year mortgage was too long for him. This is a violation of
   a. equal credit.
   b. RESPA.
   c. Truth-in-Lending.
   d. fair housing.

93. If a piece of land is being divided into five parcels, the developer must have a(n)
   a. public report.
   b. affidavit of property value.
   c. ingress and egress.
   d. affidavit of land disclosure.

94. In real estate, there are two types of assessments. What are they?
   a. foreign and domestic
   b. redemption and receiver
   c. public and private
   d. *pro rata* and *per diem*

95. When you pay something in arrears, like property taxes, it means you
   a. pay up front and use over time.
   b. use first, then pay.
   c. pay monthly.
   d. order as much as you would like.

96. Which of the following is a unilateral contract?
   a. open listing
   b. ER
   c. purchase agreement
   d. buyer-broker

97. What is the maximum fee a developer can charge for a lot reservation when a public report is pending?
   a. $1,000
   b. none
   c. $25,000
   d. $5,000

98. Using the gross rent multiplier method of evaluation, what would be the value of a three-family house that had an annual gross income of $40,000, if the average selling price of a three-family house in the community is $300,000 and the average annual gross income of the properties is $30,000?
   a. $400,000
   b. $40,000
   c. $600,000
   d. $300,000

99. An agent e-mails a prospective buyer some data on property based on the information gathered. This would be
   a. implied agency.
   b. exclusive agency
   c. fiduciary.
   d. realty agency.

100. A real estate consumer from Texas has how many years to file a complaint against a transaction in Maricopa County from the Arizona Recovery Fund?
   a. one
   b. five
   c. ten
   d. none of the above

101. Brooke wants to buy a house and have a loan with no mortgage insurance and no down payment. One option she could choose would be
   a. FHA.
   b. an 80/20 combo to 100% CLTV.
   c. a 97% flex.
   d. a kiddy condo loan.

102. The device that is used to secure real estate using a trustee as a third party is
   a. chattel.
   b. mortgage.
   c. note.
   d. deed of trust.

103. Sam is processing his paperwork for a homestead exemption. He needs to file a(n)
   a. affidavit of property value.
   b. security agreement.
   c. declaration of homestead.
   d. homestead sheriff certificate.

104. *LSR* is an acronym for
   a. loan status report.
   b. loan statistic report.
   c. leasing submission review.
   d. lenders statement record.

105. When a licensee sells his or her own listing and now represents the seller and the buyer, this is called
   a. seller agency.
   b. double agency.
   c. dual agency.
   d. triple agency.

106. A cap rate is used in what type of appraisal?
   a. reproduction
   b. income approach
   c. tax assessment
   d. competitive market analysis

107. The title number that Arizona Revised Statutes (ARS Code) uses regarding real estate and allows the commissioner to enforce laws is
   a. Title 43.
   b. Title 9.
   c. Title 21.
   d. Title 32.

108. An associate broker has which of these extra privileges over a licensee?
   a. He or she needs no written employment agreement with the designated broker.
   b. He or she has no extra privileges.
   c. He or she can do property management.
   d. He or she can appraise properties.

109. What term is used when counties and communities pass ordinances to regulate the control and use of land?
   a. subdivisions
   b. deed restrictions
   c. encumbrances
   d. zoning

110. Agency is what type of relationship?
   a. consensual
   b. in writing when it is a listing agreement
   c. fiduciary
   d. all of the above

111. Real estate is defined as
   a. land, structures, and appurtenances.
   b. rights, interests, and benefits.
   c. land only.
   d. land, structures, and any equipment.

112. The Real Estate Advisory Board consists of which of the following?
   a. two brokers who are in residential resale
   b. two brokers from different counties
   c. three people from the public with no real estate license
   d. all of the above

113. Real property has inherent rights of ownership that are known as
   a. procuring causes.
   b. bundle of legal rights.
   c. police power and rights.
   d. bundle of sticks.

114. A fully executed contract is defined as a contract signed by
a. either the buyer or seller.
b. the buyer and delivered to the seller.
c. both the buyer and seller.
d. the buyer and broker.

115. If John Doe pays his debt in full on a house loan, the lender will give title back to John Doe. This action is called
a. titling.
b. defeasance.
c. hypothecation.
d. collateral.

116. An out-of-town buyer has an interest in buying a house that has been vacant for five years. The house has had no interested parties, yet the house seems to be in good condition. There were town rumors that a murder took place in the house and that it is stigmatized. Should the licensee disclose the rumor?
a. no, not under any conditions
b. no, unless the buyer specifically inquires to investigate or affirmatively disclose
c. yes, full disclosure is an agent's responsibility
d. yes, unless the murder was actually a suicide

117. Which advertised phrase might trigger further lending disclosure?
a. The interest rate is 5.4% *per annum*.
b. We have 95% financing available.
c. Financing terms available include 5% APR with 30-year amortization.
d. We have fixed and adjustable rates.

118. If a seller is known as the client, then a person walking into an open house would be a
a. client.
b. customer.
c. principal.
d. public person.

119. Which of the following applies to a security deposit in Arizona?
a. it cannot exceed one month's rent
b. it must be deposited in an interest-bearing escrow account
c. both **a** and **b**
d. neither **a** nor **b**

120. An ad that looks as if it is from FSBO, but indeed is from a licensee, is called a(n)
a. hook.
b. non-disclosed.
c. blind.
d. owner-agent.

121. A listing in which an owner instructs a licensee NOT to sell to a woman would be classified as
a. allowable.
b. restrictive.
c. avulsion.
d. demise.

122. To give constructive notice of ownership, the buyer must
a. comply with RESPA requirements.
b. record the deed.
c. be a beneficiary.
d. sign the deed.

123. Which term describes land, tenements, improvements, appurtenances, and property?
   a. real property
   b. possession
   c. disposition
   d. bundle of rights

124. A licensee working as a listing agent
   a. must present each property honestly and accurately to the buyer.
   b. works only for the seller.
   c. works only for the buyer.
   d. is not allowed.

125. An exclusive right to sell is one of four types of listings in Arizona. It is best described as
   a. the owner employing as many brokers as he or she wants.
   b. the owner not needing to give permission for a sign.
   c. the price not being disclosed.
   d. none of the above

126. The confluence of the Gila and Salt rivers is the basis for what?
   a. ARS codes
   b. map and plat
   c. townships
   d. Hoover Dam

127. A minor
   a. is barred from making contracts.
   b. is able to make a voidable contract.
   c. is exempt from making a contract.
   d. has no business making a contract.

128. A period of time over which an asset is expected to remain economically feasible to an owner is called a(n)
   a. salvage value.
   b. cost basis.
   c. useful life.
   d. accelerated life.

129. The type of estate that has indefinite duration is
   a. leasehold.
   b. fee simple conditional.
   c. fee simple.
   d. defeasible estate.

130. Owning property in severalty would pertain to which of the following?
   a. corporation
   b. government owned
   c. three brothers buying in tenancy
   d. one person buying a sole ownership

131. RESPA is required to be given by the licensee
   a. at the signing of the purchase and sales agreement.
   b. at the time of the loan application.
   c. at the time of settlement.
   d. none of the above

132. James Gadsden negotiated $10,000,000 for 45,535 square miles of land, which included part of Arizona, in what year?
   a. 1853
   b. 1914
   c. 1804
   d. 1953

133. A buyer-agent
   a. always has to be paid directly by the buyer.
   b. is not entitled to any compensation.
   c. can be paid his or her compensation from the proceeds of the sale.
   d. can be paid his or her compensation by the lessor.

134. The term *cloud on the title* means
   a. the title is free and clear.
   b. the seller must pay the broker's commission.
   c. the title is encumbered.
   d. a title search does not have to be done.

135. Harold is an independent contractor and agent at Big Town Realty. He sold the listing of Country Time Realty to his client buyer. How will Harold be paid the 3.5% buyer's broker commission noted in the multiple-listing service compensation field?
   a. Country Time Realty will pay Harold his portion of the fee and pay his broker the remainder of the fee.
   b. Country Time Realty will pay Big Town Realty the 3.5% commission and the Big Town Realty broker will pay Harold.
   c. The escrow agent will pay Harold his fee at the closing.
   d. The fee will be paid to Harold through MLS.

136. If a person dies intestate, it means
   a. he or she died with a will.
   b. he or she died without a will.
   c. he or she is a testator.
   d. he or she is a testatrix.

137. One of the main functions of the Federal Reserve Board is to
   a. stabilize title transferring.
   b. guard agency relationships.
   c. control inflation.
   d. establish foreclosures.

138. The procedure in which a property owner's rights are taken away is a
   a. forbearance.
   b. reinstatement.
   c. certificate of sale.
   d. foreclosure.

139. A tenant offers four months of rent voluntarily to the landlord. This is
   a. legal.
   b. illegal.
   c. a form of offer to purchase.
   d. a trust contract.

140. Residential property assessor rates are which of the following?
   a. 25%
   b. 15%
   c. 6%
   d. 10%

► Answers

1. **d.** The commissioner is appointed by the governor and is not an elected position.
2. **b.** Each township is six miles long by six miles wide.
3. **d.** The Federal Housing Administration (FHA) loan is for owner occupancy only and insures lenders if a borrower defaults on the loan.
4. **b.** The trustor is for the buyer/borrower and the trustee is for the beneficiary.
5. **b.** There are many ways that listing agreements can be terminated. One option is upon death or insanity of the licensee or client principal.
6. **a.** The homestead exemption is up to $150,000 of involuntary creditors only.
7. **a.** $1,250,000 × .50 = $625,000
8. **c.** Real estate property taxes are based on assessed value of the property type: commercial or residential land.
9. **a.** Property taxes are always paid first.
10. **c.** The loan-to-value ratio would have to be below 80%.
11. **a.** Escheat is the power of the government to take title of property of a person who dies intestate.
12. **a.** A purchase money second is in second position to a first and is subordinate in position.
13. **d.** Tax lien sales are held the third Monday in February and the winner gets a certificate of purchase.
14. **b.** The landlord tenant act states that a landlord has 14 business days to return a security deposit.
15. **a.** A trust deed is a method for a lender's security in a real estate loan.
16. **a.** Once a buyer-broker agreement has expired, the licensee can do nothing about it and must uphold ethical conduct.
17. **a.** An estate for years is one that has a definite termination date with no provision for an additional period of time.
18. **c.** All landowners whose property is adjacent to a body of water have the right to it.
19. **a.** A subdivision can be improved or unimproved land fewer than 36 acres each.
20. **a.** The note is the promise to pay the lender.
21. **a.** A *cloud on the title,* depending on the situation, has the ability to stop a transaction because the seller is unable to cure.
22. **d.** A *pro forma* statement is a projected annual operating statement.
23. **b.** This would be an example of an executory contract because the parties have agreed to all of the terms.
24. **c.** $1 is considered to be valid consideration.
25. **a.** Only the operating expenses are used in the income approach to value. The operating expenses are subtracted from the effective income and divided by an appropriate capitalization rate to determine the appraiser's estimate of value. Debt service is the payment of a mortgage.
26. **d.** You must notify the commissioner within ten days of any name change, address change, or conviction.
27. **b.** You must have written permission to display a sign on a person's land.
28. **d.** $319,000 × .05 = $15,950 (total commission) $15,950 × .5 = $7,975 (which is the 50% that goes to the listing office) The broker principal is entitled to 60% of $7,975 ($7,975 × .6), which equals $4,785.

29. **a.** To obtain your salesperson's license, you must be 18 years old; to obtain your broker's license, you must be 21 years old.

30. **b.** The trustee will send the deed of reconveyance on behalf of the parties to show satisfaction of encumbrance.

31. **d.** This is a lease in which the tenant pays a fixed amount plus a percentage of the gross sales.

32. **d.** Under most consumer protection laws, *caveat emptor* (let the buyer beware) may not apply. Buyers should be strongly encouraged to hire professional inspectors as well as purchase home warranties or residential service contracts.

33. **c.** Unpaid property taxes are a lien the first Monday in January.

34. **d.** Interest-only loans do not have a set amount of principal payment.

35. **c.** The salesperson license is dependent on an active broker's license.

36. **a.** A purchaser must have access to the property he or she is buying.

37. **b.** Six months of property taxes are due every March and October.

38. **b.** FIRREA stands for Financial Institution's Reform, Recovery, and Enforcement Act of 1989, or the "Bail Out Bill," which established new regulations to become an appraiser and develop an appraisal report.

39. **c.** A material defect is a defect that is material information to a buyer in order to make a knowledgeable real estate purchase decision.

40. **d.** The commissioner must terminate his or her license upon being appointed.

41. **d.** Before anyone can depreciate real property for tax reasons, it must be improved.

42. **a.** The $5 has no effect on the answer, each tile is 256 square inches, and the area is 17,280 square inches, so 67.5 tiles are needed.

43. **d.** A listing must have all owners' signatures and beginning and ending dates with no automatic renewal clause.

44. **c.** Because the seller and buyer are related and the price was favorable to the buyer due to the relationship, this transaction is not an arm's-length transaction.

45. **a.** Any change to a contract must be initialed or signed by all principals and may not be forged.

46. **b.** A broker must keep all closed contracts for five years.

47. **d.** Alice's land serves Alex's need to cross the property for access to his property.

48. **d.** The original tenant would now be responsible to rent the property as if he or she were the landlord.

49. **b.** A bill of sale is a legally binding document.

50. **d.** The overall gross rents of a commercial office building would project the value best.

51. **c.** Lease with option to buy is not a mortgage, but it is an agreement between the seller and a potential future purchaser.

52. **b.** The lender can terminate a borrower's interest in a pledged real estate in the event that the borrower defaults on a loan.

53. **c.** A lead-based paint disclosure and the EPA pamphlet, "Protecting Your Family," must be given to tenants of residential properties built prior to 1978.

54. **a.** Sales, income, and cost approaches are required by the U.S. government as a basis for valuation and final methodology.

55. **d.** These are all terms for the mortgage company, which is also the beneficiary.

56. d. Regulation Z requires lenders to provide a truth-in-lending statement.

57. c. Landlords must give tenants two days' notice if they wish to inspect the property.

58. a. The deposit is also known as earnest money to bind an offer to purchase if both parties execute the offer.

59. c. A principal is the individual who has employed the services of a licensee to represent his or her best interests.

60. d. The Federal Fair Housing Act of 1968 prohibits discrimination in residential real estate based on race, color, religion, sex, or national origin.

61. b. The real estate department looks down upon agents overstating their own personal opinions about a home or neighborhood.

62. c. A contract is voidable until a negative action makes it void.

63. c. Taking a protected class to the same area is steering.

64. a. The term *realty* does not apply because it applies to real property and not personal property.

65. c. The client dictates how the appraisal will be delivered. It could be verbal, such as court testimony services, or it may be in writing.

66. a. Disclosure must be given at the first meeting.

67. c. A mortgage broker acts as an intermediary between borrowers and lenders for a fee. He or she does not fund or service loans. Mortgage bankers fund loans in their name and often service the loans after closing.

68. d. There is no set rate that applies for listing your home with a real estate agent.

69. a. There are 12 months in a year, so 240 months would be a 20-year loan.

70. d. The term *equitable title* does not apply because a trustee cannot hold an equitable position on that property.

71. a. The Equal Credit Opportunity Act (ECOA) prohibits discrimination based on race, color, religion, national origin, sex, marital status, or age when granting credit.

72. b. A domestic judgment occurs in the case of *Arizona Court v. an Arizona Citizen.*

73. a. The broker concealed the roof leak with a false statement from the buyer, which would be material information to the buyer's decision. Concealment is known as misrepresentation.

74. d. Interest is paid in arrears. The August payment included the interest for July. A banker's year is 360 days and a calendar year is 365 days (366 in a leap year).
$187,523 \times 6.75\% = \$12,657.80$
interest for a year
$\$12,657.80 \div 360 = \$35.16$ interest per day
$\$35.16 \times 21$ days in August $= \$738.37$
prorated interest due at closing for payoff

75. b. Calculate the annual interest of 8%, and then calculate the monthly interest charge.
$8\% = 0.08$
$\$18,000$ loan $\times 0.08 = \$1,440$ annual interest
$\$1,440 \div 12$ months $= \$120$ interest per month
$\$120 \times 2$ months $= \$240$ interest owed for two months
$\$18,000$ loan to be paid back $+ \$240$ interest $= \$18,240$ total loan payoff

76. b. $93,549. The annual gross income is $25,456 × 12 months, or $305,472. The annual rent of $305,472 − annual operating expense of $211,923 = a net operating income of $93,549.

77. c. The affidavit of property value must be signed by the buyer and the seller and is used for property taxation purposes.

78. b. The tenant has to wait ten days and can deduct from the next month's rent $300 or half a month's rent, whichever is greater.

79. c. A developer must show 100 years of water supply to be deemed an assured water supply.

80. a. When a loan is accelerated, the loan has been called in all due and payable by the lien holder.

81. a. The Telephone Consumer Protections Act (TCPA) states that calls cannot be made before 8:00 A.M. and after 9:00 P.M.

82. b. Following the statutory period of redemption, a sheriff deed is granted back to the lien holder.

83. c. The two loans add up to $262,500, which is 70% of the home's appraised value of $375,000.

84. a. 12 acres × 43,560 square feet in each acre is 522,720 square feet; subtract 22,720 for streets and divide by each lot size. 100' × 100' is 10,000 square feet each for 50 lots.

85. b. The purpose of the closing statement is to show the financial obligations of the parties.

86. a. A licensed salesperson sponsored by a broker is authorized to act on behalf of the broker who is the agent for all clients of the firm. The salesperson may bind the broker to certain specified contracts such as listing agreements and buyer representations.

87. d. 6% = 0.06
$340,000 loan amount × 0.06 interest =
$20,400 interest for one year
$20,400 interest ÷12 months =
$1,700 interest paid in first payment
$2,028 principal and interest payment –
$1,700 interest = $328 principal paid
$340,000 loan – $328 principal paid =
$339,672 loan balance after first payment

88. c. Broker Peter Eklund has violated the fiduciary duty of confidentiality and put his client at a disadvantage in negotiating.

89. c. A special assessment tax for a road is charged by the number of feet fronting the road.

90. b. The principle of highest and best use means that that value of the property will produce the greatest net return over a given period of time.

91. b. If the buyer hires an agent to perform a specific act, the agent hired is a single agent.

92. a. The Equal Credit Opportunity Act is a federal law that prohibits discrimination based on age.

93. c. Five or fewer parcels have no public report, but must have an affidavit of land disclosure with a five-day rescission period.

94. c. The two types of assessments are public and private.

95. b. Paying in arrears means you use first, then pay. In Arizona, property taxes are paid this way, along with most home loans.

96. a. A unilateral contract is unilateral because it is binding by only one party. In this type of listing, the owner can list with multiple agents.

97. d. The maximum fee a developer can charge for a lot reservation while a public report is pending is $5,000.

98. a. The gross multiplier is determined by dividing the average selling price by the annual income; $300,000 ÷ $30,000 = gross multiplier of 10; gross multiplier of 10 × $40,000 = $400,000.

99. a. Implied agency is created when an agent offers assistance to a person based on pertinent information.

100. b. Anyone has five years to file a claim against the recovery fund, as long as the transaction was in Arizona.

101. b. An 80/20 has no mortgage insurance because the first loan does not exceed 80% of the value and the 20% second loan would result in 100% financing or no down payment.

102. d. A deed of trust is a third-party instrument that consists of trustee, trustor, and beneficiary.

103. c. The declaration of homestead must be recorded for public record in order to acquire homestead exemption.

104. a. The acronym *LSR* stands for loan status report, which must be attached with the contract at submission or otherwise noted.

105. c. Dual agency is created when an agent is representing the seller and the buyer. This may be deemed a conflict of interest; therefore, a dual agency disclosure must be signed by the parties.

106. b. Capitalization rate is an analysis of how much investors are willing to spend in a certain neighborhood in return for a certain amount of income.

107. d. Title 32 of the Arizona Revised Statutes is the code regarding real estate.

108. b. An associate broker has nothing extra over a licensee when working under a designated broker.

109. d. Zoning is the term that controls use of land for real property.

110. d. All of these are aspects of the agency relationship.

111. a. Real estate includes land, structures, and appurtenances. Real estate is immobile, but tangible.

112. d. All of the above are members of the nine-person Real Estate Advisory Board. The other members must be two brokers from land development.

113. b. The inherent rights of ownership are known as the bundle of legal rights theory. The rights include the right to use, lease, sell, enter, give it away, or any combination.

114. c. A fully executed contract is a contract signed by the buyer and seller.

115. b. Defeasance clauses are used in a mortgage that states that the lender will return title to the borrower once the debt or loan has been paid in full.

116. b. There is no duty to a seller's agent unless the buyer or buyer's agent has a specific inquiry to either investigate or affirmatively disclose.

117. b. Further disclosure would need to include the loan amount, the cash amount of the down payment, the terms of repayment, and the annual percentage rate.

118. b. All third parties in a real estate transaction are customers.

119. d. In Arizona, the security deposit can exceed one month's rent and does not need to be deposited in an interest-bearing escrow account.

120. c. An ad that looks as if it were from a private party and not from a licensee is called a blind ad.

121. b. In Arizona, a restrictive listing may not be taken by a licensee.

122. b. The recording of the deed gives constructive notice of ownership.

123. a. Real property includes the bundle of rights, which falls under property rights.

124. b. A listing agent represents the seller. Additional disclosures have to be made and agreed to by the principal to change the status of agency relationship.

125. d. None of these describes an exclusive right to sell. It is the most popular type of listing in Arizona. It is when only one broker is employed as an exclusive agent and the employing broker receives a commission no matter who sells the property.

126. c. This is the basis for townships, which are every six miles from the initial point of Arizona, which is the confluence of Gila and Salt rivers.

127. b. Minors are capable of making a voidable contract.

128. c. Useful life is the period of years over which a building can be depreciated.

129. c. Fee simple gives the greatest interest possible and indefinite duration to the owner.

130. c. When three brothers buy together, that is a type of co-ownership; owning property in severalty is when there are two or more owners of the same property.

131. d. The licensee is not required to give the RESPA.

132. a. In 1853, the United States purchased a part of Arizona from Mexico in the Gadsden Purchase.

133. c. The buyer-agent can be paid by the buyer or from the proceeds of the sale.

134. c. A *cloud* means that the title is not clear.

135. a. All cooperative sales fees are paid from the listing broker. He or she collects the listing fee from the seller and pays the selling broker, who disburses fees according to his or her company policy to individual agents.

136. b. Intestate is a person who dies without a will. The court will appoint a personal representative to act as the executor of the estate.

137. c. The Federal Reserve Board's main purpose is to control inflation using supply and demand of money.

138. d. Foreclosure is the procedure in which a property owner loses rights and ownership to his or her property.

139. a. As long as the tenant volunteers more than one-and-a-half month's rent, this is legal in Arizona.

140. d. Residential property is taxed at 10%, commercial is taxed at 25%, and land is taxed at 15%.

▶ Scoring

Evaluate how you did on this practice exam by first finding the number of questions you answered correctly. Only the number of correct answers is important—questions you skipped or got wrong don't count against your score. At the time this book was printed, a passing score for the exam was 75%. On this practice exam, a passing score would be 105 correct.

Use your scores in conjunction with the Learning-Express Test Preparation System in Chapter 2 of this book to help you devise a study plan using the real estate refresher course in Chapter 4, the real estate math review in Chapter 5, and the real estate glossary in Chapter 6. You should plan to spend more time on the sections that correspond to the questions you found most difficult and less time on the lessons that correspond to areas in which you did well.

For now, what is much more important than your overall score is how you performed on each of the areas tested by the exam. You need to diagnose your strengths and weaknesses so that you can concentrate your efforts as you prepare. The different question types are mixed in the practice exam, so in order to diagnose where your strengths and weaknesses lie, you will need to compare your answer sheet with the following table, which shows the categories each question falls into.

Once you have spent some time reviewing, take the second practice exam in Chapter 7 to see how much you have improved.

EXAM 1 FOR REVIEW

Exam 1 Subject Area	Question Numbers (Questions 1–140)
Business Practice and Ethics 63% – 6	25, 38, 44, 58, 60, 61, 63, 65, 67, 68, 71, 74, 81, 92, 131, 135
Agency and Listing 92% – 1	5, 35, 39, 59, 66, 91, 96, 99, 105, 110, 118, 124
Property Characteristics, Descriptions, and Ownership Interests and Restrictions – 2 85%	2, 15, 18, 19, 41, 64, 94, 95, 109, 111, 113, 123, 129
Property Valuation and the Appraisal Process – 1 96%	3, 11, 17, 50, 54, 106, 128
Real Estate Sales Contracts 100%	16, 23, 32, 43, 49, 53, 62, 114, 127
Financing Sources 90% – 1	10, 12, 34, 55, 56, 69, 83, 88, 101, 117
Closing/Settlement and Transferring Title 100%	9, 21, 24, 30, 85, 90, 115, 136
Property Management 100% 0	22, 31, 48, 86
Real Estate Math 83% – 1	7, 28, 42, 76, 84, 98
Arizona Ownership Transfer 78% – 4	6, 36, 47, 70, 72, 77, 79, 82, 89, 93, 97, 102, 103, 122, 126, 130, 132, 134
Arizona Licensing 100% – 0	1, 26, 29, 40, 107, 112
Arizona Activities of Licensees 0 100%	14, 27, 45, 46, 73, 75, 100, 104, 108, 116, 119, 120, 121, 125, 133
Arizona Finance Settlement 100%	4, 8, 13, 20, 33, 37, 51, 52, 80, 137, 138, 140
Arizona Leasing and Property Management 1 75%	57, 78, 87, 139

OVERALL 89%

Real Estate Refresher Course

CHAPTER SUMMARY

If you want to review real estate concepts for your exam, this is the chapter you need. Using this chapter, you can review just what you need to know for the test.

HOW YOU USE this chapter is up to you. You may want to proceed through the entire course in order, or perhaps, after taking the first practice exam, you know that you need to brush up on just one or two areas. In that case, you can concentrate only on those areas. Following are the major sections of the real estate refresher course and the page on which you can begin your review of each one. This list of items covered in the Arizona real estate salesperson's or broker's exam is from the *Candidate Information Bulletin* and can be found online at www.prometric.com.

Business Practice and Ethics

Arizona-Specific Material

▶ Business Practice and Ethics

Professional Ethics

A **REALTOR**® is a member of the National Association of REALTORS®. Only those real estate agents who are members are authorized to use the REALTOR® registered trademark. REALTORS® agree to abide by the Association's Code of Ethics, which is a higher standard than law or rule.

Federal Requirements for Real Estate

Licensing, including real estate licensing, is done by each state. There are no federal real estate licensing requirements. Once licensed, however, licensees must be aware of and adhere to federal laws relating to real estate (i.e., ADA, fair housing, interstate land sales, etc.).

Fair Housing/Consumer Protection

Basic Concepts

Federal and Arizona fair housing laws were enacted to allow all people an equal opportunity to enjoy the benefits of owning real property.

A **protected class** is any group of people designated by the Department of Housing and Urban Development (HUD) in consideration of federal and state civil rights legislation. Protected classes currently include color, race, religion, national origin, gender/sex, handicap/disability, and familial status. Various state and municipal governments may have additional protected classes, but there will never be fewer than the minimum established by the Federal government. Arizona's protected classes match those of the Federal government. It is illegal to discriminate against someone in a protected class, who is perceived to be in a protected class, or because of one's association with a protected class.

Arizona's fair housing laws are substantially the same as Federal laws. Most enforcement efforts are conducted through the Arizona attorney general's office. A **complainant** alleging a violation of fair housing laws may also file a complaint with HUD. After receiving a complaint, **testers** may be sent out to confirm the validity of the complaint. When testers are used, one set of testers will usually be a member of a protected class and another set will not. Care is taken to ensure that the test is legitimate. While this practice may sound like entrapment, it has been deemed a valid method of enforcement. The **respondent** in the complaint is typically a property owner, real estate agent, broker or agency, management company, property manager, or leasing agent.

Federal Civil Rights Act of 1866

The **Civil Rights Act of 1866** prohibits discrimination on the basis of race in the sale, lease, or other transfer of real or personal property. This Act has no exceptions. It applies to individual home sellers as well as to real estate agencies.

Federal Fair Housing Act of 1968 (Title VIII)

The **Federal Fair Housing Act (Title VIII of the Civil Rights Act of 1968)** and all of its subsequent amendments broadened the prohibitions against discrimination in housing to include race, color, religion, national origin, sex/gender, familial status, and handicap/disability in connection with the sale or rental of housing or vacant land offered for residential construction or use. The law specifically prohibits the following discriminatory acts:

- refusing to sell to, rent to, or negotiate with any person who is a member of a protected class, or otherwise making a dwelling unavailable to such a person
- changing terms, conditions, or services based on inclusion in a protected class
- practicing discrimination through any statement or advertisement that restricts the sale or rental of residential property or that would indicate that people of a protected class are not welcome
- representing to any person, as a means of discrimination, that a dwelling is unavailable for sale or rental
- **blockbusting**—making a profit by inducing owners of housing to sell or rent by representing that persons of a protected class are moving into the neighborhood
- **redlining**—discriminating against an entire class of risks instead of evaluating individual risks, commonly seen via altering the terms or conditions of a home loan or availability of insurance in certain geographic areas of a community
- denying persons membership or limiting their participation in any multiple-listing service, real estate brokers' organization, or other facility related to the sale or rental of dwellings
- **steering**—the practice of directing home seekers to or away from particular neighborhoods based on protected class. Steering includes both efforts to exclude minorities from one area of a city and efforts to direct minorities to minority or changing areas.
- attributing an impact on value due to any of the prohibited practices listed above in an appraisal report
- making notations indicating discriminatory preferences
- coercing, intimidating, or interfering with any person in the exercise of his or her rights

Familial status includes prohibiting discriminations against children (those under 18), families with children (whether headed by a parent or guardian), persons who are in the process of obtaining custody of a child, and pregnant women.

The Fair Housing Act Amendment of 1988 prohibits discrimination against a handicapped person, including:

- refusal to make reasonable accommodations in policies
- refusal to permit reasonable modifications of existing premises at the handicapped person's expense

After 1991, all new (or rehab) four-family homes or larger must include adaptive design accommodations related to handicapped accessibility.

The 1968 Fair Housing Act covers only residential property, and, in fact, covers most housing.

In some circumstances, the Act exempts owner-occupied buildings with no more than four units AND that is sold or rented without the use of a broker AND without the use of discriminatory advertising AND sold by someone who is not considered to be a "dealer" in housing. In addition, housing operated by religious organizations and private clubs that limit occupancy to their own members may be exempt when certain conditions apply. When an exemption applies, one may be able to legally discriminate against some protected classes, but never by race.

The Housing for Older Persons Act allows communities that are intended for occupancy by older persons to lawfully discriminate against those in the protected class of familial status, if either all residents of the community are 62 years of age or older or at least 80% of the units are occupied by at least one person who is 55 years of age or older. At one time, the community had to provide significant facilities and services designed for the elderly, but that requirement was eliminated in 1995.

A person found guilty of a fair housing violation may face:

- civil penalties of up to $11,000 for the first offense, up to $27,500 for the second offense within a five-year period, and up to $55,000 for the third offense within seven years from the first offense
- monetary fines for actual and/or punitive damages caused by the discrimination
- an injunction to stop the sale or rental of the property to someone else, making it available to the complainant
- court costs
- criminal penalties against those who coerce, intimidate, threaten, or interfere with a person's buying, renting, or selling of housing
- state penalties including the loss of the real estate license and administrative fines from the Arizona Department of Real Estate

Risk Reduction

The broker is responsible for his or her office and the conduct of each of the agents in his or her office. Brokers can reduce their risk by establishing office policies designed to ensure that each client and customer is treated fairly and equally. Brokers should also ensure that agents periodically receive training about fair housing (and other important topics) on a regular basis.

▶ Agency

Principles of Agency

Law of Agency

An **agent** is a person (or brokerage) who represents the interest of another person or party (called the **principal**) in dealings with third persons. An agent acts as the fiduciary to his or her client.

A Mnemonic Trick

An agent's fiduciary duties to his or her client or principal (remember it as OLD CAR):

- **O**bedience
- **L**oyalty
- **D**isclosure (of material facts concerning the transaction)
- **C**onfidentiality
- **A**ccountability (of funds)
- **R**easonable <u>care</u>

Care
Obedience
Accounting
Loyalty
Disclosure
Confidentiality
OR

COLDAC

In **single agency**, a broker or brokerage is representing either the buyer or the seller. In **dual agency**, one brokerage (through one or more of its agents) is representing both the buyer and the seller in the same transaction. In Arizona, a dual agent is always required to have the prior, informed, written consent of both parties before acting as a dual agent. A dual agent's ability to give both parties all of the fiduciary duties is compromised, and therefore requires their permission before proceeding.

In Arizona, a licensee may establish an agency relationship with one or more parties to the transaction. The various agency relationships include:

- **Seller's agent**—an agent who works for the best interest of the seller (**client**) and owes the seller fiduciary duties. A seller's agent can work with a buyer, but as a **customer** only, not a client. The buyer must understand that the agent owes his or her fiduciary duties to the seller.

- **Buyer's agent**—an agent who works for the best interest of the buyer (**client**) and owes the buyer fiduciary duties. A buyer's agent can work with a seller, but as a **customer** only, not a client. The seller must understand that the agent owes his or her fiduciary duties to the buyer. A common example would be a buyer's agent showing a buyer a home that is being sold "by owner." The buyer's agent represents only the buyer, not the seller.

- **Undisclosed dual agency** is prohibited. Consequently, the written consent must also explain to both parties the limitations on/off the fiduciary duties owed to both parties. For example, normally an agent owes a client the fiduciary duty of full disclosure, but in a dual agency, the agent cannot disclose that the buyer will pay more or that the seller will take less or other information that would be adverse to the other party.

Listing Procedures
Listing Agreements

- An **open listing** is an agreement that a commission will be paid to the listing broker only if he or she is the procuring cause of the sale. A seller may enter into an open listing with an unlimited number of brokers. If the property is sold by another broker or by the sellers themselves, the listing broker is not entitled to a commission.

- An **exclusive agency listing** means that only one listing broker represents the seller. If the property sells through the efforts of the broker or through another broker who is cooperating with the listing broker (i.e., a cooperating broker in a multiple-listing service), the listing broker receives a commission. However, the seller retains the right to sell the property on his or her own without paying a commission.
- an **exclusive right to sell listing** provides the greatest protection to the listing broker, who will be paid a commission no matter who sells the property.
- a **net listing** would be structured so the listing broker takes any part of the purchase price over a predetermined amount. Net listings are not illegal in Arizona, but are risky, and are "discouraged" by the Arizona Department of Real Estate.

Multiple-listing system (MLS) is a system where all members can share information regarding the properties they have for sale. Each member of a particular MLS agrees to "cooperate" with other brokers of that same MLS and to share in the commission when a cooperating broker who is a member of that MLS effects a sale.

Buyer Representation

- an **exclusive buyer agency agreement** (also known as a buyer broker exclusive employment agreement) provides the greatest protection to the buyer's broker, who will be paid a commission no matter who finds a property for the buyer. This agreement is analogous to an exclusive right to sell listing.

There is no buyer/broker agreement analogous to a net listing. However, brokers may legally rebate a portion of their commission to their buyer client.

▶ Property

Characteristics of Property

Real versus Personal Property

Property can be divided into two classes: **real property** and **personal property**.

Real property (also known as **real estate** or **realty**) is land and that which is permanently attached to the land (i.e., buildings, shrubs, trees). **Land** includes the earth's surface, the minerals and water below the surface (**subsurface rights**), and the air space above the surface (**air rights**).

Personal property (also known as **chattel**) is all that is not real property (i.e., movable items not attached to land). Ownership of real property is transferred by a deed, and ownership of personal property is transferred by a **bill of sale**.

There are two types of real property:

- **corporeal**—land and improvements to the land
- **incorporeal**—rights such as the ability to inherit real estate, or the right to use the property of another (an easement)

There are two types of personal property:

- **tangibles** such as a car, refrigerator, or chandelier
- **intangibles** such as a patent or copyright, which are considered intellectual property

Items Affixed to the Property

Fixtures are human-made additions to real property, such as fences, lights, and other improvements. When an item of personal property is permanently attached to real estate, it becomes real property and is identified as a fixture. Fixtures are appurtenant and remain with the property when ownership transfers to a new owner. An exception occurs when a commercial tenant installs a trade fixture to be used in the business for which the space has been leased. In the absence of a contract between the landlord and tenant stating otherwise, **trade fixtures** remain the property of the tenant and may be removed by the tenant at or before the end of the lease. The tenant is obligated to repair any damage caused by the removal of a trade fixture.

The determination of a fixture is made by asking and answering the following questions:

1. How is the item attached?
2. Is the item adaptable to a different property?
3. What was the intent of the parties?
4. Is there a contractual agreement that defines the item as a fixture or as chattel?
5. What was the relationship of the parties?

Growing things can be real property or personal property. Plants and trees that occur naturally or as part of the landscaping are part of the real estate and are considered real property. If the plant or a portion of the plant is severed, it becomes personal property. For example, a pine tree that is growing would be part of the real property, if the pine tree was cut for lumber, it would become personal property. The citrus tree itself is considered real property; the lemons, after being picked, become personal property the moment they are plucked from the tree. **Emblements** are annually cultivated crops and are personal property. The Right of Emblements is the right of a tenant farmer to return after a lease has terminated to harvest a crop grown by the tenant.

Property Rights

The **bundle of rights of ownership** interest in real property includes the **rights of possession, control, enjoyment, encumbrance,** and **disposition** (transfer title to someone else by **sale, gift, will,** or **exchange**).

Ownership and Estates in Land

Estates in real property are **freehold** (an ownership interest in the property) or **non-freehold** (a rental interest in the property).

Types of Freehold Estates

Fee simple is the highest and best form of ownership. Also known as **fee simple absolute**, the owner has all of the rights in the bundle of rights of ownership mentioned previously.

A **fee simple defeasible estate** (sometimes called a defeasible fee) is a qualified estate, which means that ownership may end if a specific event happens or does not happen. There are two types of fee simple defeasible estates: fee simple subject to a condition subsequent and a fee simple subject to a special limitation.

A **fee simple subject to a condition subsequent** restricts use of the property to a specific purpose or forbids a specific use. If the condition occurs, then the former owner has the right to reacquire full ownership, but the right is not automatic; the former owner will need to go to court to reacquire title. A fee simple subject to a condition subsequent also grants to the former owner a **right of reentry**. This right of reversion means that the former owner may be able to go to court in the future and then retake possession of the property. As an example, a deed granting to the new owner (grantee) on the condition that there be no alcohol served upon the premises is a fee simple subject to a condition subsequent. If alcohol is served on the property, the former owner has a right to go to court to reacquire title to the property.

A **fee simple subject with a special limitation**, which is also known as a **fee simple determinable**, also restricts the use of the property to a specific purpose and is tied to duration. In this instance, the duration of ownership can be determined from the deed, and if a prescribed condition does not continue, then the former owner automatically reacquires title to the property, without having to go to court. As in the fee simple subject to a condition subsequent, the right of the former owner to reacquire title is called a **possibility of reverter** and is considered a **future interest**. As an example, a deed granting to the new owner (grantee), "for so long as" (may also provide "while" or "during") the property is used for educational purposes, is a fee simple with a special limitation. If the new owner stops using the property for educational purposes, ownership automatically reverts to the former owner.

A **life estate** lasts only for the lifetime of some person. In a **conventional life estate**, the holder of the estate is called the **life tenant**, and the life tenant owns the property while the life tenant is alive. In a life estate *pur autre vie* (meaning "for the life of another"), the life tenant's ownership of the property is based upon the life of someone other than the life tenant, such as the grantor or a third party. When that person dies, then the life tenant no longer owns the property and ownership either reverts to the **grantor** (known as a reversionary interest) or goes to a third party, called a **remainderman** (known as a remainder interest). Reversionary and remainder interests are also **future interests**, which means that the owner of these interests currently owns no possessory rights to the subject property, but may own a fee simple interest at some time in the future.

The holder of a life estate has all the responsibilities of ownership while the estate is in effect, and may not neglect or destroy (known as waste) the premises unless the vested holder of the life estate grants permission. The vested holder is the party who will own the property after the life estate holder is deceased.

A conventional life estate cannot be inherited by the life tenant's heirs because the life estate terminates upon the life tenant's death. As stated previously, ownership of the property either reverts to the owner or goes to a remainderman. A life estate *pur autre vie*, however, can be inherited if the life tenant dies before the person upon whom the life estate is measured (also known as the measuring life). The life tenant's heirs would inherit only a life estate, which would continue only as long as the measuring life.

Forms of Ownership

There are many different entities that can acquire ownership in real property: an individual, a group of individuals, a corporation, a government entity (at any level of government), and more. In addition, there are many different forms of ownership.

An **estate in severalty** (sole ownership) occurs when property is held by one person or a legal entity. The individual's interest is severed from everyone else's.

Concurrent ownership is ownership by more than one party.

Tenancy in common involves two or more individuals who own an undivided interest in real property without rights of survivorship. Undivided means that each tenant has the right of possession of the entire property.

The degree of interest in the estate can be equal or can vary among the tenants in common. One party can have 40%, another 25%, and another 35%. If a deed conveying property is made out to two people and does not stipulate otherwise, they are presumed to be tenants in common with equal interest. A party can freely dispose of his or her interest by sale, gift, devise, or descent without affecting the rights of the other owners. The new owner will be a **tenant in common** with the other owners.

Joint tenancy also involves two or more natural persons (i.e., not a legal entity) and includes the right of survivorship. Four unities must exist to create a valid joint tenancy:

1. Unity of time—All tenants must acquire their interest at the same moment. This means that no new joint tenants can be added at a later time.
2. Unity of title—There is only one title. All tenants must acquire their interest from the same source—the same deed, will, or other conveyance.
3. Unity of interest—Each tenant has an equal percentage ownership.
4. Unity of possession—Each tenant enjoys the same undivided interest in the whole property and right to occupy the property.

Joint tenancy is not implied and must be created by using specific language in the deed. The absence of any one of these unities at the time of taking title will prevent the grantees from taking title as joint tenants, and if one or more unities changes after taking title, then the joint tenancy for those particular members will be terminated. For example, if after three people take title as joint tenants, one of the owners transfers his or her interest to a fourth person, then the two original joint tenants remain as joint tenants, but the fourth party owns his or her share as tenants in common.

The **right of survivorship** means that a joint tenant cannot will his or her ownership interest, and when a co-owner dies, the surviving co-owners share equally in the deceased owner's interest. The last survivor becomes the sole owner.

Tenancy by the entirety is a form of joint tenancy specifically for married couples. Tenancy by the entirety is *not* legal in Arizona.

Community property is a form of joint ownership in Arizona that is based upon the idea that each spouse has an equal ownership interest in all property acquired during marriage, except for gifts or inheritance. This form of ownership is available only to a husband and wife, and it is a holdover of Spanish law and is found predominantly in the Western states. This form of ownership was unknown under English common law.

Community property with right of survivorship is the same as above, except that upon the death of either spouse, the survivor receives title in severalty (i.e., alone). This form of ownership avoids court probate and has federal income tax benefits (i.e., a step-up in basis on the value of the deceased spouse's interest as of the date of death).

Will or Inheritance

A person who dies with a will is said to have died **testate**, and will have his or her property distributed as specified in the will. A person who has died without a will has died **intestate**. When someone dies intestate, his or her possessions will be distributed based on the state **laws of descent**.

- A transfer of personal property by will is called a **bequest**
- A transfer of money is called a **legacy**
- A transfer of real estate by will is called a **devise**

Escheat is the state's right to claim ownership of real or property when a person dies and leaves no heirs and no will. Ownership of the property reverts to the state. This reversion to the state is called *escheat*, from the Anglo-French word meaning "to fall back," and ties back to the reversion of lands under ancient English feudal law to the King when there were no qualified heirs. **Adverse possession** may be used to acquire title to property against the owner's will. The occupancy must be **open**, **notorious** (not secretive), **continuous** (for a period of ten years), and **without permission**. Adverse possession can be used only against private property owners, not public property. Tacking may allow two people to combine time periods to reach the statutory requirement—a father may occupy for three years, and upon his death, an heir may occupy for seven more years to meet the ten-year requirement.

Eminent domain is the right of the government (federal or state) to take private property for a public purpose, with just compensation. Condemnation is the process used to exercise the government's power of eminent domain. The Arizona Constitution specifies the circumstances in which eminent domain can be exercised. The taking of property without compensation falls under the police power of confiscation.

Government Restrictions

The government may enact laws and enforce them to protect the safety, health, morals, and general welfare of the public. The government's right to control the owner's use of private property is called **police power**. Examples of police power are **zoning laws** and **building codes**.

Zoning ordinances designate which land parcels in a city can be used for specific property uses (i.e., single-family homes, multifamily homes, commercial uses). A **non-conforming use** is a use that was in existence before the current zoning regulation went into effect and that is allowed to remain, but is subject to strict rules regarding future modifications. A **conditional use permit** or **special permit** allows a property use that is not specified for the zoned area, but is nevertheless considered for the public good.

All new construction or modification of existing structures must comply with the **setback** requirements (the minimum distance from property boundaries or other buildings).

A **variance** may be granted for a deviation from a zoning requirement. Normally variances need approval by the local **zoning board**.

Building codes are minimum construction standards for building, framing, plumbing, electrical wiring, and other components.

These municipal regulations restrict the property owner's use of his or her land but do not constitute a taking (see **Eminent Domain**). Consequently, there is no payment to the property owner who suffers a loss of value through the exercise of police power.

Water Rights

Water rights are defined by state law and depend on the water source and use. On a navigable body of water, the property owner's boundary will extend to the water's edge, (average high water line) or the mean vegetation line. On a non-navigable body of water, the property owner's boundary will extend to the center of the body of water.

Littoral rights: Littoral rights refer to real property that borders non-flowing bodies of water, such as lakes, ponds, and oceans.

Riparian rights: Riparian rights refer to real property that borders moving waterways, such as rivers or streams. In Arizona, riparian rights will affect ownership of land, but will not include the right to divert and use the water.

Doctrine of reasonable use: Individual owners of riparian land have the right to reasonable use of the water that does not prevent use by other owners. States following this principle usually assign a higher priority to some uses, such as the domestic use of water on a residential property.

Water permits: These are issued by the state and are used to ration scarce water resources in areas of growing population, particularly in western states.

Use of underground (subterranean) water: This is vital in many states that have insufficient water from surface sources for residential, agricultural, and commercial uses.

Underground streams confined to well-defined channels can be difficult to establish. If the location of an underground stream can be determined by a non-invasive method, the type of distribution applied to surface water will be followed.

Percolating water: This water drains from the surface to underground strata. The states have modified the traditional English rule that there was no limitation on the amount of water a landowner could remove.

Doctrine of correlative rights: This limits the amount of water that can be taken to a proportionate share based on each owner's share of the surface area.

Accretion—the gradual addition of land resulting from the natural deposit of soil by streams, lakes, or rivers.

Avulsion—the sudden loss of land when a stream or other body of water suddenly changes its course, or by a sudden or violent act of nature.

Erosion—the gradual loss of land by wind, water, and other natural processes.

Reliction—the gradual uncovering of land that was once covered by water. When water recedes from its usual watermark, the new land usually belongs to the adjacent landowner.

Alluvion—the soil carried by a moving body of water that is deposited on someone's land.

Accession—acquiring ownership of land due to the deposit of soil by natural forces (wind or water).

Doctrine of prior appropriation: Ownership and use of water in states where water is not abundant may be controlled by the "doctrine of prior appropriation," which is roughly translated to mean "first in time, first in right." Water use under this doctrine is controlled by the state. Property owners that abut or include waterways *are not* entitled to use any of the water unless they apply for and receive a permit from the state. To receive such rights, the property owner must demonstrate to the state that the water will be used for some beneficial use. Priority goes to the permits that were granted first (i.e., first in time, first in right). Arizona follows the doctrine of prior appropriation.

► Property Valuation and the Appraisal Process

Principles of Valuation

Economic Principles

Many principles of value underlie the appraisal process, including the following:

Supply and demand: As the number of properties available for sale goes up relative to the number of potential buyers, prices will fall. As the number of properties declines while the number of potential buyers remains the same or increases, prices will rise.

Change: forces to which all property is subject that can either increase or decrease property values (these forces can be physical, political, economic, or social)

Substitution: the principle that the typical buyer will want to pay no more for a property than would be required to buy another, equivalent property.

Highest and best use: the legally allowed property use that makes maximum physical use of a site and generates the highest income

Conformity: Individual properties in a neighborhood tend to have a higher value when they are of similar architecture, design, age, and size.

Progression: the benefit to a property of being located in an area of more desirable properties; a small, plain house on a street of mansions will benefit from proximity to them.

Regression: the detriment to a property of being located in a neighborhood of less desirable properties; a large, over-improved house on a street of small, plain houses will have a lower value than it would in a neighborhood of comparable houses.

Anticipation (of future betterments): Value is the present worth of the expected future benefits to be derived from owning the property, operating it (if the property has a commercial aspect), and potential gains when it is sold.

Assemblage and plottage: Assemblage is the process of bringing a group of adjoining parcels under the same ownership. When the combining of adjoining parcels results in a value that is higher than merely the sum of the various parcels, then the additional value is referred to as plottage or plottage value. For example, if two lots, each worth $10,000, are combined into one parcel that is worth $25,000 (rather than $20,000—the sum of the value of the two lots), then the additional $5,000 is referred to as plottage value.

Law of decreasing returns: when property improvements no longer bring a corresponding increase in property value.

Law of increasing returns: when property improvements bring a corresponding increase in property value.

Contribution: The value of any component is measured by what it adds to the property as a whole. If an improvement is excessively expensive or excessively large for the surrounding area and land, it is called an **over-improvement.**

Competition: A potential for profit attracts competition to the market. When competition brings more sellers to the market, there is the potential for an oversupply of properties resulting in lower prices. When competition brings more buyers to the market, there is the potential for a shortage of properties resulting in higher prices.

Determining Value

Forces Affecting Value

- **social**—demographic and other trends that affect the demand for property
- **economic adjustments**—employment level, business start-ups, availability of credit, and other factors that influence the level of prosperity of a region
- **political/government regulations**—regulations that affect property use like zoning regulations, building codes, and environmental laws
- **physical**—changes caused by the elements, which can occur gradually or over a brief period of time

Appraisal

Appraisal and Value

An **appraisal** is performed by a licensed or certified appraiser who gives an unbiased estimate of a property's **value** as of a certain time, based on supporting data. The **Uniform Standards of Professional Appraisal Practice (USPAP)** set the minimum requirements for appraisals.

Market value is the most probable price that an informed buyer will be likely to pay and that an informed seller will be likely to accept in an arm's-length transaction, where neither party is acting under duress.

Establish Appraisal Purpose

Although real estate agents focus their attention on when a property owner wishes to sell, there are many other times when an owner wants to know the value of his or her property.

- **condemnation**—when the government takes private property by eminent domain, the owner must be paid fair market value for the property.
- **assessed value**—determination for property tax purposes (the basis for taxation)

- **insurance purposes**—the maximum amount that an insurer would be willing to pay for an insured loss
- **estate settlement**—the value of the sum of a person's estate (real property and personal property) when he or she dies
- **sales value for owner**—the price the property should bring in the open market
- **loan value**—the maximum loan amount that can be secured by the property
- **exchanges**—a transaction in which a property is, for IRS purposes, considered to be traded for another property, rather than sold for money or other consideration

The Appraisal Process

Following are the steps in the appraisal process:

- State the problem (i.e., scope of work)—the nature of the appraisal assignment must be clearly understood. The assignment may be to find a market value of the subject property. If so, that should be stated.
- Determine the kinds and sources of data necessary.
- What are the characteristics of the subject property?
- What economic or other factors will play a role in determining property value?
- What approach(es) will be most appropriate for this appraisal, and what kind of data will be necessary?
- Determine the highest and best use of the site.
- Estimate the value of the site.
- Estimate the property's value by each of the appropriate approaches (market data, cost, and/or income).
- Reconcile the different values reached by the different approaches to estimate the property's most probable market value. This process is called **reconciliation** or **correlation**. Reconciliation is never the result of averaging.
- Report the estimate of value to the client in writing. There are several types of documents that may be prepared.
- The **narrative appraisal report** provides a lengthy discussion of the factors considered in the appraisal and the reasons for the conclusion of value.
- The **form report** is used most often for single-family residential appraisals. A **Uniform Residential Appraisal Report** (**URAR**) is required by various agencies and organizations.

Market Data Approach (Sales Comparison Approach)

If the property being appraised is a residential property, the most important determinant of value is the price that other similar properties have commanded in the open market. In using the market data approach, the appraiser will select **comparable properties (comps)** to compare to the property being appraised (**subject property**). An appraiser would prefer to have at least three comps for a market data appraisal and typically will use sales only within the last six months. The sales price of a comparable is adjusted down to compensate for the market value of a desirable feature that is present in the comp but not the subject property. The sales price of a comp is adjusted up to allow for desirable features that are present in the subject property and not the comp.

Example: The house at 29 Milo Avenue is being appraised. Comparable A sold last month for $350,000. A comparable property has a detached garage and the subject property does not. The estimated value of the garage is $9,600, which is subtracted from the sales price of $350,000 to derive an adjusted sales price for the comp of $340,400. After analyzing the sales prices of three comps this way, and comparing the resulting adjusted figures, the appraiser estimates the value of the subject property at $340,000.

Land, whether or not it has any improvements (buildings), is often valued separately by using the market data approach.

Income Approach

If a property produces income in the form of rent and other **revenues**, its value may be estimated by analyzing the amount and stability of the income it can produce. The income approach is used to value income-producing properties.

The formula for determining value by the income approach is

$$\text{Value} = \text{Net Operating Income} \div \text{Capitalization Rate}$$

Effective gross income is found by totaling income from all sources and subtracting an allowance for vacancy and collection losses.

Net operating income is found by subtracting **maintenance and operating expenses** from effective gross income. For appraisal purposes, operating expenses include variable expenses (such as salaries and utilities), fixed expenses (such as real estate taxes and insurance), and reserves for replacement (such as set-asides for a new roof and furnace) but not the costs of financing, income tax payments, depreciation deductions, and capital improvements.

The **capitalization rate (cap rate)** is the desired return on the investment. The cap rate is found by building its component parts. An investor expects to receive a profit on the capital invested, as well as to have the capital itself returned by the time the investment is unusable.

Example: Mary wants to purchase an apartment building that has a remaining economic life of 40 years. She wants a 10% annual return on her investment, as well as the return of the amount invested. The building's net operating income is $120,000 annually. This means that each year the investment will have to have a cap rate of 10% plus $2\frac{1}{2}$% (100% divided by 40 years), or $12\frac{1}{2}$% . If we divide the net income of $120,000 by the $12\frac{1}{2}$% cap rate, the value of the property to this investor can be estimated at $960,000.

A **gross rent multiplier** (GRM) is a rule of thumb for estimating value of income-producing property based on monthly market rent. To determine the gross rent multiplier, an appraiser will determine the gross monthly rent of recently sold properties and then divide each property's sales price by the gross monthly rent.

Example: Building A produces monthly rent of $4,000 and sold recently for $400,000. Building B produces monthly rent of $3,200 and sold recently for $350,000. The GRM for Building A is $400,000 divided by $4,000 or 100. The GRM for Building B is $350,000 divided by $3,200 or $109.375. After analyzing several more properties, the appraiser concludes that a GRM of 100 is appropriate for the subject property. Applying that multiple to the subject property's monthly rent of $3,700, the appraiser reaches an estimate of value by this method of $370,000.

GRM calculations may also be annualized.

Cost Approach

When the property is not an income-producing property and it is difficult to find comparables, the cost approach to value is often used. This approach is most often used with unique properties and public service buildings (churches, a college campus, or a state capitol building).

The appraiser begins by estimating the replacement cost of the improvements. **Replacement cost** is the cost, at today's prices and using today's methods of construction, for an improvement having the same or equivalent usefulness as the subject property. Or, the appraiser may estimate the **reproduction cost**, the cost of creating an exact replica of the improvements. This would show the value of a new building. Because the subject property is not new, adjustments must be made for depreciation. There are three types of depreciation.

1. **Physical deterioration**—the effect of the elements and ordinary wear-and-tear. Physical deterioration can be curable or incurable.
2. **Functional obsolescence**—features that are no longer considered desirable in design, manner of construction, or layout. A house with four bedrooms and only one bathroom suffers from functional obsolescence. Can be curable or incurable.
3. **Economic obsolescence**—results from factors outside of the property over which the owner has no control, such as economic, locational, or environmental influences. Generally incurable.

The **value of the land** must be considered in determining value by the cost approach. The value of the land is established as though it were vacant, using the market data approach. While land value can decrease, land is not depreciable.

The formula for determining value using the cost approach is as follows:

$$\text{Value} = \text{Replacement or Reproduction Cost} - \text{Accrued Depreciation} + \text{Land Value}$$

Example: An appraiser has determined that the reproduction cost of a building is $500,000. There is $60,000 of accrued depreciation, and the land is valued at $200,000. The market value would be determined by taking $500,000 (the replacement cost) and subtracting $60,000 (the accrued depreciation) and then adding $200,000 (the land value). The appraiser would estimate the value to be $640,000.

Elements of Value

An appraisal will specify the type of value sought. The elements that establish value can be remembered by the acronym **DUST**:

Demand for the type of property

Utility (desirable use) the property offers

Scarcity of properties available

Transferability of property to a new owner (lack of impediments to a sale)

▶ Real Estate Sales Contracts

Purpose, Scope, and Elements of Real Estate Sales Contracts

General

A contract is a legally enforceable agreement between two parties to do something (**performance**) or to refrain from certain acts (**forbearance**).

Real Estate Contracts

A **listing agreement** is an employment agreement between a real estate brokerage and the owner of a property. It is a personal services contract, engaging the services of the broker to effect the sale of a specific property, and spelling out the terms and consideration due. Under the listing agreement, the broker acts as the agent for the seller, who is the principal, and owes fiduciary duties to the seller.

A **buyer-broker agreement** is an employment agreement between a real estate brokerage and a potential buyer of real property. It is also a personal services contract, spelling out the terms and consideration due. Under the buyer-broker agreement, the broker acts as the agent for the buyer, who is the principal, and owes fiduciary duties to the buyer.

Under Article XXVI of the Arizona State Constitution, real estate salespersons and brokers are expressly authorized to draft all documents (or fill in preprinted forms) related to a real estate transaction that they are handling, but must do so without charging any type of fee for drafting or preparing the documents.

"Standardized" forms are available from various sources in Arizona, but Arizona law does not require licensees to use a specific contract or listing form. A real estate agent or broker may draft an offer to purchase for a buyer. The seller may then accept the offer, reject it, or make a counteroffer. If acceptance eventually results, the offer, together with any counteroffers, constitutes the final purchase contract. Either or both parties are free to seek legal counsel regarding a real estate transaction, but the use of attorneys is not required. Most residential transactions in Arizona occur without attorneys involved.

A **lease** is a contract for the rental (possession) of property. The lessor (landlord) permits the lessee (tenant) to use the property for the period and under the terms specified in the lease.

A **deed** conveys title to real property. Deeds must be in writing, executed (signed), and delivered to transfer ownership of property. A deed does not have to be recorded to be valid, but should be recorded to give constructive notice to the world that the grantee (buyer/recipient) is the current owner of the property. A deed must be acknowledged and notarized to be recorded in the county recorder's office.

In some states, lenders use the **deed of trust** (**trust deed**) form of mortgage document whereby the borrower pledges the collateral as security for the loan. The deed of trust is a three-party instrument. The lender is the **beneficiary**, the borrower is the **trustor**, and a third party selected by the lender is the **trustee**. The borrower conveys the **power of sale** to the trustee, and upon any default by the borrower, the trustee will proceed with the foreclosure process.

This three-party system does not require a court action to proceed with foreclosure and is **nonjudicial foreclosure**. In this case, state law applies and there will be specific notice and procedural requirements. When the property is sold, a **trustee's deed** is used to convey title to the new owner.

If the proceeds of the foreclosure sale of either the mortgage or the deed of trust do not cover the amount owed on the loan, some states allow the lender to obtain a **deficiency judgment** against the borrower. This means that other assets can be claimed by the lender to satisfy the remaining indebtedness. Other states provide homeowners with anti-deficiency protection in the event that the proceeds of the sale on loan default do not cover the amount owed.

Real estate can be pledged as collateral for a loan using any of the following four methods.

1. The **standard**, or **regular mortgage**, is the most common. The borrower conveys title to the lender as security for the debt. The mortgage contains a statement that the mortgage will become void if the debt is paid in full and on time.
2. An **equitable mortgage** is a written agreement that does not follow the form of a regular mortgage, but is still considered by the courts to be one. An equitable mortgage, or **equitable lien** can arise in a number of ways. For example, a prospective buyer may give the seller a money deposit along with an offer to purchase property. If the seller refuses the offer and also refuses to return the deposit, the court will hold that the purchaser has an equitable mortgage in the amount of the deposit against the seller's property.
3. In some cases, the borrower may convey the deed to the pledged property to the lender as a **deed as security** for a loan. If the loan is repaid in full and on time, the borrower can force the lender to convey the real property back to him or her. Like the equitable mortgage, a deed used as security is treated according to its intent, not its label.
4. A **deed of trust** is a three-party agreement including a beneficiary (lender), a trustor (borrower), and a trustee (neutral third party). The key aspect of this method is that the borrower executes a deed to the trustee rather than to the lender. If the borrower pays the debt in full and on time, the trustee delivers a **release of liability** or **deed of reconveyance** to the borrower.

A promissory note is a promise to repay a loan. This document is signed by the borrower and equates to an IOU. The promissory note is evidence of the debt. A **mortgage** is a document where the borrower (mortgagor) pledges property to secure the repayment of a debt (collateral). If the debt is not repaid as agreed between the lender and borrower, the lender can force the sale of the pledged property and apply the proceeds to repayment of the debt. The mortgage is the security for the debt.

A **bilateral contract** is one in which both parties exchange promises to do or refrain from doing something which is legal, for consideration. A real estate purchase contract is bilateral because both sides have an obligation to perform—the turning over of title to the property in exchange for money or other consideration.

A **unilateral contract** is one in which one party is bound to perform. One party makes a promise and the other party does not promise, but can make the contract a binding agreement by taking some action.

A contract is **executory** when it has not yet been fully performed. Examples of executory contracts include (1) a lease during the term of the lease, and (2) a real estate purchase contract while it is in escrow (i.e., after it has been signed by all parties, but title has not yet been transferred).

A contract is **executed** when all contract terms have been met and the transaction is completed. Informal reference to an executed contract may also merely mean that the contract has been signed (i.e., "the seller has executed the contract").

Essential Elements of Contracts

A contract is a legally enforceable agreement between two parties to do something (performance) or to refrain from certain acts. A contract must:

- have an **offer** and **acceptance** (mutual assent)
- include **consideration** (does not need to be money)
- have a **lawful objective**
- involve **legally competent parties**
- be in writing and signed as required by the **Statute of Frauds** (one notable exception is a lease for one year or less)
- have a **legal description**, identifying the property to be conveyed

If a notary witnesses the parties' signatures, the notary certifies only that the persons signing have presented evidence of their identity and have signed the document in front of the notary public.

Offers and Counteroffers

The real estate sales contract begins as a written **offer** from buyer to seller and will typically include:

- identity of all parties to the transaction
- full legal description of the real estate, as well as a listing of any personal property to be included
- sales price, including the amount of down payment and an indication of how the remainder of the price will be paid at closing
- financing contingency giving details of the type of financing the buyer hopes to obtain and stipulating a deadline for release of the contingency

- statement that the transaction is contingent on a sale of other property of the buyer. (The seller will want a deadline for release of the contingency, particularly if a noncontingent offer is made while the transaction is pending.)
- name of the escrow agent for the transaction and by whom the fee for this service will be paid
- list of property inspections to be made and by whom, including deadlines for the inspections as well as the appropriate notifications to buyer and/or seller (The seller will want a limit on expenditures for any pest control treatment of necessary repairs.)
- list of applicable categories of disclosure required by state and federal law, which may include location in a flood, earthquake, or other zone, and the presence of hazardous materials, such as lead-based paint
- provision for arbitration or mediation of disputes that may arise between the parties
- remedies, including suit for specific performance, money damages, or acceptance of liquidated damages, in the event one of the parties breaches the agreement
- statement of compliance with the federal **Foreign Investment in Real Property Tax Act** (**FIRPTA**)
- state of compliance with all applicable Fair Housing Laws
- statement of compliance with any other state or federal law not already mentioned
- provision for a final walk-through by the buyer to ensure that the property has been adequately maintained before closing
- statement of who will bear the risk of loss in the event of property damage or destruction between the time the contract is signed and the transaction is closed
- statement of the agency representation and commission owed
- signature of the buyer(s) and space for signature of the seller(s)

An offer will **expire** (end) if it is not accepted by the deadline specified in its terms. If no deadline is specified, a reasonable time period will be implied. An offer can be withdrawn at any time prior to the offeror being notified of its **acceptance**.

Any change to the terms of an offer is a **counteroffer** and has the effect of rejecting the initial offer and making a new offer. The offer and acceptance must both be made voluntarily (without coercion) and without misrepresentation.

Termination of an Offer
The offer to purchase can be terminated by one of the following:

- death of either party
- expiration of the time frame listed in the offer
- revocation by the offeror before receiving notice of acceptance by offeree
- bankruptcy of either party
- condemnation or destruction of the property
- outright rejection of the offer or a counteroffer by the offeree (a counteroffer constitutes a rejection of the previous offer)

Valid/Void/Voidable Contracts

A contract can be construed by the courts to be valid, void, voidable, or unenforceable.

A **valid** contract meets all the requirements of law. It is binding upon its parties and legally enforceable in a court of law.

A **void** contract has no legal effect and, in fact, is not a contract at all. Even though the parties may have intended to enter into a contract, no legal rights are created and no party is bound. The word *void* means "the absence of something." An example of a void contract is a contract to commit a crime.

A **voidable** contract is cancellable (rescindable) by one party but not the other, but some action must be taken to void it. For example, when one party is guilty of fraud, the other party may void the contract. But if the offended party wishes to fulfill the contract, then the party who committed fraud is still bound to the terms of the contract. A contract with a minor is voidable at the option of the minor party.

Purchase and Sale Agreement

The purchase and sale agreement includes the following:

- **names** of all parties to the transaction
- **description of the land**
- **sales price** (consideration)
- amount of buyer's earnest money **deposit**, which will be held in an escrow account or in a broker's trust account (Although not legally required, inasmuch as earnest money is intended to show the buyer's good faith to consummate the transaction, the absence of any earnest money is likely to result in rejection of the offer or a counteroffer.)
- **date** of the contract
- **signatures** of the buyer(s) and seller(s)
- other material terms of the transaction (i.e., close of escrow, financing, contingencies, etc.)

The Arizona **Statute of Frauds** requires that an agreement for the sale of real property be in writing to be enforceable. Most contracts dealing with real estate must be in writing. An exception is a lease of one year or less, or leases that cannot be performed within one year of entering into them. Even then, it is in the best interests of both landlord and tenant to have a written agreement.

Once a contract to purchase has been signed by both parties, the buyer has **equitable title** in the property. Equitable title means that the buyer has a legal interest in the real property and the right to obtain legal title in the future, but that the seller still holds legal title. **Legal title** is title that is fully vested in the owner as evidenced by a deed, will, or court document. Legal title to land and its appurtenances could encompass no more than the entire bundle of rights that an owner possesses.

Most real estate contracts allow the buyer the **right to assign** the contract to another party, but that right can be restricted or prohibited altogether by language in the agreement. If the contract is assigned, the original buyer is not relieved of his or her obligations if the assignee does not fulfill the responsibilities under the contract.

Breach of Contract

When one party fails to perform as required by the contract, a breach of contract (default) has occurred. The wronged or innocent party has the following possible remedies:

- Sue for **money damages.** Money damages are damages that can be quantified in dollars. For example, if a seller cannot perform, but the buyer has already spent a large amount of money on inspections, appraisals, and so on, the buyer could sue to recover the money spent.
- Sue for **specific performance**. Specific performance means forcing the defaulting party to fulfill the terms of the contract. In the case of a defaulting seller, the buyer can sue for specific performance to force the seller to sell the subject property to the buyer.
- Accept liquidated money damages. This remedy means damages have been predetermined or preagreed upon. The language in the purchase contract may say that if the buyer defaults, the seller will receive the buyer's earnest money as liquidated damages.
- Mutually **rescind** the contract. Mutual cancellations would require agreement of both parties and could not be done solely by the wronged party. Sometimes both parties are better off just walking away from the contract and canceling the agreement.

▶ Financing

Essentials of Financing

Financing requires an understanding of the qualification process, types of financing available, the process of foreclosure and its affect upon credit, alternatives to foreclosure, and pertinent laws and regulations affecting the lending industry.

Financing/Mortgages

Real Estate Cycle

Although there are many steps to the real estate cycle, typically they include:

1. Listing the real property
2. Qualifying the buyer
3. Showing the buyer properties
4. Contracts between the buyer and seller
5. Financing—most offers have a financing contingency (i.e., contingent upon the buyer qualifying for and receiving financing)
6. Close of escrow (sometimes referred to as "passing papers" or "settlement" in some parts of the country)

Financing Procedure

The first step to obtaining financing is submitting a **loan application**.

Bank approval steps: The lender wants to make sure that the borrower is a good credit risk. To ensure this, lenders look at several items:

- the property—the bank will send an appraiser to evaluate the property and ensure that the sales price is in line with other comparable properties that have recently sold nearby
- the borrower's ability to pay
- a check of the borrower's credit

Many real estate contracts that contemplate new financing include a **financing clause**. The financing clause or contingency clause makes the purchase contract expressly contingent upon the buyer receiving approval for the new loan. If the buyer cannot qualify, the buyer receives his or her earnest money back and the transaction is canceled. If the buyer can qualify, the transaction closes, unless some other contingency is not satisfied or one or more parties commits a breach.

Types of Lending Institutions

There are many sources of financing available to the buyer of real property. The borrower's funds may come from a **savings and loan association**, a **commercial bank**, a **mutual savings bank** (owned by its depositors), a **cooperative bank**, a **credit union**, a **mortgage company** (which is different from a mortgage broker who does not actually loan money but brings borrowers and lenders together), a **life insurance company**, or a **private lender**.

Money as a Commodity

The **discount rate** is the interest rate the Federal Reserve Bank charges when it makes a loan to another financial institution. The **prime rate** is the interest rate charged by banks to their preferred borrowers. Many home equity loans are based on the prime rate published by the Federal Reserve Bank. **Interest rates** are market-driven for long-term loans and do not necessarily rise or fall with changes in either the short-term discount rate or prime rate.

Some loans include **origination fees** and/or **discount points**. Each point is calculated as 1% of the amount borrowed, so one point on a $100,000 loan would be $1,000. **Origination fees** are costs of the loan and are the usual way for mortgage brokers to be paid. When borrowers pay **discount points**, they are prepaying the lending institution money at the beginning of the loan to receive a lower interest rate over the life of the loan. This can also be called a **buydown** because the borrower is "buying down" the interest rate of the loan.

Lender Qualification Process

Each lender has its own qualification process. Generally, a lender will apply two or more ratios to the borrower's income to determine if the borrower can afford the proposed payment. The first ratio normally relates to the maximum amount of house payment and the second ratio normally relates to the house payment plus other monthly expenses. For example, if a lender applies ratios of 28% and 35% and the borrower has income of $10,000 per month, then the first ratio of 28% means that the borrower's house payment (including principal and interest and reserve account payments for property taxes and property insurance) could not exceed $2,800 and the second ratio of 35% would mean that the borrower's house payment and other monthly expenses could not exceed $3,500.

Naturally, these are guidelines, and the ratios may vary from lender to lender, and other factors will also be important (i.e., credit, length of employment, etc.).

Types of Financing

Financing is available from a myriad of sources. For the typical home buyer, loans are available from lenders that are backed by government sources (i.e., VA-guaranteed loans, FHA-insured loans, etc.) or may come from commercial lending establishments (i.e., a conventional loan from bank, a savings and loan, etc.). Types of financing will be discussed further later.

Foreclosure and Alternatives

A loan on real estate is typically secured by a mortgage or deed of trust. A mortgage must be foreclosed judicially (i.e., by filing a lawsuit in a court of law). Assuming the plaintiff prevails, the court will order that the property be sold. The sheriff will conduct a sheriff's sale, which is conducted as an auction—the highest bidder receives a Certificate of Purchase. Before the sheriff's sale, the borrower/former owner has an **Equitable Right of Redemption**, which merely means that anytime before the sheriff's sale, the borrower may pay the full amount that is due, plus all of the costs that have been incurred in the foreclosure process. After the sheriff's sale, the borrower/former owner, has a **Statutory Right of Redemption**, which, as the name suggests, is granted by Arizona Statute. The Statutory Right of Redemption is six months, unless the borrower has abandoned the subject property, in which case the redemption period is 30 days. Anytime during the redemption period, the borrower/former owner may pay the amount paid by the highest bidder and the costs of the sheriff's sale and redeem the property (i.e., retain title to the property). If the borrower/former owner does not redeem the property (either before or after the sale), then the highest bidder at the sheriff's sale, who originally only received a Certificate of Purchase, will receive a Sheriff's Deed to the subject property. It will then be up to the new owner to begin legal proceedings to remove the former owner (via eviction proceedings) from the subject property, unless the former owner has already vacated the property. If the subject property sells for less than the amount that is owed on the lien being foreclosed, then the lender may return to court and obtain a **deficiency judgment**. For example, if the first lien on a property were $100,000 and the property sold for $80,000 at the foreclosure sale brought by the first lienholder, then the lienholder may be able to obtain a deficiency judgment against the borrower for $20,000. A deficiency judgment is a **general lien**, which means that it is a lien upon all real property (if the judgment is recorded) and personal property of the borrower.

Arizona has anti-deficiency statutes that limit a lender's ability to obtain a deficiency judgment on certain property. If the foreclosed property is (1) a one- or two-family residence, (2) the residence of the borrower, (3) on 2.5 acres of land or less, and (4) the loan being foreclosed is **purchase money**, which means that it was a loan obtained for the purpose of purchasing the loan, but also applies when a purchase money loan has subsequently been refinanced. Under these conditions, the lender cannot obtain a deficiency judgment and must look exclusively to the subject property to recover its losses. The Arizona anti-deficiency statutes apply to mortgages and to deeds of trust.

A deed of trust may be foreclosed nonjudicially via a trustee's sale, which means that it may be foreclosed without going to court. A trustee's sale is faster and easier than a judicial foreclosure and, therefore, much preferred by lenders in Arizona. Upon default by the borrower, which may be a monetary default (i.e., failure to pay the monthly payment) or a nonmonetary default (i.e., failure to insure the property), the lender may send instructions to the trustee to commence a trustee's sale. The trustee then sends the borrower a Notice of Default and Intent to Sell via certified mail, must post a copy of the notice on the subject property, publish the notice in a local newspaper, and record the notice with the county recorder. Ninety days or more after the foregoing, the trustee may conduct a trustee's sale, which is conducted as an action and the property is sold to the highest bidder. Unlike a mortgage and sheriff's sale, the highest bidder receives a Trustee's Deed at the trustee's sale and there is no statutory right of redemption. The borrower may reinstate the loan anytime BEFORE the trustee's sale by paying the past due payments, late fees, and costs of initiating the trustee's sale. (Note: The lender cannot accelerate the balance due on the promissory note; to reinstate the loan, the borrower need only make up the past due payments and other charges incurred.) After the trustee's sale, it is up to the highest bidder to remove the borrower/former owner from the subject property via eviction proceedings.

An agreement for sale (also called land contract, contract for deed, etc.) is foreclosed nonjudicially in Arizona by following the forfeiture statutes. The seller, called the **vendor**, must send a notice to the buyer, called the **vendee**, via certified mail and record the notice with the county recorder. The seller/vendor must wait a specific amount of time, however, before sending/recording the notice. The amount of time the seller/vendor must wait is prescribed by statute. If the buyer/vendee has paid less than 20% of the purchase price, then the seller must wait at least 30 days; if the buyer/vendee has paid more than 20% but less than 30% of the purchase price, then the seller must wait at least 60 days; if the buyer/vendee has paid more than 30% but less than 50%, then the seller must wait 120 days; if the buyer/vendee has paid more than 50%, then the seller must wait nine months. After the notice is served and recorded, the buyer/vendee may still reinstate the loan by paying the amounts stated in the notice, which are limited to the past due payments, late fees, and costs incurred to commence forfeiture proceedings. (Note: The seller cannot accelerate the balance due on the promissory note, unless the seller wishes to foreclose the Agreement for Sale as a mortgage, in which case, the seller must then file a judicial foreclosure and follow the mortgage foreclosure statutes.) If the buyer/vendee does not reinstate the loan, then the seller/vendor records a Notice of Completion of Forfeiture and the buyer/vendee's interest in the property is forfeited. The seller must then remove the buyer/vendee from the subject property via eviction proceedings.

An alternative to any of the foregoing foreclosures is a deed-in-lieu of foreclosure, wherein the borrower voluntarily executes a deed or other document to the lender and relinquishes all interest in the subject property. When a lender accepts a deed-in-lieu of foreclosure, the lender takes the property subject to any/all junior liens (if any). Consequently, a lender is not obligated to accept a deed-in-lieu of foreclosure.

Pertinent Laws and Regulations

Real Estate Settlement and Procedures Act (RESPA)

The **Real Estate Settlement Procedures Act (RESPA)**, enacted by Congress in 1974, is the federal law that requires disclosures by lenders, mortgage brokers, and closing agents in federally related transactions involving the sale or transfer of a dwelling of one to four units. Seller financing, also known as purchase money mortgages and construction loans, are not subject to RESPA requirements. The law requires:

- The lender or mortgage broker must provide the borrower with a copy of the special information booklet prepared by HUD within three business days of the loan application.
- The lender or mortgage broker must provide the borrower with a **good-faith estimate of closing costs**.
- A **Uniform Settlement Statement** (form **HUD-1**) must be made available to the borrower and seller at least one day prior to closing. The borrower and the seller will receive a copy of the form after the closing is completed.
- Fees, kickbacks, or other such payments to persons who do not actually provide settlement services are strictly prohibited.
- Any affiliated business arrangement with an individual or entity offering settlement *Truth-in-Lending (Regulation Z)*.

The **Truth-in-Lending Act (TILA)**, enacted by Congress in 1968, is part of the Consumer Protection Act. TILA is commonly referred to as **Regulation Z**. The law applies to creditors (lenders) involved in at least one of the following:

- more than 25 consumer credit transactions per year
- more than five transactions per year with a dwelling used as security
- the credit is offered to consumers
- the credit is offered on a regular basis
- the credit is subject to a finance charge
- the arrangement requires more than four installments
- the credit is primarily for personal, family, or household purposes

If credit is extended to a business, or for a commercial or an agricultural purpose, Regulation Z does not apply. The required Truth-in-Lending disclosures must be made in a **disclosure statement** that highlights certain information by using a box, boldface type, a different type style, or a different background color. The disclosure statement must be presented to the borrower within **three business days** of making the loan application; the day the application is completed by the borrower is not counted.

The act requires certain disclosures in advertising anything that involves financing. If an advertisement contains any one of the TILA list of financing terms (called **trigger terms**), the ad must also include five disclosures. The following are some of the trigger terms.

- amount of down payment in dollars or percentage
- amount of any additional payments
- number of payments
- period of payments
- dollar amount of any finance charge
- statement that there is no interest charged

If the ad contains any one of these trigger terms, the ad must also include all of these disclosures:

- cash price or the amount of the loan
- amount of down payment or a statement that none is required
- number, amount, and frequency of repayments
- annual percentage rate (APR)
- deferred payment price or total of all payments

When a consumer is refinancing a loan that qualifies under the Truth-in-Lending Act, which is enforced through Regulation Z as a consumer credit transaction, the borrower has three business days to **rescind** (or cancel) the mortgage (**right of rescission**).

Advertisements for consumer loans covered under Regulation Z must give the APR and provide other payment terms and conditions if specific credit terms are used. Remember, this is a disclosure law, so consumers have a summary of the financial offer and can compare products available from other providers in the marketplace.

▶ Property Management

Leases

Freehold versus Non-Freehold

Estates in real property are **freehold** (an ownership interest in the property) or **non-freehold** (a rental interest in the property).

Types of Tenancy

TYPE	CHARACTERISTIC	EXAMPLE
Estate/Tenancy for Years	a lease with a definite start date and a definite end date	residential apartment lease from January 1 to June 30 (although less than a year, it has a definite start and end date)
Tenancy for Period to Period	a lease with an automatic renewal option	90-day house lease that will renew for another 90 days unless proper notice is given by either party
Tenancy at Will	a lease without a termination date. It terminates when proper notice is given by either party.	a residential apartment lease that continues indefinitely until either party gives notice (normally 30 days)
Tenancy at Sufferance	also called holdover tenant. The tenant remains in possession of the property after the termination of a lease. If the lessor accepts rent from the holdover tenant, a tenancy at will is created; otherwise, the tenant at sufferance may be evicted.	a residential apartment lease has ended, but the tenant has not vacated the property

A **non-freehold** estate gives the holder of the estate a right to occupy the property for a time, after which the property will revert to the fee simple holder. The **lessor** permits the **lessee** to use the property for the period and under the **terms** specified in the **lease**.

Common Leases

Leases for more than one year or that cannot be fully performed within one year must be written and signed by the landlord and the tenant, but need not be recorded to be enforceable. An individual who wishes to notify the public of a leasehold interest may record the lease or a memorandum of lease, which is a summary of the important terms of the lease (term, dates, rental amount, options, etc.).

A lease must include a sufficient property description. A legal description, as used in a deed, is acceptable, but most residential leases include merely a street address and apartment number and are legally sufficient.

There are several kinds of leases.

- A **gross lease** specifies that the landlord pays all expenses: property taxes, insurance, maintenance. This kind of lease is often used for apartments and other residential properties.

- A **net lease** specifies that the tenant pay a base amount of rent and certain expenses. The most common arrangement requires the tenant to pay property taxes, insurance, and maintenance. This is called a net, net, net or triple net lease.
- A **percentage lease** requires the tenant to pay a percentage of gross sales as rent in addition to a base rental amount specified in the lease. Percentage leases are often used in shopping centers.
- A **graduated lease** calls for periodic, stated changes in rent during the term of the lease.
- A **ninety-nine year lease** is a long-term land lease typically used for commercial development when the lessee prefers to spend money on capital improvements or the owner does not want to sell (often used by fast-food restaurants).

When a lease is **assigned**, the original lessee transfers the remaining interest in a lease to a new party. With a **sublet**, only a portion of the lease is transferred. In both instances, the original lessee remains responsible. With a **novation**, a new lease is substituted for the original lease, removing responsibility from the original lessee. Some leases expressly prohibit the lessee's interest to be transferred.

When a property sells and there are existing leases, the leases are **binding** on the new owner, unless the lease includes a provision that expressly permits one or both parties to terminate the lease if the subject property is sold.

Obligations of Parties

The lessor (property owner or landlord) of a residential property is normally obligated to provide:

- **utility services** (although the lessee may be required to pay for these services under the terms of the lease)
- a property that is **fit for habitation**
- a property that is free of sanitary and building code violations

The lessor of residential property will not be allowed to interfere with the tenant's **quiet enjoyment** of the leased property. This means that the lessor must recognize the tenant's right of possession of the property.

If the unit becomes unfit for habitation or the lessor interferes with the tenant's quiet enjoyment of the property, the lessee may, after giving the landlord notice and a reasonable time to cure the default, vacate the apartment because the landlord's failure to act constitutes a **constructive eviction**. Alternatively, if the noncompliance is something that may be easily remedied, the tenant may elect to hire a licensed contractor to perform the work and deduct the amount of the repair from the next month's rent up to the greater of one-half month's rent or $300. The tenant must also provide the landlord with a lien waiver from the contractor who performed the work.

The lessee is obligated to not commit or allow **waste**, which means that he or she will use the property in the proper manner. The lessee is also obligated to:

- keep the leased property clean and dispose of trash in a sanitary manner
- use fixtures and appliances in a safe and sanitary manner, and in the rooms designated for their use
- not damage, deface, or otherwise destroy the property, or permit anyone else to do so

In Arizona, if a lessor takes a **security deposit**, the total of **all** refundable deposits cannot exceed more than one and one-half month's rent. For example, if rent is $1,000, the landlord cannot lawfully collect more than $1,500 in total refundable deposits (i.e., security deposit, cleaning deposit, key deposit, etc.), but "deposits" do not include reasonable charges or fees for cleaning or redecorating or other fees, charges, or any other **nonrefundable** amounts. In the foregoing example, the landlord could also collect a $200 cleaning fee and a $100 redecorating fee (provided these amounts are reasonable), but could not also collect a $1 key deposit because the total deposits held would then equal $1,501, which would exceed the statutory limitation.

In Arizona, the landlord is not required to hold deposits in a separate account. The landlord is not required to pay the tenant interest on deposits held and, in fact, the landlord is entitled to retain any interest that is earned on deposits.

If the tenant fails to pay rent, the landlord must issue a Five-Day Notice to Pay or Quit. If the tenant fails to vacate or pay the rent within the five days, the landlord may go to court and file a Special Detainer Action. (Note: An Arizona residential landlord cannot simply lock the tenant out of the property.) A Special Detainer Action is an actual eviction—a legal proceeding that seeks to recover possession of the property. A hearing is conducted by a court. If the court finds that the tenant has failed to comply with the rental agreement (i.e., failed to pay rent or committed some other nonmonetary default), then the court may enter judgment in favor of the landlord and award the landlord possession of the rental unit, any amounts that are currently due, attorney's fees, and costs. The landlord must wait an additional five days; if the tenant has not vacated within the five days after entry of judgment, the landlord may ask the court to issue a Writ of Restitution. The Writ of Restitution is served by the sheriff or constable upon the tenant and the tenant is physically removed from the rental unit; the landlord may then enter the rental unit and change the locks. Any of the tenant's personal property remaining in the rental unit must be moved and stored by the landlord, unless (1) the value of the personal property is less than the cost to move and sell the personal property and (2) the written rental agreement includes a provision that allows disposal of personal property without conducting a sale. Otherwise, the landlord must then conduct a public auction and sell the personal property. Any time before the auction, the tenant may recover possession of the personal property by paying the moving and storage costs, but is not obligated to pay rent, late fees, or other amounts that may be due to the landlord. After the sale, the landlord may apply to sale proceeds to any amounts owed to the landlord, including moving and storage of the personal property, past due rent, late charges, etc. **Distraint** for rent is the seizure of the tenant's personal property to satisfy amounts owed to the landlord. Distraint for rent is illegal in Arizona for residential landlords, but it is still legal and, indeed, commonly done by commercial landlords.

Options

An **option** is a unilateral contract. This means that it is binding upon only one party—the giver of the option, the optionor. The holder of the option, the optionee, has the right, but not the obligation, to exercise the option. An option to purchase enables a purchaser to purchase a property at a set price and upon specified terms within a given time frame. An option may also be used with a lease. An option obligates the seller to sell, but does not obligate the buyer to buy. To create a valid option, the property owner must receive consideration (i.e., money or some other legally recognized consideration), and the option must be in writing. Options may be **assigned** without the consent of the optionor unless transfer is expressly restricted (i.e., in the option).

A **right of first refusal** gives one party the first right to purchase a property or the right to match any other offer made on the subject property.

Property Manager and Owner Relationships

Property Management

The range of services that the property manager can perform for the landlord (property owner) includes marketing, leasing, maintenance, bill payment, preparing reports on monthly income, operating expenses, and rent collection.

A person or company managing real property for another must have a real estate license, except for an on-site manager who manages a single property. For example, an on-site manager for a 1,000 unit apartment building that is constructed on a single lot is not required to have a real estate license, but a person who manages two separate single-family homes is required to have an Arizona salesperson's or broker's license.

A property manager (person or firm) is required to have a written property management agreement with the owner. The written property management agreement must include start and end dates, be signed by the owner and broker, state the compensation to be paid to the broker, state terms and conditions of the broker's services, specify the type and frequency of the broker's reports to owner, state the broker's obligations to owner, contain a mutually acceptable cancellation clause, state amount and purpose of any funds held by broker for owner's benefit, and state whether trust account earns interest and who receives interest. In addition, the property management agreement may include an automatic renewal clause, if the broker sends notice at least 30 days prior to expiration, and a liquidated damages provision. Upon termination of the property management agreement, the broker must provide owner with copies of all rental agreements and related documents: Within five days, a list of tenant deposits; within 35 days, return all money in accounts to owner; within 75 days, final bank reconciliation and list of accounts payable/receivable. Financial records must be kept for three years.

Trust Accounts

A broker may maintain one or more trust accounts, including a property management trust account. The broker and any of the broker's licensees may be a signer on the trust account, but the broker remains responsible for all trust account funds. All funds received from others that belong to the broker's clients (relating to property management) must be deposited into the property management trust account. As with other trust accounts, the broker must ensure that the broker's personal funds are not commingled with client funds, except for up to $500, which may be kept in the account to keep the account open and to cover charges for the account. The trust account must be reconciled monthly and a separate client ledger kept for each client, showing all of the deposits and withdrawals for each client.

▶ Arizona Specific Material

The remainder of this chapter covers Arizona-specific practices and principles, which will help you prepare for the exam and your career as an Arizona salesperson.

▶ Ownership/Transfer

Legal Descriptions

Arizona Fair Housing Statutes

Arizona has a statute directed specifically to real estate professionals (including real estate brokers, appraisers, and lenders) and prohibits discrimination in a "real estate transaction" on the basis of race, color, religion, sex, disability, familial status, or national origin. A "real estate transaction" is defined rather broadly and includes the sale, purchase, construction, repair, improvement, or appraising of real estate.

A separate Arizona law prohibits discrimination by anyone in the sale or rental of real property on the basis of race, color, religion, sex, disability, familial status, or national origin. This statute, however, provides some limited exemptions (the exemptions do not apply to real estate licensees); the prohibition against discrimination does not apply to:

1. The sale or rental of a single-family house sold or rented by an owner if:
   a. The owner does not:
      (i) Own more than three single-family houses at any one time.
      (ii) Own any interest in, nor is there owned or reserved on his or her behalf, under any express or voluntary agreement, title to or any right to any part of the proceeds from the sale or rental of more than three single-family houses at any one time.
   b. The house was sold or rented without either:
      (i) The use of the sales or rental facilities or services of a real estate broker, agent, or salesperson licensed under title 32, chapter 20 or the use of an employee or agent of a licensed broker, agent, or salesperson or the facilities or services of the owner of a dwelling designed or intended for occupancy by five or more families.
      (ii) The publication, posting, or mailing of a notice, statement, or advertisement prohibited by § 41-1491.15.
2. The sale or rental of rooms or units in a dwelling containing living quarters occupied or intended to be occupied by no more than four families living independently of each other if the owner maintains and occupies one of the living quarters as the owner's residence.

A person who believes he or she has been discriminated against can file a complaint with the Arizona Attorney General or file a civil action. Remedies include injunctive relief, damages, affirmative relief, civil penalties, and attorneys' fees for prevailing complainants.

A licensee who is found to have unlawfully discriminated may have his or her license revoked or suspended.

If an agent meets with a seller who expresses discriminatory preferences, the agent should first attempt to educate the seller about the law and that violation of federal and/or state fair housing laws is illegal and may result in substantial financial liability for both the licensee and the owner. If the owner persists with discriminatory preferences, the agent should discuss the matter with his or her broker; the agent's broker will ultimately decide whether the brokerage must withdraw from the listing (or refuse to take the listing, if not already listed).

Arizona Consumer Fraud Act

Sellers of real estate, real estate licensees, and others are subject to the Arizona Consumer Fraud Act. This law prohibits unfair and deceptive practices in the sale, rental, or advertising of real estate. A person found liable under this statute is subject to civil penalties and licensees are also subject to having his or her license suspended or revoked. In addition, the Real Estate Commissioner's rules require licensees to disclose any material fact about the subject property and/or the buyer of the property. This means that a buyer's agent would have to disclose that the buyer recently filed bankruptcy when presenting the buyer's offer to the seller/seller's agent, provided the offer was contingent upon the buyer obtaining a loan. Similarly, if the seller's agent knows that the subject property has termites, the seller's agent must disclose this information whether or not the seller consents to disclosure of this information.

Lead Paint Law

Sellers and real estate agents must comply with federal lead-based paint disclosure requirements. Before signing a lease or purchase agreement on a property built before 1978, a prospective purchaser must be given a federally approved lead-based paint hazard information pamphlet. The landlord/seller must disclose any "known" lead-based paint hazards, but is not required to conduct any testing. A prospective buyer has ten days (but the parties can agree to some other period) to test for the presence of lead-based paint and/or hazards.

Deeds and Legal Descriptions of Property

In order to convey real property, the deed must include an unmistakable description of the property. To satisfy the requirement for legal description in the deed, one of the following methods may be used.

- **Metes and bounds system** is one of the oldest methods of land measurement and description used in this country. The **bounds** (boundary lines) of property are measured from a specified point of beginning along measurements called **metes**, with each change of direction marked by a compass angle. **Markers** denote each turning point; in modern description, **natural monuments** (the old oak tree) have been replaced by **benchmarks** (metal pins). The description ends with the return to the **point of beginning** (POB).
- **Lot and block system** uses parcel numbers noted on a subdivision map (**plat map**). The plat is divided into blocks by streets. The blocks are then separated into lots.

- **Government survey system** (rectangular survey system) was developed to have a more uniform method of delineating property boundaries. Property is identified by reference to the intersection of a **meridian (principal meridian)** running north-south and a baseline running east-west. Land is separated into rectangles called **townships** of six miles squared (six miles to a side, or 36 square miles). Townships are counted in **tiers** north or south of a baseline and ranges east or west of a meridian. A township is divided into 36 sections. A **section** is one mile squared (one square mile) and contains 640 acres. An **acre** contains 43,560 square feet.

Deeds

In Arizona, the parties typically do not participate in a face-to-face close of escrow. Instead, closing is accomplished by the parties each signing and/or delivering the necessary funds and documents to the escrow agent in advance of the closing date. The parties give the escrow agent written instructions to record the necessary documents and to disperse the necessary funds on the close of escrow date.

A **deed** is a written document that conveys property from the **grantor** (owner/giver) to the **grantee** (buyer/recipient). The requirements for a valid deed are as follows:

- It must be in writing.
- The grantor(s) must be of sound mind (legally capable).
- It must identify the parties (grantor and grantee).
- It must identify the property adequately; preferably with a full legal description.
- It must contain a **granting clause**—also called words of conveyance—that contains the appropriate words ("I hereby grant, transfer, and convey").
- It must state the **consideration** (something of value like money or love) given.
- It must be signed by the grantor(s).
- It must be **delivered** to and **accepted** by the grantee.

In Arizona, a deed must be acknowledged and signed before a notary public in order to be valid and in order to be recorded (made a part of the public records of the county in which the property is located). However, in order to be valid, deeds **do not** have to be witnessed, signed by the grantee, or recorded. A recorded deed provides **constructive notice** (assumed or publicly available notice) of the conveyance and, therefore, although not required to be valid, recording of a deed is advisable.

There are many different types of deeds.

- A **general warranty deed** (commonly used in Arizona) carries the grantor's **express** or **implied assurances** (called **warranties** or **covenants**) regarding the validity of the title.
- A **special warranty deed** carries the grantor's assurances only as to the state of the title only for the period of time after the grantor acquired ownership.
- A **quitclaim deed** transfers whatever interest the grantor may own but does not warrant that the grantor actually has any interest in the described property.

Mortgage Note and Mortgage Deed

Note: Remember that in real estate terminology, words ending in *or* refer to the person giving something (i.e., the mortgagor/borrower gives the pledge) and the words ending in *ee* refer to the person receiving something (i.e., the mortgagee/lender receives the benefit of the pledge of the collateral). Forget about the fact that the lender gives the money; it is the pledge of collateral that is important in this discussion.

The **mortgage** pledges the property as collateral. When the loan has been paid in full, the **defeasance clause** in the mortgage deed requires the lender (mortgagee) to issue a **satisfaction of mortgage** (showing the release of the debt) that should be recorded to remove the encumbrance affecting the title to the property.

A **due-on-sale** clause (also known as **alienation**) means that the loan must be paid off in full when the property is sold and the loan cannot be assumed by another party.

A **subordination clause** states that the loan will be junior (subordinated) to another lien in the future.

A defaulting borrower faces penalties of varying severity. Late charges will be incurred if the borrower is late in making a payment. If the borrower remains in default, the lender may invoke an acceleration clause. An **acceleration clause** gives the lender the right to collect the balance of the loan immediately. Finally, if the debt remains unpaid, the **power of sale** clause in the trust deed allows the process of foreclosure to begin.

A mortgage deed, used in some parts of the country, is different from the **grantor/grantee deed**, which is the deed that transfers actual ownership (bundle of rights) from the grantor (seller) to the grantee (buyer). Arizona uses a mortgage (which creates a lien in favor of the lender), but not a mortgage deed. However, most lenders use deeds of trust in Arizona.

Liens and Judgments

Liens

Liens are claims against property that secure payment of a financial obligation owed by the property or the property owner. They come in many varieties. Liens may be created voluntarily or involuntarily (i.e., by operation of law). A mortgage is a voluntary lien because you agreed to give the lender a lien on your property in exchange for a loan. A judgment lien is an involuntary lien.

Liens may be either general or specific. A **specific lien** is a lien on one specific property, such as a mortgage or city tax lien. A **general lien**, such as a judgment from a court of law or an IRS tax lien, is a lien on all of a person's real and property.

A **mechanic's lien** is an example of both a specific lien and an involuntary lien. In general, a mechanic's lien is available to anyone who provides material or labor for an improvement to real estate if he or she has not been paid for services rendered. Unlike most other liens, where lien priority is based upon the date the lien is recorded, the priority of a mechanic's lien is based upon the date work commenced or materials were furnished. For example, if work commenced January 1, but was not completed until May 31 (five months later), and the contractor recorded the notice of lien on June 30, then the priority of the contractor's lien dates back to January 1. In order to obtain a mechanic's lien, however, the contractor must meet certain requirements: (1) if the value of the goods and services exceeds $750, the person must be a licensed contractor; (2) the contractor must have a signed agreement with the owner; (3) the contractor must send via certified mail a preliminary 20-day notice within

20 days of commencing work and/or supplying materials to the owner; (4) the contractor must record a notice and claim of lien with the county recorder and serve a copy upon the owner within 120 days after work is complete; and (5) the contractor must file a lawsuit to foreclose the mechanic's lien within six months after the notice and claim of lien are recorded.

Foreclosure (sale) of the real estate may be postponed by the property owner during a court hearing on the merits of the case, provided the property owner posts a bond to ensure payment to the claimant.

A **judgment** is a determination of a court that may impose an obligation for payment on a property owner. If the judgment is unpaid, a **writ of attachment** specifies the property that the sheriff will be ordered to sell by a **writ of execution**.

Tax liens are available to federal, state, and local taxing authorities. Enforcement is usually by tax sale. The purchaser receives a tax deed.

- **Property tax or special assessment tax lien** is imposed for nonpayment of state or local property taxes. These taxes take precedence over all other liens.
- A **federal tax lien** is imposed by the IRS for nonpayment of federal income tax, gift tax, or other taxes.
- A **state tax lien** is imposed for nonpayment of state income tax, sales tax, use tax, or other tax.

Encumbrances and Liens

An **encumbrance** is a right or interest in a property that does not belong to an owner or tenant. An encumbrance is **voluntary** if it is imposed with the consent of the owner. A mortgage is a voluntary encumbrance because the owner agreed to allow the lender to file a lien upon the property in exchange for receiving a loan. An encumbrance is **involuntary** if it can be imposed without the consent of the owner. Property tax liens are involuntary encumbrance. Encumbrances consist of **liens** (a claim to property to ensure payment of a debt to another) and items which affect the use and physical condition of the property such as **encroachments** or **easements**.

An **encroachment** occurs when a property improvement extends onto an adjoining parcel of land. An encroachment may be so slight as to be unnoticeable or unobjectionable, as with a fence line that deviates by only one or a few inches from the defined property boundary. The remedy may be removal of the encroachment or money damages. If no legal action is taken (or permission granted) by the owner of the burdened land, such action may become a **claim of adverse possession**.

Easements grant a right to use a portion of a property owner's land for a specific purpose. The **dominant tenement** is a parcel of land that benefits from an easement over an adjoining or adjacent parcel. An **easement appurtenant** is one that runs with the land because it is transferred when title to the dominant tenement is transferred. The **servient tenement** is the parcel of land that is burdened with the easement; that is, the parcel over which the owner of the dominant tenement is allowed to travel.

A **commercial easement in gross** does not benefit any one parcel of real estate but rather benefits a number of parcels to bring such things as utilities. A **personal easement in gross** is granted to a person and is not appurtenant, which means that it does not attach to the land and cannot be transferred.

An easement may be acquired by:

- **express grant** in a deed
- **easement by necessity**, which is when a parcel is landlocked and there is no method of ingress or egress other than over someone else's land
- **easement by prescription**—obtained in a manner similar to that of adverse possession. The right to be obtained is a right of use rather than ownership, but the use must be without the permission of the property owner, open and notorious, and must continue for a statutory number of years (ten years in Arizona).

Unlike an easement, which is permanent, a **license** is the temporary permission to come onto someone's land. The holder of a ticket for a baseball game has a license to enter the stadium for the game. A license can be revoked by the licensor and, generally, cannot be transferred by the holder of the license to another person.

If a married person owns property in his or her name only, upon death, the surviving spouse is entitled to a one-third life interest in the property. If the surviving spouse is the wife, the right is called **dower**. If the surviving spouse is the husband, the right is called **courtesy** (sometimes spelled curtesy).

Title/Recordation

Title Search

A title search will reveal the chain of title, the history of conveyances, and encumbrances that can be found in the public records. The title search begins with the name of the present owner and the instrument that establishes title in that owner as the grantee. Working back through what is called the **grantee index**, the name of the grantor to the present owner is found on the deed in which that owner is the grantee. In this way, the person examining the title can go back to the first recorded document of the property. The **chain of title** is an account of the successive owners of the property. An **abstract of title** is a certified summary of the history of the recorded documents affecting the title.

In Arizona, evidence of marketable title is presented via title insurance. Arizona does not recognize an Abstract of Title or a Certificate of Title or an attorney's opinion of title as evidence of marketable title.

Torrens System

Torrens system is a system of registering land. When purchasing registered land, instead of a deed, the grantee is given a numbered **certificate of title**. The Torrens system is not used in Arizona.

Tax Stamps

Arizona does not use **tax stamps**. Instead, Arizona requires that an Affidavit of Value be recorded with every deed transferring real property (there are some exceptions, such as deeds between family members, deeds of trust, reconveyance deeds, etc.). The Affidavit of Value is used by the county assessor for purposes of determining the full cash value of the property and, thereby, calculating the assessed value of the property. Real property taxes in Arizona are based on the assessed value of the property and the calculation of the real property taxes is based upon the category of use: 10% for residential, 16% for raw land, and 25% for commercial.

Community Property

Community property states do not recognize dower and courtesy rights. In a community property state, all property acquired during the marriage is community property, except for gifts and inheritance, which are considered sole and separate property. Sole and separate property also includes property that was acquired before marriage and property acquired after marriage if the other spouse executes a disclaimer deed. Under community property law, each spouse has a one-half interest in all community property, including real property. If one spouse dies, the surviving spouse automatically owns one-half of the real property. The other half, which belonged to the deceased spouse, is then distributed according to will or, if the spouse died intestate, then according to the laws of intestate succession, which vary from state to state. Arizona is a community property state.

Community property with right of survivorship is much like joint tenants with right of survivorship, except that it is a method of holding title that is available only to married couples. Upon the death of either spouse, the surviving spouse becomes the owner of the entire property. In addition, the surviving spouse receives the deceased person's share of the property with a "step-up" in basis.

For example, a husband and wife acquire a property for $100,000. The husband dies at a time when the property is worth $500,000. If held as joint tenants with right of survivorship or if held in some other manner and the surviving spouse inherits the other one-half by will or intestate succession, then the wife owns her one-half with a value of $250,000 and a basis of $50,000 (half of the original $100,000), plus the other half with a value of $250,000 and a basis of $50,000 (the other half of the original $100,000). If, however, the couple hold title as community property with right of survivorship, then the wife owns her one-half with a value of $250,000 and a basis of $50,000 (half of the original $100,000), plus the other half with a value of $250,000 and a "step-up" in basis on the other half of $250,000. The wife still owns all of the property, but her basis is $300,000 (her $50,000 plus the $250,000 step-up in basis on the other half). Capital gain is calculated by subtracting the adjusted basis of the property from the net selling price.

Homestead Exemptions

The homestead exemption is state law. In Arizona, the homestead exemption is $150,000, and it applies automatically (i.e., no documents need be completed or filed). The exemption amount is the same if the homeowner is married or single. A person may have only one homestead exemption at a time. The exemption means that the homeowner is entitled to retain the first $150,000 of equity if the owner's home is sold by a judgment creditor to satisfy a debt owed by the owner to the judgment creditor. If there is less than $150,000 in equity, the judgment creditor cannot force the sale of the homestead property. A judgment creditor is someone who holds a judgment that awards a monetary amount against someone else. A judgment is valid in Arizona for five years. After four and one-half years, but before the expiration of five years, the judgment may be renewed by filing a renewal of judgment with the court that issued the original judgment. A judgment remains valid until it is paid, expired, declared invalid, or discharged in bankruptcy.

Subdivided and Unsubdivided Lands

Subdivided land refers to land that is under a common plan and is divided (or proposed to be divided) into six or more parcels of fewer than 36 acres each. A Commissioner's Public Report is required before any of the subdivided parcels may be sold. The purpose of the Commissioner's Public Report is to protect the public. It must be given to the purchaser at or before the purchaser signs the contract to purchase subdivided land, and a receipt for the Commissioner's Public Report must be kept for five years. Once obtained, the subdivider is prohibited from advertising or representing to prospective purchasers that the subdivision is "endorsed by the real estate commissioner" or other similar language or that the investment is without risk. The subdivider also cannot include language in the purchase contract that prohibits the buyer from testifying at future zoning hearings.

If the Commissioner's Public Report is not given to the buyer, the contract is voidable by the buyer for three years.

While the subdivider is awaiting approval of the Commissioner's Public Report, the subdivider may take **lot reservations**. Lot reservations are not a binding contract and must be refundable to the proposed purchaser. The maximum lot reservation is $5,000.

Unsubdivided land is six or more parcels of 36 acres or more, but fewer than 160 acres. The buyer has a six-month rescission period if the land was not inspected, but only a seven-day rescission period if the land was inspected.

Arizona regulations establish the criteria when a public report is required for time-shares, for condos/condo coversions, and on resale properties.

▶ Common Interest Ownerships

Condominiums/Cooperatives/Time-Sharing Leases and Options

Condominiums

In Arizona, a condominium is created by recording a **declaration**. A declaration is a document prepared by the condominium developer and provides specific information that is required by law (i.e., name of development, legal description of each unit, description of common elements, etc.). The declaration must be recorded in the county where the condominium(s) are located. A deed is used for the sale and/or transfer of a condominium. Each unit owner agrees to be bound by the **bylaws** and rules and regulations of the condominium. The **bylaws** establish the condominium association and define its legal authority. The condominium association may thereafter adopt rules for the day-to-day administration of the association.

Condominium fees are determined by the annual operating **budget** of the condominium. Fees are normally due monthly and are based on the unit's percentage of ownership.

Some of the **common areas** are for the use of all of the unit owners (such as the foundation, elevator, pool) while some of the common areas will be defined as limited common elements and will be designated for the exclusive use of a specific unit (such as a balcony).

An advantage of condominium ownership over cooperative ownership is that a default in payment of taxes, mortgage payment, or monthly assessment affects only the specific unit. Each unit is defined as a separate parcel of real estate and is owned in fee simple.

If a unit owner fails to pay his or her monthly condominium fee, the association has a statutory lien against the condominium.

Upon receipt of notice of a pending sale of a condominium, certain information must be provided to the new buyer. If the development includes less than 50 condominiums, then the owner/seller of the condominium must provide the information; if the development includes 50 or more condominiums, then the association must provide the information. The information must include a copy of the declaration, bylaws and rules, any known violations of the foregoing by the owner/seller, the amount of the periodic assessment, any current or pending special assessments, copies of the current budget, financial statement, and reserve study for the association.

Cooperatives

Cooperatives are apartments owned by a corporation that holds titles to the entire cooperative property, holds a blanket mortgage on the entire property, and is responsible for the *ad valorem* taxes for the entire property. The cooperative is taxed as one entity.

Each purchaser of an apartment unit is a stockholder in the corporation and receives a **stock certificate in the corporation**. The purchaser obtains the right to occupy through a **proprietary unit lease for the life of the corporation**. Each block of stock is tied to a specific right to occupy and carries a lease payment financial obligation that represents a *pro rata* share of the total cost of the operations expense and mortgage payments on the building.

A disadvantage of cooperative ownership over condominium ownership is that default of the monthly payment by a shareholder affects the entire cooperative and the other shareholders must make up the deficiency.

Time-Sharing

Time-shares are when multiple owners own a proportional interest in a single condominium unit with the exclusive right to use and occupy the unit for a specified period of time each year. The individual owners pay common expense, maintenance costs, and management fees based on the ratio between the ownership period and the total number of ownership periods available in the property. This type of ownership can be either a fee simple or leasehold interest. If owned in fee simple, the owner owns a specified period(s) each and every year and may use, sell, rent, or exchange this right. If a leasehold interest is held, then the holder may use one specific period(s). The right to transfer that right to another may be limited. Time-share owners can participate in an **exchange program** (either in-house for affiliated resorts or external) and exchange their time-share for another location.

▶ Licensing

Activities Requiring a License

Licensing Requirements

The following activities, when performed for another person and for a fee, require a real estate license in the state of Arizona:

- sales
- exchanges
- purchases
- rentals/leases
- negotiations
- offers
- listing
- options
- advertisement agency
- prospecting
- loan negotiating
- apartment searching

Types of Licenses

A **real estate broker** is any person who, for another person and for a fee, performs any of the previously mentioned activities.

A **real estate salesperson** also has the right to perform any of the previously mentioned activities, except that they must work for and on behalf of a real estate broker, which may be either a self-employed broker (i.e., sole proprietor) or a brokerage (i.e., a partnership, corporation, limited liability company, etc.). The self-employed broker and the brokerage entity are known as the **employing broker**. A salesperson cannot be self-employed, but must act under an employing broker.

When a corporation, partnership, or limited liability company applies for a broker's license, a licensed broker must be appointed to act as the designated broker for the company. The designated broker must be an officer of the corporation, a partner in the partnership, or a managing member of the limited liability company.

A **nonresident** can hold an Arizona real estate salesperson or broker license. The licensee must provide the Arizona Department of Real Estate (ADRE) with a current residence address.

Issuance, Renewal, Revocation, and Suspension Procedures

Arizona License Law

The ADRE has extensive information about qualifying for and the process of obtaining a real estate license (both salesperson and broker) on its website: www.AZRE.gov.

ADRE contracts with a private company to administer the state real estate examination for salespersons and brokers. Presently, that company is Thomson Prometric, which publishes the *Candidate Information Bulletin* that includes information about requirements, education and licensing. You may obtain a copy of the *Candidate Information Bulletin* by calling 800-347-9242 or by visiting its website at www.prometric.com.

General Licensing Requirements and Recovery Fund

Eligibility for Licensing

In order to receive a **salesperson's** license, a person must:

- be more than 18 years old
- complete 90 hours of classroom instruction
- pass a real estate school examination
- pass the state real estate examination

To receive a **broker's** license, a person must:

- be actively employed by a licensed real estate broker for three of the last five years
- complete 90 hours of classroom instruction
- pass a real estate school examination
- pass the state real estate examination

In the event of the death, severe illness, incompetence, or insanity of a licensed broker who is the sole proprietor of a real estate company, ADRE may issue a temporary broker's license to a spouse, next of kin, administrator, personal representative, or other eligible person. A temporary broker's license is valid for 90 days, but under limited circumstances may be extended to 15 months.

As of July 1, 2007, real estate licenses are valid for four years. A licensee must take 24 hours of continuing education classes (classroom or distance learning) every two-year period prior to renewing either a salesperson or broker's license. Designated and self-employed brokers must also complete a three-hour broker management clinic every renewal period. If a person does not complete his or her continuing education requirements and does not timely renew his or her license, the license automatically becomes inactive and the licensee must cease all real estate activity. A licensee may, however, collect real estate income (i.e., commissions) if the licensee's license was active at the time the real estate income was earned (i.e., if a transaction is put into escrow while the licensee's license is active and closes during the time the license is inactive).

Currently, the fee for renewing a salesperson's license is $60 and the fee for renewing a broker's license is $125. A complete list of current fees is available at ADRE's website: www.re.state.az.us.

There are some people who do not need a real estate license. They include:

- any individual acting for himself or herself
- a salaried employee or property manager employed by the property owner
- a trustee
- a public official or public employee performing official duties
- a person acting as an attorney-in-fact under a power of attorney
- an attorney performing duties for a client
- a court appointee
- a bank, insurance company, or credit union and its employees

Powers and Duties of the Real Estate Commissioner

Real Estate Advisory Board

The Real Estate Advisory Board gives recommendations to the Commissioner of Real Estate regarding issues confronting the ADRE. The Real Estate Advisory Board is made up of nine members: two members must be real estate brokers; two members must be residential real estate salespersons or brokers; two members must be engaged in real estate subdividing; and three members must be from the public (not real estate related).

Each member is appointed by the governor and each serves without salary for six years; the six-year terms of the members are staggered to ensure continuity. The Board provides the governor with an annual evaluation of the commissioner of real estate.

The commissioner of real estate is charged with the responsibility of running ADRE. ADRE handles licensing of real estate agents and brokers, renewal of real estate licenses, approval of real estate schools, approval of real estate courses for continuing education for licensees, auditing of real estate brokers and companies, investigation of complaints against licensees, administrative actions against licensees (i.e., suspension or revocation of real estate license), and approval of subdivision reports. In addition, the commissioner establishes rules to accomplish the foregoing and to implement the Arizona real estate statutes. The commissioner's rules are found in the Arizona Administrative Code, Sections R4-28-101 through R4-28-1313. The commissioner's rules may be reviewed at www.azsos.gov/public_services/Title_04/4-28.htm?.

There are many ways for an agent to lose his or her license either temporarily or permanently. According to Arizona license law, ADRE may suspend, revoke, or refuse to renew a license on the following grounds:

1. Pursued a course of misrepresentation or made false promises, either directly or through others, whether acting in the role of a licensee or a principal in a transaction.

2. Acted for more than one party in a transaction without the knowledge or consent of all parties in the transaction.

3. Disregarded or violated any of the provisions of this chapter or any rules adopted by the commissioner.

4. Knowingly authorized, directed, connived at or aided in the publication, advertisement, distribution, or circulation of any material false or misleading statement or representation concerning the licensee's business or any land, cemetery property, subdivision, or membership campground or camping contract offered for sale in this or any other state.

5. Knowingly used the term *real estate broker*, *cemetery broker*, or *membership camping broker* without legal right to do so.

6. Employed any unlicensed salesperson or unlicensed associate broker.

7. Accepted compensation as a licensee for the performance of any of the acts specified in this chapter from any person other than the licensed broker to whom the licensee is licensed, the licensed professional corporation of which the licensee is an officer and shareholder, or the licensed professional limited liability company of which the licensee is a member or manager.

8. Represented or attempted to represent a broker other than the broker to whom the salesperson or associate broker is licensed.

9. Failed, within a reasonable time, to account for or to remit any monies, to surrender to the rightful owner any documents or other valuable property coming into the licensee's possession and that belongs to others, or to issue an appraisal report on real property or cemetery property in which the licensee has an interest, unless the nature and extent of the interest are fully disclosed in the report.

10. Paid or received any rebate, profit, compensation, or commission in violation of this chapter.

11. Induced any party to a contract to break the contract for the purpose of substituting a new contract with the same or a different principal, if the substitution is motivated by the personal gain of the licensee.

12. Placed a sign on any property offering it for sale or for rent without the written authority of the owner or the owner's authorized agent.

13. Solicited, either directly or indirectly, prospects for the sale, lease, or use of real property, cemetery property, or membership camping contracts through a promotion of a speculative nature involving a game of chance or risk or through conducting lotteries or contests that are not specifically authorized under the provisions of this chapter.

14. Failed to pay to the commissioner the biennial renewal fee as specified in this chapter promptly and before the time specified.

15. Failed to keep an escrow or trust account or other record of funds deposited with the licensee relating to a real estate transaction.

16. Commingled the money or other property of the licensee's principal or client with the licensee's own or converted that money or property to the licensee or another.

17. Failed or refused upon demand to produce any document, contract, book, record, information, compilation, or report that is in the licensee's possession or that the licensee is required by law to maintain concerning any real estate, cemetery, or membership camping business, services, activities, or transactions involving or conducted by the licensee for inspection by the commissioner or the commissioner's representative.

18. Failed to maintain a complete record of each transaction which comes within the provisions of this chapter.

19. Violated the federal fair housing law, the Arizona civil rights law, or any local ordinance of a similar nature.

20. Tendered to a buyer a wood infestation report in connection with the transfer of residential real property or an interest in residential real property knowing that wood infestation exists or that the wood infestation report was inaccurate or false as of the date of the tender or that an inspection was not done in conjunction with the preparation of the wood infestation report.

21. As a licensed broker, failed to exercise reasonable supervision over the activities of salespersons, associate brokers or others under the broker's employ or failed to exercise reasonable supervision and control over the activities for which a license is required of a corporation, limited liability company or partnership on behalf of which the broker acts as designated broker under § 32-2125.

22. Demonstrated negligence in performing any act for which a license is required.

23. Sold or leased a property to a buyer or lessee that was not the property represented to the buyer or lessee.

24. Violated any condition or term of a commissioner's order.

25. Signed the name of another person on any document or form without the express written consent of the person.

26. Procured or attempted to procure a license under the provisions of this chapter for the holder or applicant or another by fraud, misrepresentation, or deceit, or by filing an original or renewal application which is false or misleading.

27. Been convicted in a court of competent jurisdiction in this or any other state of a felony or of any crime of forgery, theft, extortion, conspiracy to defraud, a crime of moral turpitude, or any other like offense.

28. Made any substantial misrepresentation.

29. Made any false promises of a character likely to influence, persuade, or induce.

30. Been guilty of any conduct, whether of the same or a different character than specified in this section, which constitutes fraud or dishonest dealings.

31. Engaged in the business of a real estate, cemetery, or membership camping broker or real estate, cemetery, or membership camping salesperson without holding a license as prescribed in this chapter.

32. Not shown that the holder or applicant is a person of honesty, truthfulness, and good character.

33. Demonstrated incompetence to perform any duty or requirement of a licensee under or arising from this chapter. For the purposes of this paragraph, "incompetence" means a lack of basic knowledge or skill

appropriate to the type of license the person holds or a failure to appreciate the probable consequences of the licensee's action or inaction.

34. Violated the terms of any criminal or administrative order, decree, or sentence.

35. Violated any federal or state law, regulation or rule that relates to real estate or securities or that involves forgery, theft, extortion, fraud, substantial misrepresentation, dishonest dealings, or violence against another person or failure to deal fairly with any party to a transaction that materially and adversely affected the transaction. This paragraph applies equally to violations of which the licensee was convicted in any lawful federal or state tribunal and to any admissions made in any settlement agreement by the licensee to violations.

36. Failed to respond in the course of an investigation or audit by providing documents or written statements.

When ADRE investigates and/or holds a hearing regarding a licensee, the department may summon witnesses and records. If ADRE believes sufficient evidence exists to warrant further proceedings, it refers the matter to the Arizona attorney general. A Notice of Hearing and Complaint is prepared and served upon the licensee. The licensee is given an opportunity to provide a written response and may appear with counsel at all hearings. An administrative law judge is appointed to hear the matter. The hearing is conducted by the Arizona Office of Administrative Hearings. After the hearing, the administrative law judge prepares Findings of Fact and Conclusions of Law. These are sent to the commissioner with a recommended Order. The commissioner either adopts, modifies or rejects the findings and conclusions, and enters a commissioner's Order. In issuing an order, the commissioner may take any one or a combination of actions, which may include the following:

- Dismissal of all charges: No sanctions are imposed upon nor penalties assessed upon the respondent.
- Revocation (of license, approval, or certificate): The individual or entity is not eligible to conduct business activities unless granted a new license at some future date.
- Suspension (of license, sales, approval or certificate): The individual's or entity's license is suspended for a specific period of time or until some condition is met. During this period, the individual is not allowed to conduct business.
- Civil penalty: A respondent may be assessed a civil penalty in an amount not to exceed $1,000 per violation. Funds collected as a result of a civil penalty are placed in the State's general fund.
- Issue a provisional license.
- Order developer to offer rescission of sales.

If the individual or entity does not comply with the order, the commissioner may pursue further administrative sanctions.

▶ Activities of Licensees

Employment Contracts

Employment contracts may refer to agreements between the broker and clients (i.e., listing agreements, buyer/broker agreements) and may also refer to agreements between the broker and employees of the broker (i.e., staff, agents hired as employees rather than independent contractors, etc.). In Arizona, even a licensee who is hired by a broker as an independent contractor for IRS purposes is considered to be an "employee" of the broker by ADRE, because the broker has a statutory duty to supervise. As a note, state law ARS 32-2151.02 indicates that employment contracts are listings and buyer-broker employment agreements.

Independent contractor status for IRS purposes is very important for Arizona brokers. Failure to include the appropriate language in the broker-agent agreement will result in the agent being deemed an "employee," for purposes of requiring the broker to withhold social security taxes, unemployment, workman's compensation, etc. The ADRE regards all agents of the designated broker or self-employed broker, whether designated as employees or independent contractors, to be **employed** by the **employing broker**, thus requiring the broker to supervise and train all agents.

Advertising

The following are the statutory requirements regarding **advertising**:

- A broker shall not advertise in any way that is false or misleading.
- **blind advertising**—No broker may advertise real property to purchase, sell, rent, mortgage or exchange through classified advertisement or otherwise unless he or she affirmatively discloses that he or she is a real estate broker.
- All advertisements shall include the name of the **employing broker**. The employing broker is: (1) the name of a self-employed broker, (2) the name of the business entity (i.e., corporation, partnership, LLC), or (3) the "doing business as" (d/b/a) name that appears on the employing broker's license. Salespersons and associate brokers are prohibited from advertising the purchase, sale, rental or exchange of any real property without identifying the name of the employing broker.
- No broker shall advertise to purchase, sell, rent, mortgage, or exchange any real property in any manner that indicates directly or indirectly unlawful **discrimination** against any individual or group.

Offers

Licensees are prohibited from advising against the use of an attorney in any real property transaction and, in fact, are required by the Commissioner's Rules to take affirmative action and advise clients to seek appropriate counseling from legal, tax, insurance, and accounting professionals when considering a prepossession or postpossession agreement.

Purchase Contracts

There is no state-required purchase contract form. Various private organizations (i.e., the Arizona Association of REALTORS®) make forms available for use, but the decision as to which form to use is left to the broker of each office.

Disclosures

Disclosure of material information is required by Arizona law by both parties to the transaction (i.e., sellers and buyers). Case law and commissioner's standards impose similar duties for the agents of both parties. Consequently, even though a listing broker has a fiduciary duty of confidentiality to the broker's client (the seller), the broker is nevertheless required by law to disclose material facts that the broker knows (i.e., termite infestation) or should have known.

Handling of Funds

Promotional Sales of Out-of-State Real Property

Brokers who are not licensed in Arizona are prohibited from advertising, renting, or selling real estate located in Arizona, but under certain circumstances (i.e., written agreement, appropriate supervision, compliance with Arizona requirements, and other requirements), an out-of-state broker may be able to enter into a cooperating agreement with an Arizona broker whereby the out-of-state broker would perform very limited real estate functions and receive some portion of the commission. The out-of-state broker may not list, market, advertise, place a sign, or conduct negotiations on Arizona property.

Record Keeping and Documentation

Property managers must keep financial records for three years. They must keep terminated lease agreements for one year, unless they have already returned the lease to the owner after termination of the property management agreement.

A broker must keep employment status records for five years, which includes listing agreements, buyer-broker agreements and broker-agent agreements. A broker must keep terminated transactions (i.e., closed, cancelled, etc.) for five years. A broker must keep rejected offers to purchase for one year, unless a contract ultimately results, in which case the broker must keep all rejected offers for five years.

A broker must review and initial all transaction documents (i.e., listings, buyer-broker agreements, sales contracts, etc.) within five days.

Agencies

Creation of Agency

The employment agreement is one way to establish an **agency** relationship between an agent and his or her principal. These employment agreements can either be a listing agreement for the right to sell a property or a buyer agency agreement for the right to help a buyer find a property. A written or oral listing agreement will establish an **express agency** (a hiring). **Implied agency** can be inferred by the conduct of the principal and agent (the parties act as if there had been an actual hiring). **Ostensible agency** may occur when a principal gives a third party reason to believe that another person is the principal's agent even though that person is unaware of the appointment. If the third party accepts the principal's representation as true, the principal may have established ostensible authority and therefore may be bound by the acts of his or her agent. This may happen, for example, when a seller gives the keys for a property to an agent. Other agents may reasonably rely upon the first agent's statement that authority exists for the first agent to show the property.

Listing agreements in Arizona do not have to be in writing to establish agency, but must be in writing if the agent/broker wishes to enforce payment of the commission. The statute of frauds prevents enforcement of a listing or buyer broker agreement unless it is in writing.

Duties of an Agent

The real estate listing agent owes the property owner (**principal**) the duties of a **fiduciary** if they are acting as a seller's agent. The agent must act in the owner's best interest. The buyer's agent owes the same responsibilities to the buyer.

When agents have a **personal interest in a property** and are selling or buying property for themselves, they must disclose, in writing, that they are licensed real estate agents to the other party.

If the broker intends to hold earnest money and/or other client money, then the broker must have a trust account. Most Arizona brokers have earnest money checks made out to a title company; and the checks are placed in the title/escrow company's neutral escrow account. These funds must be kept separate from the broker's personal or business account and not commingled.

Many properties sell through the cooperation offered in MLS. The broker working with the buyer is called a **cooperating broker**.

Subagency is normally found in a co-broke situation when a seller's agent works with a buyer as a customer. While legal, subagency is rarely done in Arizona. A **subagent** owes fiduciary duties to the seller and can only offer the buyer customer level services (fairness and honesty).

Termination of Agency

An agency contract can be terminated by:

- **completion of the objective**—either the property is sold or the buyer client has bought a house
- **expiration of the time limit** specified in the contract
- **mutual consent (rescission)**
- **revocation/renunciation**—by either principal or agent
- **death of the principal or broker** (because the agency contract is between the broker owner of the real estate company and the principal, the agency relationship is not affected by the death of the agent. If the agency agreement is with a self-employed broker, the agency is terminated. If the agency agreement is with a brokerage that employs a designated broker and the designated broker dies, the agency is not terminated.
- **destruction of the property**
- **bankruptcy of either party**

Broker-Salesperson Relationships

Broker versus Salesperson

A real estate salesperson can be hired by a real estate broker as an **employee** or as an **independent contractor**. A salesperson cannot be self-employed; he or she must be affiliated with a broker (and only one broker at a time). A salesperson can only accept a payment, fee, or commission from his or her broker. The broker is responsible for the actions of his or her agents.

All employment agreements (i.e., a listing agreement or a buyer-broker agreement) belong to the broker, not the salesperson. If a client (i.e., a seller under a listing agreement or a buyer under a buyer-broker agreement) fails to pay a commission, a broker may file a civil lawsuit to recover the commission. Alternatively, the broker may assign the right to collect the commission to the salesperson and the salesperson may file a civil lawsuit directly against the client to recover the commission.

Two kinds of agency relationships are common in real estate practice.

- **General agency**—Real estate brokers typically have real estate agents who act as the broker's general agents when working with clients/principals of the brokerage. A real estate agent is a general agent for a real estate broker (i.e., the real estate agent has broad authority to act on behalf of the broker).
- **Special agency**—A principal to a transaction (the seller or buyer) secures the advice and assistance of a real estate broker and the broker's agents. Although one of the broker's real estate agents signs the agency contract with the buyer or seller, the real estate agent is acting on behalf of the real estate broker and, under the law, the agency contract is between the broker of the real estate company and the principal. A real estate broker is a special agent for a client/principal (i.e., hired to sell a particular property on behalf of a seller or hired to find a particular property on behalf of a buyer).

Brokerage Definition

Arizona law defines a **Real estate broker** as anyone who, for another and for compensation:
  (a)   Sells, exchanges, purchases, rents, or leases real estate or time-share interests.
  (b)   Offers to sell, exchange, purchase, rent, or lease real estate or time-share interests.
  (c)   Negotiates or offers, attempts or agrees to negotiate the sale, exchange, purchase, rental, or leasing of real estate or timeshare interests.
  (d)   Lists or offers, attempts or agrees to list real estate or timeshare interests for sale, lease or exchange.
  (e)   Auctions or offers, attempts or agrees to auction real estate or time-share interests.
  (f)   Buys, sells, offers to buy or sell, or otherwise deals in options on real estate or time-share interests or improvements to real estate or time-share interests.
  (g)   Collects or offers, attempts or agrees to collect rent for the use of real estate or time-share interests.
  (h)   Advertises or holds himself or herself out as being engaged in the business of buying, selling, exchanging, renting or leasing real estate or time-share interests or counseling or advising regarding real estate or time-share interests.

(i) Assists or directs in the procuring of prospects, calculated to result in the sale, exchange, leasing, or rental of real estate or time-share interests.

(j) Assists or directs in the negotiation of any transaction calculated or intended to result in the sale, exchange, leasing, or rental of real estate or time-share interests.

(k) Incident to the sale of real estate negotiates or offers, attempts, or agrees to negotiate a loan secured or to be secured by any mortgage or other encumbrance upon or transfer of real estate or time-share interests subject to § 32-2155, subsection C.

(l) Engages in the business of assisting or offering to assist another in filing an application for the purchase or lease of, or in locating or entering upon, lands owned by the state or federal government.

(m) Claims, demands, charges, receives, collects, or contracts for the collection of an advance fee in connection with any employment enumerated in this section, including employment undertaken to promote the sale or lease of real property by advance fee listing, by furnishing rental information to a prospective tenant for a fee paid by the prospective tenant, by advertisement or by any other offering to sell, lease, exchange, or rent real property or selling kits connected therewith. This shall not include the activities of any communications media of general circulation or coverage not primarily engaged in the advertisement of real estate or any communications media activities that are specifically exempt from applicability of this article under § 32-2121.

(n) Engages in any of the acts listed in subdivisions (a) through (m) of this paragraph for the sale or lease of other than real property if a real property sale or lease is a part of, contingent on or ancillary to the transaction.

(o) Performs any of the acts listed in subdivisions (a) through (m) of this paragraph as an employee of, or in behalf of, the owner of real estate, or interest in the real estate, or improvements affixed on the real estate, for compensation.

Compensation/Commissions

Commissions

The best way to ensure that an agent will be paid for the work he or she performs is to make sure that he or she is always working under an employment agreement, a listing agreement, or a buyer agency representation agreement.

Commissions are negotiable and are established through an agreement of the parties. The Sherman Anti-Trust Law prohibits price fixing among real estate offices. Nevertheless, a broker can establish or fix a minimum or maximum commission amount within that broker's own office.

Sometimes there is a dispute over a commission if a buyer has worked with more than one agent. The commission will be paid to the broker who is found to be the **procuring cause** in producing a ready, willing, and able buyer. Determining procuring cause can be a difficult task because it is not necessarily the agent who was the first to show the property or the agent who wrote the offer.

Commission Splits

Commissions may be split into many pieces when a property is sold. When a listing office submits a listing to MLS, the listing office includes the amount of commission it will offer to a cooperating broker who procures a buyer that successfully completes the transaction.

The remaining commission may then be split between the real estate company/broker and the real estate agent. The way a broker shares a commission with an agent varies among different offices. Some offices take a percentage of the commission to cover operating expenses, advertising, and administrative help. Other offices charge agents a set monthly desk fee to cover overhead, and the agent receives all or most of the commission.

▶ Settlement

Property Taxation

The government has the right to collect property taxes from property owners to provide funds for services such as schools, fire and police protection, parks, and libraries. The federal government does not tax property, relying on income taxes for operating revenues, but cities levy taxes on real property. These taxes are levied according to the value of the property and are called *ad valorem* taxes. Arizona property taxes are assessed once each year and, by statute, become a lien on all real property on the first day of January each year. The tax bill, however, is not prepared and sent until mid-year, and the first one-half of the taxes is not due until October 1 (delinquent if not paid by November 1) and the second one-half is not due until March 1 of the following year (delinquent if not paid by May 1). If the property taxes are not paid, the county treasurer sells the property at a tax sale. Tax sales are conducted in February, once a year. After the tax sale, all other liens on that property are extinguished, including first liens and IRS tax liens. Real property tax liens have the highest priority of all liens. Special assessment liens, which are a type of property taxes, have second priority. Other liens have priority according to the date recorded, except for mechanic's liens, which have priority according to the date work commenced. The successful bidder at a property tax sale receives a Certificate of Purchase. The owner has three years within which to redeem the property by paying the back taxes and other amounts paid by the successful bidder. If not redeemed, the successful bidder will receive a treasurer's deed.

Foreclosure and Forfeiture

Foreclosure is the legal act of a creditor or lender selling property (the collateral) because the terms of a note were not met (normally for nonpayment).

Lenders require that borrowers pledge the real estate as collateral for a mortgage loan. If the borrower defaults on the loan, the lender can terminate the borrower's interest in a property through a judicial process called foreclosure. Traditionally, because the borrower had possession of the property, this process was the only way for a lender to seek satisfaction in the event of a default. However, a judicial foreclosure requiring court action can be time-consuming and very costly.

5 ▶ Real Estate Math Review

CHAPTER SUMMARY

Real estate mathematics accounts for almost 10% of the Arizona real estate sales exam, so you should take this topic seriously. But even if math is not your favorite subject, this chapter will help you do your best. It not only covers arithmetic, algebra, geometry, and word problems, but also has practice problems for each of the real estate math topics.

ERE ARE THE types of math questions you will encounter on the exam:

- Percents
- Areas
- Property Tax
- Loan-to-Value Ratios
- Points
- Equity
- Qualifying Buyers
- Prorations
- Commissions

- Sale Proceeds
- Transfer Tax/Conveyance Tax/Revenue Stamps
- Competitive Market Analyses (CMA)
- Income Properties
- Depreciation

Keep in mind that although the math topics are varied, you will be using the same math skills to complete each question. But before you review your math skills, take a look at some helpful strategies for doing your best.

▶ Strategies for Math Questions

Answer Every Question

You should answer every single question, even if you don't know the answer. There is no penalty for a wrong answer, and you have a 25% chance of guessing correctly. If one or two answers are obviously wrong, the odds of selecting the correct one may be even higher.

Bring a Calculator

You are allowed to bring a calculator to your exam, but it must be silent, handheld, solar- or battery-operated, and non-programmable. As a precaution, you should bring an extra battery with you to your exam. Try not to rely entirely on the calculator. Although using one can prevent simple adding and subtracting errors, it may take longer for you to use the calculator than to figure it out yourself.

Use Scratch Paper

Resist the temptation to "save time" by doing all your work on your calculator. The main pitfall with calculators is the temptation to work the problem all the way through to the end on the calculator. At this point, if none of the answers provided is correct, there is no way to know where the mistake lies. Use scratch paper to avoid this problem.

Check Your Work

Checking your work is always good practice, and it's usually quite simple. Even if you come up with an answer that is one of the answer choices, you should check your work. Test writers often include answer choices that are the results of common errors, which you may have made.

▶ Real Estate Math Review

Here's a quick review of some basic arithmetic, algebra, geometry, and word problem skills you will need for your exam.

Arithmetic Review

Symbols of Multiplication

When two or more numbers are being multiplied, they are called **factors**. The answer that results is called the **product**.

> *Example:*
> $5 \times 6 = 30$ 5 and 6 are **factors** and 30 is the **product**.

There are several ways to represent multiplication in the above mathematical statement.

- A dot between factors indicates multiplication:

  $5 \cdot 6 = 30$

- Parentheses around one or more factors indicates multiplication:

  $(5)6 = 30, 5(6) = 30,$ and $(5)(6) = 30$

- Multiplication is also indicated when a number is placed next to a variable:

  $5a = 30$ In this equation, 5 is being multiplied by a.

Divisibility

Like multiplication, division can be represented in a few different ways:

$$8 \div 3 \qquad 3\overline{)8} \qquad \frac{8}{3}$$

In each of the above, 3 is the **divisor** and 8 is the **dividend**.

If the number after the one you need to round to is 5 or more, make the preceding number one higher. If it is less than 5, drop it and leave the preceding number the same. (Information about rounding is usually provided in the exam instructions or in the exam bulletin.)

Example:
0.0135 = .014 or .01

Decimals

The most important thing to remember about decimals is that the first place value to the right begins with tenths. The place values are as follows:

1	2	6	8	•	3	4	5	7
THOUSANDS	HUNDREDS	TENS	ONES	DECIMAL POINT	TENTHS	HUNDREDTHS	THOUSANDTHS	TEN THOUSANDTHS

In expanded form, this number can also be expressed as:

$1{,}268.3457 = (1 \times 1{,}000) + (2 \times 100) + (6 \times 10) + (8 \times 1) + (3 \times .1) + (4 \times .01) + (5 \times .001) + (7 \times .0001)$

Fractions

To do well when working with fractions, it is necessary to understand some basic concepts. Here are some math rules for fractions using variables:

$$\frac{a}{b} \times \frac{c}{d} = \frac{a \times c}{b \times d}$$

$$\frac{a}{b} + \frac{c}{b} = \frac{a + c}{b}$$

$$\frac{a}{b} \div \frac{c}{d} = \frac{a}{b} \times \frac{d}{c} = \frac{a \times d}{b \times c}$$

$$\frac{a}{b} + \frac{c}{d} = \frac{ad + bc}{bd}$$

Multiplication of Fractions

Multiplying fractions is one of the easiest operations to perform. To multiply fractions, simply multiply the numerators and the denominators, writing each in the respective place over or under the fraction bar.

Example:

$$\frac{4}{5} \times \frac{6}{7} = \frac{24}{35}$$

Division of Fractions

Dividing fractions is the same thing as multiplying fractions by their **reciprocals**. To find the reciprocal of any number, flip its numerator and denominator. For example, the reciprocals of the following numbers are:

$$\frac{1}{3} \rightarrow \frac{3}{1} = 3$$

$$x \rightarrow \frac{1}{x}$$

$$\frac{4}{5} \rightarrow \frac{5}{4}$$

$$5 \rightarrow \frac{1}{5}$$

When dividing fractions, simply multiply the dividend (the number being divided) by the divisor's (the number doing the dividing) reciprocal to get the answer.

Example:

$$\frac{12}{21} \div \frac{3}{4} = \frac{12}{21} \times \frac{4}{3} = \frac{48}{63} = \frac{16}{21}$$

Adding and Subtracting Fractions

To add or subtract fractions with like denominators, just add or subtract the numerators and leave the denominator as it is. For example,

$$\frac{1}{7} + \frac{5}{7} = \frac{6}{7} \quad \text{and} \quad \frac{5}{8} - \frac{2}{8} = \frac{3}{8}$$

To add or subtract fractions with unlike denominators, you must find the **least common denominator**, or LCD.

For example, if given the denominators 8 and 12, 24 would be the LCD because $8 \times 3 = 24$, and $12 \times 2 = 24$. In other words, the LCD is the smallest number divisible by each of the denominators.

Once you know the LCD, convert each fraction to its new form by multiplying both the numerator and denominator by the necessary number to get the LCD, and then add or subtract the new numerators.

Example:

$$\frac{1}{3} + \frac{2}{5} = \frac{5(1)}{5(3)} + \frac{3(2)}{3(5)} = \frac{5}{15} + \frac{6}{15} = \frac{11}{15}$$

Percent

A **percent** is a measure of a part to a whole, with the whole being equal to 100.

- To change a decimal to a percentage, move the decimal point two units to the right and add a percentage symbol.

    Example:
    $.45 = 45\%$ $.07 = 7\%$ $.9 = 90\%$

- To change a fraction to a percentage, first change the fraction to a decimal. To do this, divide the numerator by the denominator. Then change the decimal to a percentage.

    Example:
    $\frac{4}{5} = .80 = 80\%$

    $\frac{2}{5} = .4 = 40\%$

    $\frac{1}{8} = .125 = 12.5\%$

- To change a percentage to a decimal, simply move the decimal point two places to the left and eliminate the percentage symbol.

    Example:
    $64\% = .64$ $87\% = .87$ $7\% = .07$

- To change a percentage to a fraction, divide by 100 and reduce.

    Example:
    $64\% = \frac{64}{100} = \frac{16}{25}$

    $75\% = \frac{75}{100} = \frac{3}{4}$

    $82\% = \frac{82}{100} = \frac{41}{50}$

- Keep in mind that any percentage that is 100 or greater will need to reflect a whole number or mixed number when converted.

    Example:
    $125\% = 1.25$ or $1\frac{1}{4}$

    $350\% = 3.5$ or $3\frac{1}{2}$

Here are some conversions you should be familiar with:

Fraction	Decimal	Percentage
$\frac{1}{2}$	.5	50%
$\frac{1}{4}$	.25	25%
$\frac{1}{3}$	.333 . . .	33.$\overline{3}$%
$\frac{2}{3}$	.666 . . .	66.$\overline{6}$%
$\frac{1}{10}$	.1	10%
$\frac{1}{8}$	.125	12.5%
$\frac{1}{6}$	.1666 . . .	16.$\overline{6}$%
$\frac{1}{5}$	.2	20%

Algebra Review

Equations

An **equation** is solved by finding a number that is equal to an unknown variable.

Simple Rules for Working with Equations

1. The equal sign separates an equation into two sides.
2. Whenever an operation is performed on one side, the same operation must be performed on the other side.
3. Your first goal is to get all of the variables on one side and all of the numbers on the other.
4. The final step often will be to divide each side by the coefficient, leaving the variable equal to a number.

Checking Equations

To check an equation, substitute the number equal to the variable in the original equation.

Example:

To check the following equation, substitute the number 10 for the variable x.

$$\frac{x}{6} = \frac{x + 10}{12}$$

$$\frac{10}{6} = \frac{10 + 10}{12}$$

$$\frac{10}{6} = \frac{20}{12}$$

$$1\frac{2}{3} = 1\frac{2}{3}$$

$$\frac{10}{6} = \frac{10}{6}$$

Because this statement is true, you know the answer $x = 10$ must be correct.

Special Tips for Checking Equations

1. If time permits, be sure to check all equations.
2. Be careful to answer the question that is being asked. Sometimes, this involves solving for a variable and then performing an operation.

Example:

If the question asks the value of $x - 2$, and you find $x = 2$, the answer is not 2, but $2 - 2$. Thus, the answer is 0.

Algebraic Fractions

Algebraic fractions are very similar to fractions in arithmetic.

Example:

Write $\frac{x}{5} - \frac{x}{10}$ as a single fraction.

Solution:

Just like in arithmetic, you need to find the LCD of 5 and 10, which is 10. Then change each fraction into an equivalent fraction that has 10 as a denominator.

$$\frac{x}{5} - \frac{x}{10} = \frac{x(2)}{5(2)} - \frac{x}{10}$$
$$= \frac{2x}{10} - \frac{x}{10}$$
$$= \frac{x}{10}$$

Geometry Review

Area	the space inside a two-dimensional figure
Circumference	the distance around a circle
Perimeter	the distance around a figure
Radius	the distance from the center point of a circle to any point on the arc of a circle

Area

Area is the space inside of the lines defining the shape.

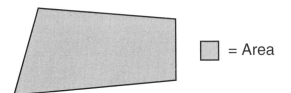

= Area

This geometry review will focus on the area formula for three main shapes: circles, rectangles/squares, and triangles.

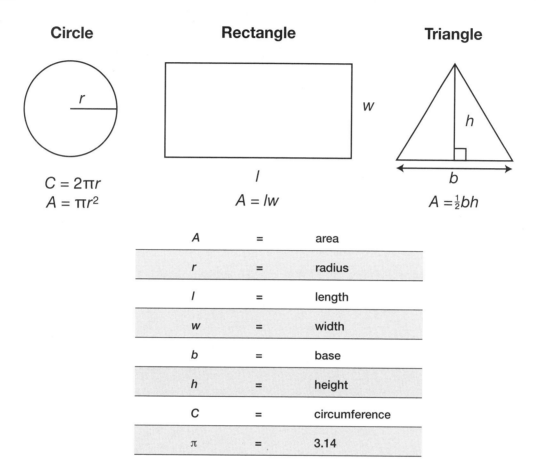

Circle	**Rectangle**	**Triangle**
$C = 2\pi r$		
$A = \pi r^2$	$A = lw$	$A = \frac{1}{2}bh$

A	=	area
r	=	radius
l	=	length
w	=	width
b	=	base
h	=	height
C	=	circumference
π	=	3.14

Perimeter

The **perimeter** of an object is simply the sum of all of its sides.

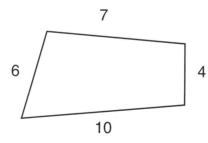

Perimeter = 6 + 7 + 4 + 10 = 27

The **circumference** is the perimeter of a circle.

$C = 2\pi r$

Word Problem Review

Because many of the math problems on the Arizona real estate sales exam will be word problems, pay extra attention to the following review.

Translating Words into Numbers

The most important skill needed for word problems is being able to translate words into mathematical operations. The following will assist you by giving you some common examples of English phrases and their mathematical equivalents.

- "Increase" means add.

    Example:
    A number increased by five = $x + 5$.

- "Less than" means subtract.

    Example:
    10 less than a number = $x - 10$.

- "Times" or "product" means multiply.

    Example:
    Three times a number = $3x$.

- "Times the sum" means to multiply a number by a quantity.

    Example:
    Five times the sum of a number and three = $5(x + 3)$.

- Two variables are sometimes used together.

    Example:
    A number y exceeds five times a number x by ten.
    $y = 5x + 10$

- "Of" means multiply.

    Example:
    10% of 100 is 10 = 10% × 100 = 10.

- "Is" means equals.

Example:
15 is 14 plus 1 becomes 15 = 14 + 1.

Assigning Variables in Word Problems

It may be necessary to create and assign variables in a word problem. To do this, first identify an unknown and a known. You may not actually know the exact value of the "known," but you will know at least something about its value.

Examples:
Max is three years older than Ricky.
Unknown = Ricky's age = x.
Known = Max's age is three years older.
Therefore,
Ricky's age = x and Max's age = $x + 3$.

Heidi made twice as many cookies as Rebecca.
Unknown = number of cookies Rebecca made = x.
Known = number of cookies Heidi made = $2x$.

Jessica has five more than three times the number of books that Becky has.
Unknown = the number of books Becky has = x.
Known = the number of books Jessica has = $3x + 5$.

Percentage Problems

There is one formula that is useful for solving the three types of percentage problems:

$$\frac{\#\ \text{part}}{\text{whole}} = \frac{\%}{100}$$

When reading a percentage problem, substitute the necessary information into the above formula based on the following:

- 100 is always written in the denominator of the percentage sign column.
- If given a percentage, write it in the numerator position of the number column. If you are not given a percentage, then the variable should be placed there.
- The denominator of the number column represents the number that is equal to the whole, or 100%. This number always follows the word *of* in a word problem.

- The numerator of the number column represents the number that is the percent.
- In the formula, the equal sign can be interchanged with the word *is*.

Examples:

- Finding a percentage of a given number:
  What number is equal to 40% of 50?

$$\frac{\overset{\#}{x}}{50} = \frac{\overset{\%}{40}}{100}$$

Cross multiply:

$100(x) = (40)(50)$

$100x = 2{,}000$

$\frac{100x}{100} = \frac{2{,}000}{100}$

$x = 20$ Therefore, 20 is 40% of 50.

- Finding a number when a percentage is given:
  40% of what number is 24?

$$\frac{\overset{\#}{24}}{x} = \frac{\overset{\%}{40}}{100}$$

Cross multiply:

$(24)(100) = (40)(x)$

$2{,}400 = 40x$

$\frac{2{,}400}{40} = \frac{40x}{40}$

$60 = x$ Therefore, 40% of 60 is 24.

- Finding what percentage one number is of another:
  What percentage of 75 is 15?

$$\frac{\overset{\#}{15}}{75} = \frac{\overset{\%}{x}}{100}$$

$$\text{Rate} = \frac{x \text{ units}}{y \text{ units}}$$

A percentage problem simply means that *y* units are equal to 100. It is important to remember that a percentage problem may be worded using the word *rate*.

Cross multiply:

$15(100) = (75)(x)$

$1{,}500 = 75x$

$\frac{1{,}500}{75} = \frac{75x}{75}$

$20 = x$ Therefore, 20% of 75 is 15.

Rate Problems

You may encounter a couple of different types of rate problems on the Arizona real estate sales exam: cost per unit, interest rate, and tax rate. **Rate** is defined as a comparison of two quantities with different units of measure.

$$\textbf{Rate} = \frac{x \text{ units}}{y \text{ units}}$$

Examples: $\frac{\text{dollars}}{\text{square foot}}$, $\frac{\text{interest}}{\text{year}}$

Cost Per Unit

Some problems on your exam may require that you calculate the cost per unit.

Example:

If 100 square feet cost $1,000, how much does 1 square foot cost?

Solution:

$\frac{\text{Total Cost}}{\text{\# of square feet}} = \frac{1{,}000}{100} = \$10$ per square foot

Interest Rate

The formula for simple interest is Interest = Principal × Rate × Time, or $I = PRT$. If you know certain values, but not others, you can still find the answer using algebra. In simple interest problems, the value of T is usually 1, as in 1 year. There are three basic kinds of interest problems, depending on which number is missing.

Equivalencies

Here are some equivalencies you may need to use to complete some questions. Generally, any equivalencies you will need to know for your exam are provided to you.

Equivalencies

12 inches (in. or ") = 1 foot (ft. or ')

3 feet or 36 inches = 1 yard (yd.)

1,760 yards = 1 mile (mi)

5,280 feet = 1 mile

144 square inches (sq. in. or in.^{2}) = 1 square foot (sq. ft. or ft.^{2})

9 square feet = 1 square yard

43,560 feet = 1 acre

640 acres = 1 square mile

Percents

You may be asked a basic percentage problem.

Example:

What is 86% of 1,750?

Solution:

Start by translating words into math terms.

$x = (86\%)(1,750)$

Change the percent into a decimal by moving the decimal point two spaces to the left.

86% = .86

Now you can solve.

$x = (.86)(1,750)$

$x = 1,505$

Other percentage problems you may find on the Arizona real estate sales exam will come in the form of rate problems. Keep reading for more examples of these problems.

Interest Problems

Let's take a look at a problem in which you have to calculate the interest rate (*R*). Remember, the rate is the same as the percentage.

Example:

Mary Valencia borrowed $5,000, for which she is paying $600 interest per year. What is the rate of interest being charged?

Solution:

Start with the values you know.

Principal = $5,000

Interest = $600

Rate = x

Time = 1 year

Using the formula $I = PRT$, insert the values you know, and solve for x.

$600 = $5,000($x$)(1)

$600 = $5,000$x$

$\frac{\$600}{\$5,000} = \frac{x}{\$5,000}$

$.12 = x$

To convert .12 to a percent, move the decimal point two places to the right.

$.12 = 12\%$

Area

Some of the problems on your exam may ask you to calculate the area of a piece of land, a building, or some other figure. Here are some formulas and how to use them.

Rectangles

Remember the formula, Area = (length)(width).

Example:

A man purchased a lot that is 50 feet by 10 feet for a garden. How many square feet of land does he have?

Solution:

Using the formula, Area = (length)(width), you have:

$A = (50)(10) = 500$ square feet

Example:

The Meyers bought a piece of land for a summer home that was 2.75 acres. The lake frontage was 150 feet. What was the length of the lot?

Solution:

When you take your sales exam, you may be provided with certain equivalencies. You will need to refer to the "Equivalencies" list on the previous page to answer this question. First, find the area of the land in square feet.

$(2.75)(43,560) = 119,790$ square feet

In the previous example, you were given the length and the width. In this example, you are given the area and the width, so you are solving for the length. Because you know the area and the width of the lot, use the formula to solve.

Area = (length)(width)

119,790 = (x)(150)

Divide both sides by 150.

$$\frac{119,790}{150} = \frac{(x)(150)}{150}$$

$$x = \frac{119,790}{150}$$

$x = 798.6$ feet

Triangles

Although it may not be as common, you may be asked to find the area of a triangle. If you don't remember the formula, see the section on Area.

Example:

The Baroms are buying a triangular piece of land for a gas station. It is 200 feet at the base, and the side perpendicular to the base is 200 feet. They are paying $2 per square foot for the property. What will it cost?

Solution:

Start with the formula Area = $\frac{1}{2}$(base)(height).

Now, write down the values you know.

Area = x

Base = 200

Height = 200

If it's easier, you can change $\frac{1}{2}$ to a decimal.

$\frac{1}{2} = .5$

Now you can plug these values into the formula.

$x = (.5)(200)(200)$

$x = (.5)(40,000)$

$x = 20,000$ square feet

Don't forget that the question is not asking for the number of square feet, but for the *cost* of the property per square foot. This is a rate problem, so you need to complete one more step:

(20,000 square feet)($2 per square foot) = $40,000

Example:

Victor and Evelyn Robinson have an outlot that a neighbor wants to buy. The side of the outlot next to their property is 86 feet. The rear line is perpendicular to their side lot, and the road frontage is 111 feet. Their plat shows they own 3,000 square feet in the outlot. What is the length of the rear line of the outlot? Round your answer to the nearest whole number.

Solution:

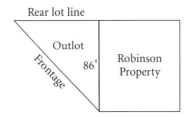

It helps to draw the figure to conceive shapes. The rear lot line is perpendicular to the side lot line. This makes the side lot line the base and the rear lot line the height (altitude).

Area = $\frac{1}{2}$(base)(height)

Area = 3,000 square feet

Base = 86 feet

Height = x

If it's easier, you can change $\frac{1}{2}$ to a decimal.

$\frac{1}{2}$ = .5

Now you can plug these values into the formula.

$3,000 = (.5)(86)(x)$

$3,000 = (43)(x)$

Divide both sides by 43.

$\frac{3,000}{43} = \frac{(43)(x)}{43}$

$x = 69.767$ feet

Don't forget the question says to round your answer to the nearest whole number. The answer is 70 feet.

Circles

Remember the formula, Area = πr^2.

Example:

Murray Brodman, a contractor, has been awarded the job to put up a circular bandstand in the town square. The radius of the circular area for the bandstand is 15 feet. What is the area of the bandstand? Use 3.14 for π.

Solution:

Area = πr^2

Start with the values you know.

Area = x

$\pi = 3.14$

radius = 15

Now plug these values into the formula.

Area = $(3.14)(15)(15) = 706.5$ sq. ft.

▶ Property Tax

To solve property tax questions, you will be using percents and rates.

Example:

The tax rate in your county is $4.17 per hundred of assessed valuation, and Mr. Brown, a possible client, has told you his taxes are $1,100. What is his property assessment? (Round your answer to the nearest ten cents.)

Solution:

Start off with the values you know.

Taxes = $1,100

Assessment = x

Tax rate = $4.17 per hundred (%)

If you remember the definition of percent as being an amount per hundred, then $4.17 per hundred is actually 4.17%. To make this equation more manageable, convert this percent to a decimal by moving the decimal point two spaces to the left. Now the tax rate is .0417.

.0417 of the assessed value of the house is $1,100. Translate the words into math terms. This means: $(.0417)(x) = \$1,100$.

To solve the equation, divide both sides by .0417.

$$\frac{.0417x}{.0417} = \frac{\$1,100}{.0417}$$

$x = \$26,378.896$

Remember, the question asks you to round to the nearest ten cents. That means that .896 needs to be rounded up to 90. So the answer is $26,378.90.

Example:

Mr. Smith knew his own taxes were $975 and his property assessment was $17,000 for the house and $6,000 for the land. He wanted to know the tax rate (%).

Tip

Note that you may be asked for monthly amounts in certain problems. Most calculations are on an annual basis—unless you divide by 12.

Solution:

Start with the values you know.

Tax = $975

Assessment for house = $17,000 plus assessment for land = $6,000. Therefore, total = $23,000.

Rate (%) = x

According to the question, $23,000 at a rate of x is $975. Convert this statement into an equation.

($23,000)($x$) = $975.

Solve the equation by dividing both sides by 23,000.

$$\frac{\$23{,}000x}{\$23{,}000} = \frac{\$975}{\$23{,}000}$$

x = .0423913

To make this equation more simple, round the answer to .0424.

Remember that you are looking for the rate. Therefore, you need to convert this decimal to a percent by moving the decimal point two places to the right. The rate is 4.24%. (This can also be expressed as $4.24 per hundred.)

Loan-to-Value Ratios

These problems often deal with percentages.

Example:

A mortgage loan for 10% is at a 75% loan-to-value ratio. The interest on the original balance for the first year is $6,590. What is the value of the property securing the loan? Round to the nearest one cent.

Solution:

First, find out the loan amount.

$6,590 is 10% of the loan amount. Let x equal the loan amount. Now, translate these words into math terms.

$6,590 = (10%)($x$)

Change 10% into a decimal by moving the decimal point two places to the left.

10% = .1

Now you have:

$6,590 = (.1)($x$)

Divide both sides by (.1).

x = $65,900

Now that you know the loan amount ($65,900), use this information to find the value of the property.

Write down the values you know.

Loan amount = $65,900

Loan-to-value ratio = 75%

Value = x

We know that 75% of the value is $65,900.

Translate this into math terms.

$(75\%)(x) = \$65,900$

Change the percent into a decimal (75% = .75) and solve.

$(.75)(x) = \$65,900$

Divide both sides by .75.

$$\frac{(.75)(x)}{(.75)} = \frac{\$65,900}{(.75)}$$

$x = \$87,866.66666$

When rounded to the nearest one cent, the answer is $87,866.67.

Points

Loan discounts are often called **points**, or loan placement fees, *one point* meaning 1% of the face amount of the loan. The service fee of 1% paid by buyers of government-backed loans is called a **loan origination fee**.

Example:

A homebuyer may obtain a $50,000 FHA mortgage loan, provided the seller pays a discount of five points. What is the amount of the discount?

Solution:

The definition of one point is 1% of the face amount of the loan.

Therefore, 5 points = 5% of the face of the loan. First, change the percent to a decimal.

5% = .05

Now you can use these values to solve.

Amount of discount = x

Points = .05

Amount of loan = $50,000

So, $x = (.05)(\$50,000)$.

$x = \$2,500$

Example:

A property is listed at $74,000. An offer is made for $72,000, provided the seller pays three points on a loan for 80% of the purchase price. The brokerage commission rate is 7%. How much less will the seller receive if he accepts the offer than he would have received if he sold at all cash at the original terms?

Solution:

Here are the values you know:

Sold for original terms—price	$74,000	
Less 7% commission	− 5,180	(.07)($74,000) = $5,180
Seller's net	$68,820	

This question becomes more difficult, because in order to find the seller's net on the offered price, you must calculate the discount. The provision is that the seller pays three points (or .03) on a loan for 80% (or .8) of the price.

Start by finding 80% of the price.

(.8)($72,000) = $57,600

Now, the points are applied to this amount. This means .03 of $57,600 is the discount.

So, (.03)($57,600) = discount = $1,728.

You know these values:

Sold at offered terms—price	$72,000	
Less 7% commission	− 5,040	(.07)($72,000) = $5,040
Less discount	− 1,728	
Seller's net	$65,232	

$72,000	Sales price		Net at original	$68,820
× .80	Loan-to-value ratio		Net at offered	− 65,232
$57,600	Loan amount		Difference	$3,588
× .03	Points			
$1,728	Discount			

Equity

Example:

If a homeowner has a first mortgage loan balance of $48,350, a second mortgage loan balance of $18,200, and $26,300 equity, what is the value of her home?

Solution:

In this case, the value of the home is determined by the total loan balance plus the equity. Add the three numbers to find the value of the home.

$48,350 loan balance + $18,200 loan balance + $26,300 = value of the home

$92,850 = value of the home

Qualifying Buyers

Example:

A buyer is obtaining a conventional loan that requires 29/33 ratios. He earns $66,000 a year, and has a $1,350 car payment. What is his maximum principal, interest, taxes, and insurance (PITI) payment?

  a. $1,612.50

  b. $1,812.50

  c. $465

  d. $2,475

Solution:

$66,000 divided by 12 = $5,500 monthly income

($5,500)(.29) = $1,595 front-end qualifier

($5,500)(.33) = $1,815 − $1,350 debt = $465 back-end qualifier

Maximum PITI is the lower of these two qualifiers, $465.

Prorations

At the time of settlement, there must be a reconciliation or adjustment of any monies owed by either party as of that date. The important fact to bear in mind is that *the party who used the service pays for it.* If you will keep this firmly in mind, you will not have any difficulty deciding who to credit and who to debit.

Example:

Mr. Seller's taxes are $1,200 a year paid in advance on a calendar year. He is settling on the sale of his house to Mr. Buyer on August 1. Which of them owes how much to the other?

Solution:

Ask yourself some questions:

How many months has the seller paid for?	12	($1,200)
How many months has the seller used?	7	($700)
How many months should the seller be reimbursed for?	5	($500)
How many months will the buyer use?	5	($500)
How many months has he paid for?	0	($0)
How many months should he reimburse the seller for?	5	($500)

Credit Mr. Seller $500

Debit Mr. Buyer $500

What would the answer be if the taxes were paid in arrears? In other words, the seller has used the service for seven months but hasn't paid anything. The buyer will have to pay it all at the end of the year. In that case, the seller owes the buyer for seven months, or $700.

In working proration problems, be sure you have the right dates when you subtract. Sometimes, the termination date for the policy is not given, and the tendency is to subtract the date the policy was written from the date of settlement. This will not give you the unused portion. You must subtract the date of settlement from the date of termination of the policy, which will be exactly the same date one, three, or five years after written, depending on the term of the policy. Most problems use either a one- or three-year term.

Remember!

Use a 30-day month and a 360-day year in all calculations unless you are told otherwise. Assume a calendar year, unless a fiscal or school year is specified.

Commissions

Let's look at a commission problem. They are typically rate (percentage) problems.

Example:
Broker Jones sold the Smith house for $65,000. The total commission came to $4,000. What was Jones's commission rate? Round to the nearest whole percent.

Solution:
You see the word *rate* and decide this is solved using percentages.
Start with the values you know.
Price of house = $65,000
Commission rate = x
Commission = $4,000

Now, translate the word problem into an equation.
$65,000x = $4,000

Divide both sides by 65,000.
$$x = \frac{\$4,000}{\$65,000}$$
$x = 0.061$
Convert the decimal to a percent by moving the decimal two places to the right. 0.061 becomes 6.1%.

Example:
An agent received a 3% commission on $\frac{1}{4}$ of her total sales. On the remainder, she received a 6% commission. What was her average commission for all of her sales?

Solution:

Start off by asking yourself: How many fourths (parts) were there? Four, naturally.

3%   6%   6%   6%

To find the average, you add up all the numbers, and divide by the number of items you add together. In this case, there are four numbers.
So, 3 + 6 + 6 + 6 = 21.
And 21% ÷ 4 = 5.25%.

Sale Proceeds

Example:

Salesman Garcia was trying to list a house. The owner said he wanted to clear (net) $12,000 from the sale of the house. The balance of the mortgage was $37,000. It would cost about $1,200 to fix up the house to sell. How much would the owner have to sell the house for if the 7% commission was included? (Round your answer to the nearest cent.)

Solution:

Use a chart to clarify the problem.

Expenses	In Dollars	In Percents
Seller's net	$12,000	
Loan balance	$37,000	
Repairs	$1,200	
Commission		%
	$50,200	7%

If the sales price is 100% and the commission is 7% of the sales price, all the remaining items added together must make 93% of the sales price. The place where most people go wrong is in not including the seller's net when they add the expenses. The seller's net has to come out of the sales price. (Where else would it come from?) Therefore, it is part of the remaining 93%. You now have a percentage problem. As always, convert your percents to decimals.

Start with the values you know:

Expenses = $50,200

Sales price = x

Seller's net, loan balance, repairs = .93 of sales price

.93 of the sales price is $50,200.

Convert this statement into an equation.

$(.93)(x) = \$50,200$

Divide both sides by .93.

$\frac{(.93)(x)}{.93} = \frac{\$50,200}{.93}$

$x = \frac{\$50,200}{.93}$

$x = \$53,978.4945$

Don't forget to round to the nearest cent!

$x = \$53,978.49$

Transfer Tax/Conveyance Tax/Revenue Stamps

Here is a transfer tax question.

Example:

A property is sold for $135,800 in cash. The transfer tax is $441.35. If transfer taxes are calculated per $200 of value, what was the rate (per $200) of the transfer tax?

Solution:

Start with the values you know.

Selling price = $135,800

Transfer tax rate = x per $200

Transfer tax = $441.35

It's probably easiest to begin by dividing by $200 because the rate is calculated per $200 of value.

So, $\frac{\$135,800}{\$200} = \$679$.

You know that $441.35 is produced by multiplying $679 by some rate. Translate this into math terms.

$\$441.35 = (x)(\$679)$

Divide both sides by $679.

$\frac{\$441.35}{(\$679)} = \frac{(x)(\$679)}{(\$679)}$

$.65 = x$

Therefore, the transfer tax rate is $.65 per $200.

Competitive Market Analyses (CMA)

To solve these problems, you will use measurements and other hypothetical features of the comparable property to arrive at a value. Remember, a CMA is not an appraisal.

Example:

If Building A measures 52' by 106' and Building B measures 75' by 85', how much will B cost if A costs $140,000 and both cost the same per square foot to build?

Solution:

Area = (length)(width)

Area of Building A = (52)(106) = 5,512 square feet

Area of Building B = (75)(85) = 6,375 square feet

Cost of Building A per square foot = $\frac{\$140,000}{5,512}$ = \$25.40

Cost of Building B = (6,375)(\$25.40) = \$161,925

Example:

Carson's house (B), which is being appraised, is an exact twin of the houses on either side of it, built by the same builder at the same time. House A was appraised for \$45,000, but it has a 14' × 20' garage, which was added at a cost of about \$18 per square foot. House C was recently sold for \$43,000, with central air valued at \$3,000. What would be a fair estimate of the value of Carson's house?

Solution:

Comparable C	\$43,000
– Air Conditioning	– 3,000
	\$40,000

Comparable A	\$45,000	Garage: 14' × 20' = 280 sq. ft.
– Cost of Garage	– 5,040	280 sq. ft. × \$18 = \$5,040
	\$39,960	

Answer: \$40,000

Income Properties

Example:

An investor is considering the purchase of an income property generating a gross income of \$350,000. Operating expenses constitute 70% of gross income. If the investor wants a return of 14%, what is the maximum he can pay?

Solution:

Gross income = \$350,000

Expenses = 70% of gross income

Net income = Gross income – Expenses

Desired return = 14%

Maximum buyer can pay = x

This is a multistep problem. Start by calculating the expenses, but remember, you will need to stop to calculate the net income. First, change the percent to a decimal.

70% = .70

Now, you know that expenses are 70% of the gross income of $350,000. Change the words to mathematical terms.

Expenses = (.7)($350,000) = $245,000

Gross income – Expenses = Net income

$350,000 – $245,000 = $105,000

The buyer wants the net income ($105,000) to be 14% of what he pays for the property.

Change the percent to a decimal (14% = .14) and then convert this statement to an equation.

$105,000 = (.14)(x)

Divide both sides by .14.

$$\frac{\$105,000}{.14} = \frac{(.14)(x)}{.14}$$

$105,000 ÷ .14 = x

$750,000 = x

Depreciation

There are several methods of depreciation, but the only one you are likely to meet on your exam is the straight-line method. This method spreads the total depreciation over the useful life of the building in equal annual amounts. It is calculated by dividing the replacement cost by the years of useful life left.

$$\frac{\text{replacement cost}}{\text{years of useful life}} = \text{annual depreciation}$$

The depreciation rate may be given or may have to be calculated by the straight-line method. This means dividing the total depreciation (100%) by the estimated useful life given for the building.

$$\frac{100\%}{\text{years of useful life}} = \text{depreciated rate}$$

If a building has 50 years of useful life left, the depreciation rate would be computed as follows:

$$\frac{100\%}{50} = 2\%$$

In other words, it has a 2% depreciation rate annually.

Example:

The replacement cost of a building has been estimated at $80,000. The building is 12 years old and has an estimated 40 years of useful life left. What can be charged to annual depreciation? What is the total depreciation for 12 years? What is the present value of this building?

Solution:

Calculate the annual depreciation.

$$\frac{\text{replacement cost}}{\text{years of useful life}} = \text{annual depreciation}$$

$$\frac{\$80,000}{40} = \$2,000$$

Find the total depreciation over the 12 years.

Annual depreciation of $2,000 × 12 years = $24,000.

Find the current value: replacement − depreciation = current value.

$80,000 − $24,000 = $56,000

▶ Summary

Hopefully, with this review, you have realized that real estate math is not as bad as it seems. If you feel you need more practice, check out LearningExpress's *Practical Math Success in 20 Minutes a Day* or *1001 Math Problems*. Use the exams in the books to practice even more real estate math.

CHAPTER

6 ▶ Real Estate Glossary

CHAPTER SUMMARY

One of the most basic components in preparing for the Arizona real estate sales exam is making sure you know all the terminology. This glossary provides a list of the most commonly used real estate terms and their definitions.

T HESE TERMS WILL help you not only as you study for your real estate exam, but also after you pass your exam and are practicing in the field. The terms are listed in alphabetical order for easy reference.

▶ A

abandonment the voluntary surrender of a right, claim, or interest in a piece of property without naming a successor as owner or tenant.

abstract of title a certified summary of the history of a title to a particular parcel of real estate that includes the original grant and all subsequent transfers, encumbrances, and releases.

abutting sharing a common boundary; adjoining.

acceleration clause a clause in a note, mortgage, or deed of trust that permits the lender to declare the entire amount of principal and accrued interest due and payable immediately in the event of default.

acceptance the indication by a party receiving an offer that he or she agrees to the terms of the offer. In most states, the offer and acceptance must be reduced to writing when real property is involved.

accretion the increase or addition of land resulting from the natural deposit of sand or soil by streams, lakes, or rivers.

accrued depreciation (1) the amount of depreciation, or loss in value, that has accumulated since initial construction; (2) the difference between the current appraised value and the cost to replace the building new.

accrued items a list of expenses that have been incurred but have not yet been paid, such as interest on a mortgage loan, which are included on a closing statement.

acknowledgment a formal declaration before a public official, usually a notary public, by a person who has signed a deed, contract, or other document that the execution was a voluntary act.

acre a measure of land equal to 43,560 square feet or 4,840 square yards.

actual eviction the result of legal action brought by a landlord against a defaulted tenant, whereby the tenant is physically removed from rented or leased property by a court order.

actual notice the actual knowledge that a person has of a particular fact.

addendum any provision added to a contract, or an addition to a contract that expands, modifies, or enhances the clarity of the agreement. To be a part of the contract and legally enforceable, an addendum must be referenced within the contract.

adjacent lying near to but not necessarily in actual contact with.

adjoining contiguous or attached; in actual contact with.

adjustable-rate mortgage (ARM) a mortgage in which the interest changes periodically, according to corresponding fluctuations in an index. All ARMs are tied to indexes. For example, a seven-year, adjustable-rate mortgage is a loan in which the rate remains fixed for the first seven years, then fluctuates according to the index to which it is tied.

adjusted basis the original cost of a property, plus acquisition costs, plus the value of added improvements to the property, minus accrued depreciation.

adjustment date the date the interest rate changes on an adjustable-rate mortgage.

administrator a person appointed by a court to settle the estate of a person who has died without leaving a will.

ad valorem tax tax in proportion to the value of a property.

adverse possession a method of acquiring title to another person's property through court action after taking actual, open, hostile, and continuous possession for a statutory period of time; may require payment of property taxes during the period of possession.

affidavit a written statement made under oath and signed before a licensed public official, usually a notary public.

agency the legal relationship between principal and agent that arises out of a contract wherein an agent is employed to do certain acts on behalf of the principal who has retained the agent to deal with a third party.

agent one who has been granted the authority to act on behalf of another.

agreement of sale a written agreement between a seller and a purchaser whereby the purchaser agrees to buy a certain piece of property from the seller for a specified price.

air rights the right to use the open space above a particular property.

alienation the transfer of ownership of a property to another, either voluntarily or involuntarily.

alienation clause the clause in a mortgage or deed of trust that permits the lender to declare all unpaid principal and accrued interest due and payable if the borrower transfers title to the property.

allodial system in the United States, a system of land ownership in which land is held free and clear of any rent or services due to the government; commonly contrasted with the feudal system, in which ownership is held by a monarch.

amenities features or benefits of a particular property that enhance the property's desirability and value, such as a scenic view or a pool.

amortization the method of repaying a loan or debt by making periodic installment payments composed of both principal and interest. When all principal has been repaid, it is considered fully amortized.

amortization schedule a table that shows how much of each loan payment will be applied toward principal and how much toward interest over the lifespan of the loan. It also shows the gradual decrease of the outstanding loan balance until it reaches zero.

amortize to repay a loan through regular payments that are composed of principal and interest.

annual percentage rate (APR) the total or effective amount of interest charged on a loan, expressed as a percentage, on a yearly basis. This value is created according to a government formula intended to reflect the true annual cost of borrowing.

anti-deficiency laws laws used in some states to limit the claim of a lender on default on payment of a purchase money mortgage on owner-occupied residential property to the value of the collateral.

anti-trust laws laws designed to protect free enterprise and the open marketplace by prohibiting certain business practices that restrict competition. In reference to real estate, these laws would prevent such practices as price fixing or agreements by brokers to limit their areas of trade.

apportionments adjustment of income, expenses, or carrying charges related to real estate, usually computed to the date of closing so that the seller pays all expenses to date, then the buyer pays all expenses beginning on the closing date.

appraisal an estimate or opinion of the value of an adequately described property, as of a specific date.

appraised value an opinion of a property's fair market value, based on an appraiser's knowledge, experience, and analysis of the property, based on comparable sales.

appraiser an individual qualified by education, training, and experience to estimate the value of real property. Appraisers may work directly for mortgage lenders, or they may be independent contractors.

appreciation an increase in the market value of a property.

appurtenance something that transfers with the title to land even if not an actual part of the property, such as an easement.

arbitration the process of settling a dispute in which the parties submit their differences to an impartial third party, on whose decision on the matter is binding.

ARELLO the Association of Real Estate License Law Officials.

assessed value the value of a property used to calculate real estate taxes.

assessment the process of assigning value on property for taxation purposes.

assessor a public official who establishes the value of a property for taxation purposes.

asset items of value owned by an individual. Assets that can be quickly converted into cash are considered "liquid assets," such as bank accounts and stock portfolios. Other assets include real estate, personal property, and debts owed.

assignment the transfer of rights or interest from one person to another.

assumption of mortgage the act of acquiring the title to a property that has an existing mortgage and agreeing to be liable for the payment of any debt still existing on that mortgage. However, the lender must accept the transfer of liability for the original borrower to be relieved of the debt.

attachment the process whereby a court takes custody of a debtor's property until the creditor's debt is satisfied.

attest to bear witness by providing a signature.

attorney-in-fact a person who is authorized under a power of attorney to act on behalf of another.

avulsion the removal of land from one owner to another when a stream or other body of water suddenly changes its channel.

▶ B

balloon mortgage a loan in which the periodic payments do not fully amortize the loan, so that a final payment (a balloon payment) is substantially larger than the amount of the periodic payments that must be made to satisfy the debt.

balloon payment the final, lump-sum payment that is due at the termination of a balloon mortgage.

bankruptcy an individual or individuals can restructure or relieve themselves of debts and liabilities by filing in federal bankruptcy court. There are many types of bankruptcies, and the most common for an individual is "Chapter 7 No Asset," which relieves the borrower of most types of debts.

bargain and sale deed a deed that conveys title, but does not necessarily carry warranties against liens or encumbrances.

baseline one of the imaginary east-west lines used as a reference point when describing property with the rectangular or government survey method of property description.

benchmark a permanently marked point with a known elevation, used as a reference by surveyors to measure elevations.

beneficiary (1) one who benefits from the acts of another; (2) the lender in a deed of trust.

bequest personal property given by provision of a will.

betterment an improvement to property that increases its value.

bilateral contract a contract in which each party promises to perform an act in exchange for the other party's promise also to perform an act.

bill of sale a written instrument that transfers ownership of personal property. A bill of sale cannot be used to transfer ownership of real property, which is passed by deed.

binder an agreement, accompanied by an earnest money deposit, for the purchase of a piece of real estate to show the purchaser's good faith intent to complete a transaction.

biweekly mortgage a mortgage in which payments are made every two weeks instead of once a month. Therefore, instead of making 12 monthly payments during the year, the borrower makes the equivalent of 13 monthly payments. The extra payment reduces the principal, thereby reducing the time it takes to pay off a 30-year mortgage.

blanket mortgage a mortgage in which more than one parcel of real estate is pledged to cover a single debt.

blockbusting the illegal and discriminatory practice of inducing homeowners to sell their properties by suggesting or implying the introduction of members of a protected class into the neighborhood.

bona fide in good faith, honest.

bond evidence of personal debt secured by a mortgage or other lien on real estate.

boot money or property provided to make up a difference in value or equity between two properties in an exchange.

branch office a place of business secondary to a principal office. The branch office is a satellite office generally run by a licensed broker, for the benefit of the broker running the principal office, as well as the associate broker's convenience.

breach of contract violation of any conditions or terms in a contract without legal excuse.

broker the term *broker* can mean many things, but in terms of real estate, it is the owner-manager of a business that brings together the parties to a real estate transaction for a fee. The roles of brokers and brokers' associates are defined by state law. In the mortgage industry, *broker* usually refers to a company or individual who does not lend the money for the loans directly, but who brokers loans to larger lenders or investors.

brokerage the business of bringing together buyers and sellers or other participants in a real estate transaction.

broker's price opinion (BPO) a broker's opinion of value based on a competitive market analysis, rather than a certified appraisal.

building code local regulations that control construction, design, and materials used in construction that are based on health and safety regulations.

building line the distance from the front, rear, or sides of a building lot beyond which no structures may extend.

building restrictions limitations listed in zoning ordinances or deed restrictions on the size and type of improvements allowed on a property.

bundle of rights the concept that ownership of a property includes certain rights regarding the property, such as possession, enjoyment, control of use, and disposition.

buydown usually refers to a fixed-rate mortgage where the interest rate is "bought down" for a temporary period, usually one to three years. After that time and for the remainder of the term, the borrower's payment is calculated at the note rate. In order to buy down the initial rate for the temporary payment, a lump sum is paid and held in an account used to supplement the borrower's monthly payment. These funds usually come from the seller as a financial incentive to induce someone to buy his or her property.

buyer's broker real estate broker retained by a prospective buyer; this buyer becomes the broker's client to whom fiduciary duties are owed.

bylaws rules and regulations adopted by an association—for example, a condominium.

► C

cancellation clause a provision in a lease that confers on one or all parties to the lease the right to terminate the parties' obligations, should the occurrence of the condition or contingency set forth in the clause happen.

canvassing the practice of searching for prospective clients by making unsolicited phone calls and/or visiting homes door to door.

cap the limit on fluctuation rates regarding adjustable-rate mortgages. Limitations, or caps, may apply to how much the loan may adjust over a six-month period, an annual period, and over the life of the loan. There is also a limit on how much that payment can change each year.

capital money used to create income, or the net worth of a business as represented by the amount by which its assets exceed its liabilities.

capital expenditure the cost of a betterment to a property.

capital gains tax a tax charged on the profit gained from the sale of a capital asset.

capitalization the process of estimating the present value of an income-producing piece of property by dividing anticipated future income by a capitalization rate.

capitalization rate the rate of return a property will generate on an owner's investment.

cash flow the net income produced by an investment property, calculated by deducting operating and fixed expenses from gross income.

caveat emptor a phrase meaning "let the buyer beware."

CC&R covenants, conditions, and restrictions of a cooperative or condominium development.

certificate of discharge a document used when the security instrument is a mortgage.

certificate of eligibility a document issued by the Veterans Administration that certifies a veteran's eligibility for a VA loan.

certificate of reasonable value (CRV) once the appraisal has been performed on a property being bought with a VA loan, the Veterans Administration issues a CRV.

certificate of sale the document given to a purchaser of real estate that is sold at a tax foreclosure sale.

certificate of title a report stating an opinion on the status of a title, based on the examination of public records.

chain of title the recorded history of conveyances and encumbrances that affect the title to a parcel of land.

chattel personal property, as opposed to real property.

chattel mortgage a loan in which personal property is pledged to secure the debt.

city a large municipality governed under a charter and granted by the state.

clear title a title that is free of liens and legal questions as to ownership of a property that is a requirement for the sale of real estate; sometimes referred to as *just title*, *good title*, or *free and clear title.*

closing the point in a real estate transaction when the purchase price is paid to the seller and the deed to the property is transferred from the seller to the buyer.

closing costs there are two kinds: (1) nonrecurring closing costs and (2) prepaid items. Nonrecurring closing costs are any items paid once as a result of buying the property or obtaining a loan. Prepaid items are items that recur over time, such as property taxes and homeowners insurance. A lender makes an attempt to estimate the amount of nonrecurring closing costs and prepaid items on the good faith estimate, which is issued to the borrower within three days of receiving a home loan application.

closing date the date on which the buyer takes over the property.

closing statement a written accounting of funds received and disbursed during a real estate transaction. The buyer and seller receive separate closing statements.

cloud on the title an outstanding claim or encumbrance that can affect or impair the owner's title.

clustering the grouping of home sites within a subdivision on smaller lots than normal, with the remaining land slated for use as common areas.

codicil a supplement or addition to a will that modifies the original instrument.

coinsurance clause a clause in an insurance policy that requires the insured to pay a portion of any loss experienced.

collateral something of value hypothecated (real property) or pledged (personal property) by a borrower as security for a debt.

collection when a borrower falls behind, the lender contacts the borrower in an effort to bring the loan current. The loan goes to "collection."

color of title an instrument that gives evidence of title, but may not be legally adequate to actually convey title.

commercial property property used to produce income, such as an office building or a restaurant.

commingling the illegal act of an agent mixing a client's monies, which should be held in a separate escrow account, with the agent's personal monies; in some states, it means placing funds that are separate property in an account containing funds that are community property.

commission the fee paid to a broker for services rendered in a real estate transaction.

commitment letter a pledge in writing affirming an agreement.

common areas portions of a building, land, and amenities owned (or managed) by a planned unit development or condominium project's homeowners association or a cooperative project's cooperative corporation. These areas are used by all of the unit owners, who share in the common expenses of their operation and maintenance. Common areas may include swimming pools, tennis courts, and other recreational facilities, as well as common corridors of buildings, parking areas, and lobbies.

common law the body of laws derived from local custom and judicial precedent.

community property a system of property ownership in which each spouse has equal interest in property acquired during the marriage; recognized in nine states.

comparable sales recent sales of similar properties in nearby areas that are used to help estimate the current market value of a property.

competent parties people who are legally qualified to enter a contract, usually meaning that they are of legal age, of sound mind, and not under the influence of drugs or other mind-altering substances.

competitive market analysis (CMA) an analysis intended to assist a seller or buyer in determining a property's range of value.

condemnation the judicial process by which the government exercises its power of eminent domain.

condominium a form of ownership in which an individual owns a specific unit in a multiunit building and shares ownership of common areas with other unit owners.

condominium conversion changing the ownership of an existing building (usually a multi-dwelling rental unit) from single ownership to condominium ownership.

conformity an appraisal principle that asserts that property achieves its maximum value when a neighborhood is homogeneous in its use of land; the basis for zoning ordinances.

consideration something of value that induces parties to enter into a contract, such as money or services.

construction mortgage a short-term loan used to finance the building of improvements to real estate.

constructive eviction action or inaction by a landlord that renders a property uninhabitable, forcing a tenant to move out with no further liability for rent.

constructive notice notice of a fact given by making the fact part of the public record. All persons are responsible for knowing the information, whether or not they have actually seen the record.

contingency a condition that must be met before a contract is legally binding. A satisfactory home inspection report from a qualified home inspector is an example of a common type of contingency.

contract an agreement between two or more legally competent parties to do or to refrain from doing some legal act in exchange for a consideration.

contract for deed a contract for the sale of a parcel of real estate in which the buyer makes periodic payments to the seller and receives title to the property only after all, or a substantial part, of the purchase price has been paid, or regular payments have been made for one year or longer.

conventional loan a loan that is neither insured nor guaranteed by an agency of government.

conversion option an option in an adjustable-rate mortgage to convert it to a fixed-rate mortgage.

convertible ARM an adjustable-rate mortgage that allows the borrower to change the ARM to a fixed-rate mortgage at a specific time.

conveyance the transfer of title from the grantor to the grantee.

cooperative a form of property ownership in which a corporation owns a multiunit building and stockholders of the corporation may lease and occupy individual units of the building through a proprietary lease.

corporation a legal entity with potentially perpetual existence that is created and owned by shareholders who appoint a board of directors to direct the business affairs of the corporation.

cost approach an appraisal method whereby the value of a property is calculated by estimating the cost of constructing a comparable building, subtracting depreciation, and adding land value.

counteroffer an offer submitted in response to an offer. It has the effect of overriding the original offer.

credit an agreement in which a borrower receives something of value in exchange for a promise to repay the lender.

credit history a record of an individual's repayment of debt.

cul-de-sac a dead-end street that widens at the end, creating a circular turnaround area.

curtesy the statutory or common law right of a husband to all or part of real estate owned by his deceased wife, regardless of will provisions, recognized in some states.

curtilage area of land occupied by a building, its outbuildings, and yard, either actually enclosed or considered enclosed.

► **D**

damages the amount of money recoverable by a person who has been injured by the actions of another.

datum a specific point used in surveying.

DBA the abbreviation for "doing business as."

debt an amount owed to another.

decedent a person who dies.

dedication the donation of private property by its owner to a governmental body for public use.

deed a written document that, when properly signed and delivered, conveys title to real property from the grantor to the grantee.

deed-in-lieu a foreclosure instrument used to convey title to the lender when the borrower is in default and wants to avoid foreclosure.

deed of trust a deed in which the title to property is transferred to a third-party trustee to secure repayment of a loan; three-party mortgage arrangement.

deed restriction an imposed restriction for the purpose of limiting the use of land, such as the size or type of improvements to be allowed. Also called a *restrictive covenant.*

default the failure to perform a contractual duty.

defeasance clause a clause in a mortgage that renders it void where all obligations have been fulfilled.

deficiency judgment a personal claim against a borrower when mortgaged property is foreclosed and sale of the property does not produce sufficient funds to pay off the mortgage. Deficiency judgments may be prohibited in some circumstances by anti-deficiency protection.

delinquency failure to make mortgage or loan payments when payments are due.

density zoning a zoning ordinance that restricts the number of houses or dwelling units that can be built per acre in a particular area, such as a subdivision.

depreciation a loss in value due to physical deterioration, functional, or external obsolescence.

descent the transfer of property to an owner's heirs when the owner dies intestate.

devise the transfer of title to real estate by will.

devisee one who receives a bequest of real estate by will.

devisor one who grants real estate by will.

directional growth the direction toward which certain residential sections of a city are expected to grow.

discount point 1% of the loan amount charged by a lender at closing to increase a loan's effective yield and lower the fare rate to the borrower.

discount rate the rate that lenders pay for mortgage funds—a higher rate is passed on to the borrower.

dispossess to remove a tenant from property by legal process.

dominant estate (tenement) property that includes the right to use an easement on adjoining property.

dower the right of a widow in the property of her husband upon his death in noncommunity property states.

down payment the part of the purchase price that the buyer pays in cash and is not financed with a mortgage or loan.

dual agency an agent who represents both parties in a transaction.

due-on-sale clause a provision in a mortgage that allows the lender to demand repayment in full if the borrower sells the property that serves as security for the mortgage.

duress the use of unlawful means to force a person to act or to refrain from an action against his or her will.

► E

earnest money down payment made by a buyer of real estate as evidence of good faith.

easement the right of one party to use the land of another for a particular purpose, such as to lay utility lines.

easement by necessity an easement, granted by law and requiring court action, that is deemed necessary for the full enjoyment of a parcel of land. An example would be an easement allowing access from landlocked property to a road.

easement by prescription a means of acquiring an easement by continued, open, and hostile use of someone else's property for a statutorily defined period of time.

easement in gross a personal right granted by an owner with no requirement that the easement holder own adjoining land.

economic life the period of time over which an improved property will generate sufficient income to justify its continued existence.

effective age an appraiser's estimate of the physical condition of a building. The actual age of a building may be different from its effective age.

emblements cultivated crops; generally considered to be personal property.

eminent domain the right of a government to take private property for public use upon payment of its fair market value. Eminent domain is the basis for condemnation proceedings.

encroachment a trespass caused when a structure, such as a wall or fence, invades another person's land or air space.

encumbrance anything that affects or limits the title to a property, such as easements, leases, mortgages, or restrictions.

equitable title the interest in a piece of real estate held by a buyer who has agreed to purchase the property, but has not yet completed the transaction; the interest of a buyer under a contract for deed.

equity the difference between the current market value of a property and the outstanding indebtedness due on it.

equity of redemption the right of a borrower to stop the foreclosure process.

erosion the gradual wearing away of land by wind, water, and other natural processes.

escalation clause a clause in a lease allowing the lessor to charge more rent based on an increase in costs; sometimes called a *pass-through clause*.

escheat the claim to property by the state when the owner dies intestate and no heirs can be found.

escrow the deposit of funds and/or documents with a disinterested third party for safekeeping until the terms of the escrow agreement have been met.

escrow account a trust account established to hold escrow funds for safekeeping until disbursement.

escrow analysis annual report to disclose escrow receipts, payments, and current balances.

escrow disbursements money paid from an escrow account.

estate an interest in real property. The sum total of all the real property and personal property owned by an individual.

estate for years a leasehold estate granting possession for a definite period of time.

estate tax federal tax levied on property transferred upon death.

estoppel certificate a document that certifies the outstanding amount owed on a mortgage loan, as well as the rate of interest.

et al. abbreviation for the Latin phrase *et alius,* meaning "and another."

et ux. abbreviation for Latin term *et uxor,* meaning "and wife."

et vir. Latin term meaning "and husband."

eviction the lawful expulsion of an occupant from real property.

evidence of title a document that identifies ownership of property.

examination of title a review of an abstract to determine current condition of title.

exchange a transaction in which property is traded for another property, rather than sold for money or other consideration.

exclusive agency listing a contract between a property owner and one broker that gives only the broker the right to sell the property for a fee within a specified period of time but does not obligate the owner to pay the broker a fee if the owner produces his own buyer without the broker's assistance. The owner is barred only from appointing another broker within this time period.

exclusive right to sell a contract between a property owner and a broker that gives the broker the right to collect a commission regardless of who sells the property during the specified period of time of the agreement.

executed contract a contract in which all obligations have been fully performed.

execution the signing of a contract.

executor/executrix a person named in a will to administer an estate. The court will appoint an administrator if no executor is named. "Executrix" is the feminine form.

executory contract a contract in which one or more of the obligations have yet to be performed.

express contract an oral or written contract in which the terms are expressed in words.

extension agreement an agreement between mortgagor and mortgagee to extend the maturity date of the mortgage after it is due.

external obsolescence a loss in value of a property due to factors outside the property, such as a change in surrounding land use.

▶ F

fair housing law a term used to refer to federal and state laws prohibiting discrimination in the sale or rental of residential property.

fair market value the highest price that a buyer, willing but not compelled to buy, would pay, and the lowest a seller, willing but not compelled to sell, would accept.

Federal Housing Administration (FHA) an agency within the U.S. Department of Housing and Urban Development (HUD) that insures mortgage loans by FHA-approved lenders to make loans available to buyers with limited cash.

Federal National Mortgage Association (Fannie Mae) a privately owned corporation that buys existing government-backed and conventional mortgages.

Federal Reserve System the central banking system of the United States, which controls the monetary policy and, therefore, the money supply, interest rates, and availability of credit.

fee simple the most complete form of ownership of real estate.

FHA-insured loan a loan insured by the Federal Housing Administration.

fiduciary relationship a legal relationship with an obligation of trust, as that of agent and principal.

finder's fee a fee or commission paid to a mortgage broker for finding a mortgage loan for a prospective borrower.

first mortgage a mortgage that has priority to be satisfied over all other mortgages.

fixed-rate loan a loan with an interest rate that does not change during the entire term of the loan.

fixture an article of personal property that has been permanently attached to the real estate so as to become an integral part of the real estate.

foreclosure the legal process by which a borrower in default of a mortgage is deprived of interest in the mortgaged property. Usually, this involves a forced sale of the property at public auction, where the proceeds of the sale are applied to the mortgage debt.

forfeiture the loss of money, property, rights, or privileges due to a breach of legal obligation.

franchise in real estate, an organization that lends a standardized trade name, operating procedures, referral services, and supplies to member brokerages.

fraud a deliberate misstatement of material fact or an act or omission made with deliberate intent to deceive (active fraud) or gross disregard for the truth (constructive fraud).

freehold estate an estate of ownership in real property.

front foot a measurement of property taken by measuring the frontage of the property along the street line.

functional obsolescence a loss in value of a property due to causes within the property, such as faulty design, outdated structural style, or inadequacy to function properly.

future interest ownership interest in property that cannot be enjoyed until the occurrence of some event; sometimes referred to as a *household* or *equitable interest.*

▶ **G**

general agent an agent who is authorized to act for and obligate a principal in a specific range of matters, as specified by their mutual agreement.

general lien a claim on all property, real and personal, owned by a debtor.

general warranty deed an instrument in which the grantor guarantees the grantee that the title being conveyed is good and free of other claims or encumbrances.

government-backed mortgage a mortgage that is insured by the Federal Housing Administration (FHA) or guaranteed by the Department of Veterans Affairs (VA) or the Rural Housing Service (RHS). Mortgages that are not government loans are identified as conventional loans.

Government National Mortgage Association (Ginnie Mae) a government-owned corporation within the U.S. Department of Housing and Urban Development (HUD). Ginnie Mae manages and liquidates government-backed loans and assists HUD in special lending projects.

government survey system a method of land description in which meridians (lines of longitude) and baselines (lines of latitude) are used to divide land into townships and sections.

graduated lease a lease that calls for periodic, stated changes in rent during the term of the lease.

grant the transfer of title to real property by deed.

grant deed a deed that includes three warranties: (1) that the owner has the right to convey title to the property, (2) that there are no encumbrances other than those noted specifically in the deed, and (3) that the owner will convey any future interest that he or she may acquire in the property.

grantee one who receives title to real property.

grantor one who conveys title to real property; the present owner.

gross income the total income received from a property before deducting expenses.

gross income multiplier a rough method of estimating the market value of an income property by multiplying its gross annual rent by a multiplier discovered by dividing the sales price of comparable properties by their annual gross rent.

gross lease a lease in which a tenant pays only a fixed amount for rental and the landlord pays all operating expenses and taxes.

gross rent multiplier similar to *gross income multiplier,* except that it looks at the relationship between sales price and monthly gross rent.

ground lease a lease of land only, on which a tenant already owns a building or will construct improvements.

guaranteed sale plan an agreement between a broker and a seller that the broker will buy the seller's property if it does not sell within a specified period of time.

guardian one who is legally responsible for the care of another person's rights and/or property.

► H

***habendum* clause** the clause in a deed, beginning with the words *to have and to hold*, that defines or limits the exact interest in the estate granted by the deed.

hamlet a small village.

heir one who is legally entitled to receive property when the owner dies intestate.

highest and best use the legally permitted use of a parcel of land that will yield the greatest return to the owner in terms of money or amenities.

holdover tenancy a tenancy where a lessee retains possession of the property after the lease has expired, and the landlord, by continuing to accept rent, agrees to the tenant's continued occupancy.

holographic will a will that is entirely handwritten, dated, and signed by the testator.

home equity conversion mortgage (HECM) often called a *reverse-annuity mortgage*; instead of making payments to a lender, the lender makes payments to you. It enables older homeowners to convert the equity they have in their homes into cash, usually in the form of monthly payments. Unlike traditional home equity loans, a borrower does not qualify on the basis of income but on the value of his or her home. In addition, the loan does not have to be repaid until the borrower no longer occupies the property.

home equity line of credit a mortgage loan that allows the borrower to obtain cash drawn against the equity of his or her home, up to a predetermined amount.

home inspection a thorough inspection by a professional that evaluates the structural and mechanical condition of a property. A satisfactory home inspection is often included as a contingency by the purchaser.

homeowners insurance an insurance policy specifically designed to protect residential property owners against financial loss from common risks such as fire, theft, and liability.

homeowners warranty an insurance policy that protects purchasers of newly constructed or pre-owned homes against certain structural and mechanical defects.

homestead the parcel of land and improvements legally qualifying as the owner's principal residence.

HUD an acronym for the Department of Housing and Urban Development, a federal agency that enforces federal fair housing laws and oversees agencies such as FHA and GNMA.

► I

implied contract a contract where the agreement of the parties is created by their conduct.

improvement human-made addition to real estate.

income capitalization approach a method of estimating the value of income-producing property by dividing the expected annual net operating income of the property by a capitalization rate.

income property real estate developed or improved to produce income.

incorporeal right intangible, non-possessory rights in real estate, such as an easement or right of way.

independent contractor one who is retained by another to perform a certain task and is not subject to the control and direction of the hiring person with regard to the end result of the task. Individual contractors receive a fee for their services, but pay their own expenses and taxes and receive no employee benefits.

index a number used to compute the interest rate for an adjustable-rate mortgage (ARM). The index is a published number or percentage, such as the average yield on Treasury bills. A margin is added to the index to determine the interest rate to be charged on the ARM. This interest rate is subject to any caps that are associated with the mortgage.

industrial property buildings and land used for the manufacture and distribution of goods, such as a factory.

inflation an increase in the amount of money or credit available in relation to the amount of goods or services available, which causes an increase in the general price level of goods and services.

initial interest rate the beginning interest rate of the mortgage at the time of closing. This rate changes for an adjustable-rate mortgage (ARM).

installment the regular, periodic payment that a borrower agrees to make to a lender, usually related to a loan.

installment contract see *contract for deed.*

installment loan borrowed money that is repaid in periodic payments, known as *installments.*

installment sale a transaction in which the sales price is paid to the seller in two or more installments over more than one calendar year.

insurance a contract that provides indemnification from specific losses in exchange for a periodic payment. The individual contract is known as an *insurance policy*, and the periodic payment is known as an *insurance premium.*

insurance binder a document that states that temporary insurance is in effect until a permanent insurance policy is issued.

insured mortgage a mortgage that is protected by the Federal Housing Administration (FHA) or by private mortgage insurance (PMI). If the borrower defaults on the loan, the insurer must pay the lender the insured amount.

interest (1) a fee charged by a lender for the use of the money loaned; (2) a share of ownership in real estate.

interest accrual rate the percentage rate at which interest accrues on the mortgage.

interest rate the rent or rate charged to use funds belonging to another.

interest rate buydown plan an arrangement where the property seller (or any other party) deposits money to an account so that it can be released each month to reduce the mortgagor's monthly payments during the early years of a mortgage. During the specified period, the mortgagor's effective interest rate is "bought down" below the actual interest rate.

interest rate ceiling the maximum interest rate that may be charged for an adjustable-rate mortgage (ARM), as specified in the mortgage note.

interest rate floor the minimum interest rate for an adjustable-rate mortgage (ARM), as specified in the mortgage note.

interim financing a short-term loan made during the building phase of a project; also known as a *construction mortgage.*

intestate to die without having authored a valid will.

invalid not legally binding or enforceable.

investment property a property not occupied by the owner.

▶ J

joint tenancy co-ownership that gives each tenant equal interest and equal rights in the property, including the right of survivorship.

joint venture an agreement between two or more parties to engage in a specific business enterprise.

judgment a decision rendered by a court determining the rights and obligations of parties to an action or lawsuit.

judgment lien a lien on the property of a debtor resulting from a court judgment.

judicial foreclosure a proceeding that is handled as a civil lawsuit and conducted through court; used in some states.

jumbo loan a loan that exceeds Fannie Mae's mortgage amount limits. Also called a *non-conforming loan.*

junior mortgage any mortgage that is inferior to a first lien and that will be satisfied only after the first mortgage; also called a *secondary mortgage.*

▶ L

laches a doctrine used by a court to bar the assertion of a legal claim or right, based on the failure to assert the claim in a timely manner.

land the earth from its surface to its center, and the air space above it.

landlocked property surrounded on all sides by property belonging to another.

lease a contract between a landlord and a tenant wherein the landlord grants the tenant possession and use of the property for a specified period of time and for a consideration.

leased fee the landlord's interest in a parcel of leased property.

leasehold a tenant's right to occupy a parcel of real estate for the term of a lease.

lease option a financing option that allows homebuyers to lease a home with an option to buy. Each month's rent payment may consist of rent, plus an additional amount that can be applied toward the down payment on an already specified price.

legal description a description of a parcel of real estate specific and complete enough for an independent surveyor to locate and identify it.

lessee the one who receives that right to use and occupy the property during the term of the leasehold estate.

lessor the owner of the property who grants the right of possession to the lessee.

leverage the use of borrowed funds to purchase an asset.

levy to assess or collect a tax.

license (1) a revocable authorization to perform a particular act on another's property; (2) authorization granted by a state to act as a real estate broker or salesperson.

lien a legal claim against a property to secure payment of a financial obligation.

life estate a freehold estate in real property limited in duration to the lifetime of the holder of the life estate or another specified person.

life tenant one who holds a life estate.

liquidity the ability to convert an asset into cash.

lis pendens a Latin phrase meaning "suit pending"; a public notice that a lawsuit has been filed that may affect the title to a particular piece of property.

listing agreement a contract between the owner and a licensed real estate broker where the broker is employed to sell real estate on the owner's terms within a given time, for which service the owner agrees to pay the broker an agreed-upon fee.

listing broker a broker who contracts with a property owner to sell or lease the described property; the listing agreement typically may provide for the broker to make property available through a multiple-listing system.

littoral rights landowner's claim to use water in large, navigable lakes and oceans adjacent to property; ownership rights to land-bordering bodies of water up to the high-water mark.

loan a sum of borrowed money, or principal, that is generally repaid with interest.

loan officer or *lender*, serves several functions and has various responsibilities, such as soliciting loans; a loan officer both represents the lending institution and represents the borrower to the lending institution.

lock-in an agreement in which the lender guarantees a specified interest rate for a certain amount of time.

lock-in period the time period during which the lender has guaranteed an interest rate to a borrower.

lot and block description a method of describing a particular property by referring to a lot and block number within a subdivision recorded in the public record.

▶ **M**

management agreement a contract between the owner of an income property and a firm or individual who agrees to manage the property.

margin the difference between the interest rate and the index on an adjustable-rate mortgage. The margin remains stable over the life of the loan, while the index fluctuates.

marketable title title to property that is free from encumbrances and reasonable doubts and that a court would compel a buyer to accept.

market data approach a method of estimating the value of a property by comparing it to similar properties recently sold and making monetary adjustments for the differences between the subject property and the comparable property.

market value the amount that a seller may expect to obtain for merchandise, services, or securities in the open market.

mechanic's lien a statutory lien created to secure payment for those who supply labor or materials for the construction of an improvement to land.

metes and bounds a method of describing a parcel of land using direction and distance.

mill one-tenth of one cent; used by some states to express or calculate property tax rates.

minor a person who has not attained the legal age of majority.

misrepresentation a misstatement of fact, either deliberate or unintentional.

modification the act of changing any of the terms of the mortgage.

money judgment a court order to settle a claim with a monetary payment, rather than specific performance.

month-to-month tenancy tenancy in which the tenant rents for only one month at a time.

monument a fixed, visible marker used to establish boundaries for a survey.

mortgage a written instrument that pledges property to secure payment of a debt obligation as evidenced by a promissory note. When duly recorded in the public record, a mortgage creates a lien against the title to a property.

mortgage banker an entity that originates, funds, and services loans to be sold into the secondary money market.

mortgage broker an entity that, for a fee, brings borrowers together with lenders.

mortgage lien an encumbrance created by recording a mortgage.

mortgagee the lender who benefits from the mortgage.

mortgagor the borrower who pledges the property as collateral.

multi-dwelling units properties that provide separate housing units for more than one family that secure only a single mortgage. Apartment buildings are also considered multi-dwelling units.

multiple-listing system (MLS—also multiple-listing service) the method of marketing a property listing to all participants in the MLS.

mutual rescission an agreement by all parties to a contract to release one another from the obligations of the contract.

► **N**

negative amortization occurs when an adjustable-rate mortgage is allowed to fluctuate independently of a required minimum payment. A gradual increase in mortgage debt happens when the monthly payment is not large enough to cover the entire principal and interest due. The amount of the shortfall is added to the remaining balance to create negative amortization.

net income the income produced by a property, calculated by deducting operating expenses from gross income.

net lease a lease that requires the tenant to pay maintenance and operating expenses, as well as rent.

net listing a listing in which the broker's fee is established as anything above a specified amount to be received by the seller from the sale of the property.

net worth the value of all of a person's assets.

no cash-out refinance a refinance transaction in which the new mortgage amount is limited to the sum of the remaining balance of the existing first mortgage.

non-conforming use a use of land that is permitted to continue, or grandfathered, even after a zoning ordinance is passed that prohibits the use.

nonliquid asset an asset that cannot easily be converted into cash.

notarize to attest or certify by a notary public.

notary public a person who is authorized to administer oaths and take acknowledgments.

note a written instrument acknowledging a debt, with a promise to repay, including an outline of the terms of repayment.

note rate the interest rate on a promissory note.

notice of default a formal written notice to a borrower that a default has occurred on a loan and that legal action may be taken.

novation the substitution of a new contract for an existing one; the new contract must reference the first and indicate that the first is being replaced and no longer has any force and effect.

▶ O

obligee person on whose favor an obligation is entered.

obligor person who is bound to another by an obligation.

obsolescence a loss in the value of a property due to functional or external factors.

offer to propose as payment; bid on property.

offer and acceptance two of the necessary elements for the creation of a contract.

open-end mortgage a loan containing a clause that allows the mortgagor to borrow additional funds from the lender, up to a specified amount, without rewriting the mortgage.

open listing a listing contract given to one or more brokers in which a commission is paid only to the broker who procures a sale. If the owner sells the house without the assistance of one of the brokers, no commission is due.

opinion of title an opinion, usually given by an attorney, regarding the status of a title to property.

option an agreement that gives a prospective buyer the right to purchase a seller's property within a specified period of time for a specified price.

optionee one who receives or holds an option.

optionor one who grants an option; the property owner.

ordinance a municipal regulation.

original principal balance the total amount of principal owed on a loan before any payments are made; the amount borrowed.

origination fee the amount charged by a lender to cover the cost of assembling the loan package and originating the loan.

owner financing a real estate transaction in which the property seller provides all or part of the financing.

ownership the exclusive right to use, possess, control, and dispose of property.

▶ **P**

package mortgage a mortgage that pledges both real and personal property as collateral to secure repayment of a loan.

parcel a lot or specific portion of a large tract of real estate.

participation mortgage a type of mortgage in which the lender receives a certain percentage of the income or resale proceeds from a property, as well as interest on the loan.

partition the division of property held by co-owners into individual shares.

partnership an agreement between two parties to conduct business for profit. In a partnership, property is owned by the partnership, not the individual partners, so partners cannot sell their interest in the property without the consent of the other partners.

party wall a common wall used to separate two adjoining properties.

payee one who receives payment from another.

payor one who makes payment to another.

percentage lease a lease in which the rental rate is based on a percentage of the tenant's gross sales. This type of lease is most often used for retail space.

periodic estate tenancy that automatically renews itself until either the landlord or tenant gives notice to terminate it.

personal property (hereditaments) all items that are not permanently attached to real estate; also known as *chattels.*

physical deterioration a loss in the value of a property due to impairment of its physical condition.

PITI principal, interest, taxes, and insurance—components of a regular mortgage payment.

planned unit development (PUD) a type of zoning that provides for residential and commercial uses within a specified area.

plat a map of subdivided land showing the boundaries of individual parcels or lots.

plat book a group of maps located in the public record showing the division of land into subdivisions, blocks, and individual parcels or lots.

plat number a number that identifies a parcel of real estate for which a plat has been recorded in the public record.

PMI private mortgage insurance.

point a point is 1% of the loan.

point of beginning the starting point for a survey using the "metes and bounds" method of description.

police power the right of the government to enact laws, ordinances, and regulations to protect the public health, safety, welfare, and morals.

power of attorney a legal document that authorizes someone to act on another's behalf. A power of attorney can grant complete authority or can be limited to certain acts and/or certain periods of time.

preapproval condition where a borrower has completed a loan application and provided debt, income, and savings documentation that an underwriter has reviewed and approved. A preapproval is usually done at a certain loan amount, making assumptions about what the interest rate will actually be at the time the loan is actually made, as well as estimates for the amount that will be paid for property taxes, insurance, and so on.

prepayment amount paid to reduce the outstanding principal balance of a loan before the due date.

prepayment penalty a fee charged to a borrower by a lender for paying off a debt before the term of the loan expires.

prequalification a lender's opinion on the ability of a borrower to qualify for a loan, based on furnished information regarding debt, income, and available capital for down payment, closing costs, and prepaids. Prequalification is less formal than preapproval.

prescription a method of acquiring an easement to property by prolonged, unauthorized use.

primary mortgage market the financial market in which loans are originated, funded, and serviced.

prime rate the short-term interest rate that banks charge to their preferred customers. Changes in prime rate are used as the indexes in some adjustable-rate mortgages, such as home equity lines of credit.

principal (1) one who authorizes another to act on his or her behalf; (2) one of the contracting parties to a transaction; (3) the amount of money borrowed in a loan, separate from the interest charged on it.

principal meridian one of the 36 longitudinal lines used in the rectangular survey system method of land description.

probate the judicial procedure of proving the validity of a will.

procuring cause the action that brings about the desired result. For example, if a broker takes actions that result in a sale, the broker is the procuring cause of the sale.

promissory note details the terms of the loan and is the debt instrument.

property management the operating of an income property for another.

property tax a tax levied by the government on property, real or personal.

prorate to divide ongoing property costs such as taxes or maintenance fees proportionately between buyer and seller at closing.

pur autre vie a phrase meaning "for the life of another." In a life estate *pur autre vie*, the term of the estate is measured by the life of a person other than the person who holds the life estate.

purchase agreement a written contract signed by the buyer and seller stating the terms and conditions under which a property will be sold.

purchase money mortgage a mortgage given by a buyer to a seller to secure repayment of any loan used to pay part or all of the purchase price.

▶ Q

qualifying ratios calculations to determine whether a borrower can qualify for a mortgage. There are two ratios. The "top" ratio is a calculation of the borrower's monthly housing costs (principal, taxes, insurance, mortgage insurance, homeowners association fees) as a percentage of monthly income. The "bottom" ratio includes housing costs as well as all other monthly debt.

quitclaim deed a conveyance where the grantor transfers without warranty or obligations whatever interest or title he or she may have.

▶ R

range an area of land six miles wide, numbered east or west from a principal meridian in the rectangular survey system.

ready, willing, and able one who is able to pay the asking price for a property and is prepared to complete the transaction.

real estate land, the earth below it, the air above it, and anything permanently attached to it.

real estate agent a real estate broker who has been appointed to market a property for and represent the property owner (listing agent), or a broker who has been appointed to represent the interest of the buyer (buyer's agent).

real estate board an organization whose members primarily consist of real estate sales agents, brokers, and administrators.

real estate broker a licensed person, association, partnership, or corporation who negotiates real estate transactions for others for a fee.

Real Estate Settlement Procedures Act (RESPA) a consumer protection law that requires lenders to give borrowers advance notice of closing costs and prohibits certain abusive practices against buyers using federally related loans to purchase their homes.

real property the rights of ownership to land and its improvements.

REALTOR® a registered trademark for use by members of the National Association of REALTORS® and affiliated state and local associations.

recording entering documents, such as deeds and mortgages, into the public record to give constructive notice.

rectangular survey system a method of land description based on principal meridians (lines of longitude) and baselines (lines of latitude). Also called the *government survey system*.

redemption period the statutory period of time during which an owner can reclaim foreclosed property by paying the debt owed plus court costs and other charges established by statute.

redlining the illegal practice of lending institutions refusing to provide certain financial services, such as mortgage loans, to property owners in certain areas.

refinance transaction the process of paying off one loan with the proceeds from a new loan using the same property as security or collateral.

Regulation Z a Federal Reserve regulation that implements the federal Truth-in-Lending Act.

release clause a clause in a mortgage that releases a portion of the property upon payment of a portion of the loan.

remainder estate a future interest in an estate that takes effect upon the termination of a life estate.

remaining balance in a mortgage, the amount of principal that has not yet been repaid.

remaining term the original amortization term minus the number of payments that have been applied to it.

rent a periodic payment paid by a lessee to a landlord for the use and possession of leased property.

replacement cost the estimated current cost to replace an asset similar or equivalent to the one being appraised.

reproduction cost the cost of building an exact duplicate of a building at current prices.

rescission canceling or terminating a contract by mutual consent or by the action of one party on default by the other party.

restriction (restrict covenant) a limitation on the way a property can be used.

reverse annuity mortgage when a homeowner receives monthly checks or a lump sum with no repayment until property is sold; usually an agreement between mortgagor and elderly homeowners.

reversion the return of interest or title to the grantor of a life estate.

revision a revised or new version, as in a contract.

right of egress (or ingress) the right to enter or leave designated premises.

right of first refusal the right of a person to have the first opportunity to purchase property before it is offered to anyone else.

right of redemption the statutory right to reclaim ownership of property after a foreclosure sale.

right of survivorship in joint tenancy, the right of survivors to acquire the interest of a deceased joint tenant.

riparian rights the rights of a landowner whose property is adjacent to a flowing waterway, such as a river, to access and use the water.

▶ S

safety clause a contract provision that provides a time period following expiration of a listing agreement, during which the agent will be compensated if there is a transaction with a buyer who was initially introduced to the property by the agent.

sale-leaseback a transaction in which the owner sells improved property and, as part of the same transaction, signs a long-term lease to remain in possession of its premises, thus becoming the tenant of the new owner.

sales contract a contract between a buyer and a seller outlining the terms of the sale.

salesperson one who is licensed to sell real estate in a given territory.

salvage value the value of a property at the end of its economic life.

satisfaction an instrument acknowledging that a debt has been paid in full.

secondary mortgage a mortgage that is in less than first lien position; see *junior mortgage.*

section as used in the rectangular survey system, an area of land measuring one square mile, or 640 acres.

secured loan a loan that is backed by property or collateral.

security property that is offered as collateral for a loan.

selling broker the broker who secures a buyer for a listed property; the selling broker may be the listing agent, a subagent, or a buyer's agent.

separate property property owned individually by a spouse, as opposed to community property.

servient tenement a property on which an easement or right of way for an adjacent (dominant) property passes.

setback the amount of space between the lot line and the building line, usually established by a local zoning ordinance or restrictive covenants; see *deed restrictions.*

settlement statement (HUD-1) the form used to itemize all costs related to closing of a residential transaction covered by RESPA regulations.

severalty the ownership of a property by only one legal entity.

special assessment a tax levied against only the specific properties that will benefit from a public improvement, such as a street or sewer; an assessment by a homeowners association for a capital improvement to the common areas for which no budgeted funds are available.

special warranty deed a deed in which the grantor guarantees the title only against the defects that may have occurred during the grantor's ownership and not against any defects that occurred prior to that time.

specific lien a lien, such as a mortgage, that attaches to one defined parcel of real estate.

specific performance a legal action in which a court compels a defaulted party to a contract to perform according to the terms of the contract, rather than awarding damages.

standard payment calculation the method used to calculate the monthly payment required to repay the remaining balance of a mortgage in equal installments over the remaining term of the mortgage at the current interest rate.

Statute of Frauds the state law that requires certain contracts to be in writing to be enforceable.

Statute of Limitations the state law that requires that certain actions be brought to court within a specified period of time.

statutory lien a lien imposed on property by statute, such as a tax lien.

steering the illegal practice of directing prospective homebuyers to or away from particular areas.

straight-line depreciation a method of computing depreciation by decreasing value by an equal amount each year during the useful life of the property.

subdivision a tract of land divided into lots as defined in a publicly recorded plat that complies with state and local regulations.

sublet the act of a lessee transferring part or all of his or her lease to a third party while maintaining responsibility for all duties and obligations of the lease contract.

subordinate to voluntarily accept a lower priority lien position than that to which one would normally be entitled.

subrogation the substitution of one party into another's legal role as the creditor for a particular debt.

substitution the principle in appraising that a buyer will be willing to pay no more for the property being appraised than the cost of purchasing an equally desirable property.

suit for possession a lawsuit filed by a landlord to evict a tenant who has violated the terms of the lease or retained possession of the property after the lease expired.

suit for specific performance a lawsuit filed for the purpose of compelling a party to perform particular acts to settle a dispute, rather than pay monetary damages.

survey a map that shows the exact legal boundaries of a property, the location of easements, encroachments, improvements, rights of way, and other physical features.

syndicate a group formed by a syndicator to combine funds for real estate investment.

▶ **T**

tax deed in some states, an instrument given to the purchaser at the time of sale.

tax lien a charge against a property created by law or statute. Tax liens take priority over all other types of liens.

tax rate the rate applied to the assessed value of a property to determine the property taxes.

tax sale the court-ordered sale of a property after the owner fails to pay *ad valorem* taxes owed on the property.

tenancy at sufferance the tenancy of a party who unlawfully retains possession of a landlord's property after the term of the lease has expired.

tenancy at will an indefinite tenancy that can be terminated by either the landlord or the tenant at any time by giving notice to the other party one rental period in advance of the desired termination date.

tenancy by the entirety ownership by a married couple of property acquired during the marriage with right of survivorship; not recognized by community property states.

tenancy in common a form of co-ownership in which two or more persons hold an undivided interest in property without the right of survivorship.

tenant one who holds or possesses the right of occupancy title.

tenement the space that may be occupied by a tenant under the terms of a lease.

testate to die having created a valid will directing the testator's desires with regard to the disposition of the estate.

"time is of the essence" a phrase in a contract that requires strict adherence to the dates listed in the contract as deadlines for the performance of specific acts.

time-sharing undivided ownership of real estate for only an allotted portion of a year.

title a legal document that demonstrates a person's right to, or ownership of, a property. **Note:** Title is *not* an instrument. The instrument, such as a deed, gives evidence of title or ownership.

title insurance an insurance policy that protects the holder from defects in a title, subject to the exceptions noted in the policy.

title search a check of public records to ensure that the seller is the legal owner of the property and that there are no liens or other outstanding claims.

Torrens system a system of registering titles to land with a public authority, who is usually called a *registrar*.

township a division of land, measuring 36 square miles, in the government survey system.

trade fixtures an item of personal property installed by a commercial tenant and removable upon expiration of the lease.

transfer tax a state or municipal tax payable when the conveyancing instrument is recorded.

trust an arrangement in which title to property is transferred from a grantor to a trustee, who holds title but not the right of possession for a third party, the beneficiary.

trustee a person who holds title to property for another person designated as the beneficiary.

Truth-in-Lending Law also known as *Regulation Z*; requires lenders to make full disclosure regarding the terms of a loan.

▶ U

underwriting the process of evaluating a loan application to determine the risk involved for the lender.

undivided interest the interest of co-owners to use an entire property despite the fractional interest owned.

unilateral contract a one-sided contract in which one party is obligated to perform a particular act completely, before the other party has any obligation to perform.

unsecured loan a loan that is not backed by collateral or security.

useful life the period of time a property is expected to have economic utility.

usury the practice of charging interest at a rate higher than that allowed by law.

► V

VA-guaranteed loan a mortgage loan made to a qualified veteran that is guaranteed by the Department of Veterans Affairs.

valid contract an agreement that is legally enforceable and binding on all parties.

valuation estimated worth.

variance permission obtained from zoning authorities to build a structure that is not in complete compliance with current zoning laws. A variance does not permit a non-conforming use of a property.

vendee a buyer.

vendor a seller; the property owner.

village an incorporated minor municipality usually larger than a hamlet and smaller than a town.

voidable contract a contract that appears to be valid but is subject to cancellation by one or both of the parties.

void contract a contract that is not legally enforceable; the absence of a valid contract.

► W

waiver the surrender of a known right or claim.

warranty deed a deed in which the grantor fully warrants a good clear title to the property.

waste the improper use of a property by a party with the right to possession, such as the holder of a life estate.

will a written document that directs the distribution of a deceased person's property, real and personal.

wraparound mortgage a mortgage that includes the remaining balance on an existing first mortgage plus an additional amount. Full payments on both mortgages are made to the wraparound mortgagee who then forwards the payments on the first mortgage to the first mortgagee.

writ of execution a court order to the sheriff or other officer to sell the property of a debtor to satisfy a previously rendered judgment.

► Z

zone an area reserved by authorities for specific use that is subject to certain restrictions.

zoning ordinance the exercise of regulating and controlling the use of a property in a municipality.

7 ▶ Arizona Real Estate Sales Exam 2

CHAPTER SUMMARY

This is the second of the four practice tests in this book. Because you have taken one practice test already, you should feel more confident with your test-taking skills. Use this test to see how knowing what to expect can make you feel better prepared.

LIKE THE FIRST exam in this book, this test is based on the Arizona real estate sales exam. If you are following the advice in this book, you have done some studying between the first exam and this one. This second exam will give you a chance to see how much you've improved. The answer sheet follows this page, and the test is followed by the answer key and explanations.

▶ Arizona Real Estate Sales Exam 2 Answer Sheet

1.	ⓐ ⓑ ⓒ ⓓ	48.	ⓐ ⓑ ⓒ ⓓ	95.	ⓐ ⓑ ⓒ ⓓ
2.	ⓐ ⓑ ⓒ ⓓ	49.	ⓐ ⓑ ⓒ ⓓ	96.	ⓐ ⓑ ⓒ ⓓ
3.	ⓐ ⓑ ⓒ ⓓ	50.	ⓐ ⓑ ⓒ ⓓ	97.	ⓐ ⓑ ⓒ ⓓ
4.	ⓐ ⓑ ⓒ ⓓ	51.	ⓐ ⓑ ⓒ ⓓ	98.	ⓐ ⓑ ⓒ ⓓ
5.	ⓐ ⓑ ⓒ ⓓ	52.	ⓐ ⓑ ⓒ ⓓ	99.	ⓐ ⓑ ⓒ ⓓ
6.	ⓐ ⓑ ⓒ ⓓ	53.	ⓐ ⓑ ⓒ ⓓ	100.	ⓐ ⓑ ⓒ ⓓ
7.	ⓐ ⓑ ⓒ ⓓ	54.	ⓐ ⓑ ⓒ ⓓ	101.	ⓐ ⓑ ⓒ ⓓ
8.	ⓐ ⓑ ⓒ ⓓ	55.	ⓐ ⓑ ⓒ ⓓ	102.	ⓐ ⓑ ⓒ ⓓ
9.	ⓐ ⓑ ⓒ ⓓ	56.	ⓐ ⓑ ⓒ ⓓ	103.	ⓐ ⓑ ⓒ ⓓ
10.	ⓐ ⓑ ⓒ ⓓ	57.	ⓐ ⓑ ⓒ ⓓ	104.	ⓐ ⓑ ⓒ ⓓ
11.	ⓐ ⓑ ⓒ ⓓ	58.	ⓐ ⓑ ⓒ ⓓ	105.	ⓐ ⓑ ⓒ ⓓ
12.	ⓐ ⓑ ⓒ ⓓ	59.	ⓐ ⓑ ⓒ ⓓ	106.	ⓐ ⓑ ⓒ ⓓ
13.	ⓐ ⓑ ⓒ ⓓ	60.	ⓐ ⓑ ⓒ ⓓ	107.	ⓐ ⓑ ⓒ ⓓ
14.	ⓐ ⓑ ⓒ ⓓ	61.	ⓐ ⓑ ⓒ ⓓ	108.	ⓐ ⓑ ⓒ ⓓ
15.	ⓐ ⓑ ⓒ ⓓ	62.	ⓐ ⓑ ⓒ ⓓ	109.	ⓐ ⓑ ⓒ ⓓ
16.	ⓐ ⓑ ⓒ ⓓ	63.	ⓐ ⓑ ⓒ ⓓ	110.	ⓐ ⓑ ⓒ ⓓ
17.	ⓐ ⓑ ⓒ ⓓ	64.	ⓐ ⓑ ⓒ ⓓ	111.	ⓐ ⓑ ⓒ ⓓ
18.	ⓐ ⓑ ⓒ ⓓ	65.	ⓐ ⓑ ⓒ ⓓ	112.	ⓐ ⓑ ⓒ ⓓ
19.	ⓐ ⓑ ⓒ ⓓ	66.	ⓐ ⓑ ⓒ ⓓ	113.	ⓐ ⓑ ⓒ ⓓ
20.	ⓐ ⓑ ⓒ ⓓ	67.	ⓐ ⓑ ⓒ ⓓ	114.	ⓐ ⓑ ⓒ ⓓ
21.	ⓐ ⓑ ⓒ ⓓ	68.	ⓐ ⓑ ⓒ ⓓ	115.	ⓐ ⓑ ⓒ ⓓ
22.	ⓐ ⓑ ⓒ ⓓ	69.	ⓐ ⓑ ⓒ ⓓ	116.	ⓐ ⓑ ⓒ ⓓ
23.	ⓐ ⓑ ⓒ ⓓ	70.	ⓐ ⓑ ⓒ ⓓ	117.	ⓐ ⓑ ⓒ ⓓ
24.	ⓐ ⓑ ⓒ ⓓ	71.	ⓐ ⓑ ⓒ ⓓ	118.	ⓐ ⓑ ⓒ ⓓ
25.	ⓐ ⓑ ⓒ ⓓ	72.	ⓐ ⓑ ⓒ ⓓ	119.	ⓐ ⓑ ⓒ ⓓ
26.	ⓐ ⓑ ⓒ ⓓ	73.	ⓐ ⓑ ⓒ ⓓ	120.	ⓐ ⓑ ⓒ ⓓ
27.	ⓐ ⓑ ⓒ ⓓ	74.	ⓐ ⓑ ⓒ ⓓ	121.	ⓐ ⓑ ⓒ ⓓ
28.	ⓐ ⓑ ⓒ ⓓ	75.	ⓐ ⓑ ⓒ ⓓ	122.	ⓐ ⓑ ⓒ ⓓ
29.	ⓐ ⓑ ⓒ ⓓ	76.	ⓐ ⓑ ⓒ ⓓ	123.	ⓐ ⓑ ⓒ ⓓ
30.	ⓐ ⓑ ⓒ ⓓ	77.	ⓐ ⓑ ⓒ ⓓ	124.	ⓐ ⓑ ⓒ ⓓ
31.	ⓐ ⓑ ⓒ ⓓ	78.	ⓐ ⓑ ⓒ ⓓ	125.	ⓐ ⓑ ⓒ ⓓ
32.	ⓐ ⓑ ⓒ ⓓ	79.	ⓐ ⓑ ⓒ ⓓ	126.	ⓐ ⓑ ⓒ ⓓ
33.	ⓐ ⓑ ⓒ ⓓ	80.	ⓐ ⓑ ⓒ ⓓ	127.	ⓐ ⓑ ⓒ ⓓ
34.	ⓐ ⓑ ⓒ ⓓ	81.	ⓐ ⓑ ⓒ ⓓ	128.	ⓐ ⓑ ⓒ ⓓ
35.	ⓐ ⓑ ⓒ ⓓ	82.	ⓐ ⓑ ⓒ ⓓ	129.	ⓐ ⓑ ⓒ ⓓ
36.	ⓐ ⓑ ⓒ ⓓ	83.	ⓐ ⓑ ⓒ ⓓ	130.	ⓐ ⓑ ⓒ ⓓ
37.	ⓐ ⓑ ⓒ ⓓ	84.	ⓐ ⓑ ⓒ ⓓ	131.	ⓐ ⓑ ⓒ ⓓ
38.	ⓐ ⓑ ⓒ ⓓ	85.	ⓐ ⓑ ⓒ ⓓ	132.	ⓐ ⓑ ⓒ ⓓ
39.	ⓐ ⓑ ⓒ ⓓ	86.	ⓐ ⓑ ⓒ ⓓ	133.	ⓐ ⓑ ⓒ ⓓ
40.	ⓐ ⓑ ⓒ ⓓ	87.	ⓐ ⓑ ⓒ ⓓ	134.	ⓐ ⓑ ⓒ ⓓ
41.	ⓐ ⓑ ⓒ ⓓ	88.	ⓐ ⓑ ⓒ ⓓ	135.	ⓐ ⓑ ⓒ ⓓ
42.	ⓐ ⓑ ⓒ ⓓ	89.	ⓐ ⓑ ⓒ ⓓ	136.	ⓐ ⓑ ⓒ ⓓ
43.	ⓐ ⓑ ⓒ ⓓ	90.	ⓐ ⓑ ⓒ ⓓ	137.	ⓐ ⓑ ⓒ ⓓ
44.	ⓐ ⓑ ⓒ ⓓ	91.	ⓐ ⓑ ⓒ ⓓ	138.	ⓐ ⓑ ⓒ ⓓ
45.	ⓐ ⓑ ⓒ ⓓ	92.	ⓐ ⓑ ⓒ ⓓ	139.	ⓐ ⓑ ⓒ ⓓ
46.	ⓐ ⓑ ⓒ ⓓ	93.	ⓐ ⓑ ⓒ ⓓ	140.	ⓐ ⓑ ⓒ ⓓ
47.	ⓐ ⓑ ⓒ ⓓ	94.	ⓐ ⓑ ⓒ ⓓ		

▶ Arizona Real Estate Sales Exam 2

1. A specific tract of land is called
   a. an acre.
   b. a lot.
   c. a parcel.
   d. a subdivision.

2. How many years must a broker keep his or her records?
   a. one
   b. five
   c. forever
   d. 12

3. Ownership of chattels is most likely transferred by which of the following?
   a. special warranty deed
   b. bill of sale
   c. quitclaim deed
   d. chattel mortgage

4. Who is responsible for advertising?
   a. the designated broker
   b. the sales associate
   c. the seller
   d. the listing agent

5. The Arizona homestead exemption only covers which of the following?
   a. mechanic's lien
   b. mortgage
   c. pool loan
   d. judgment

6. An issue with a property that affects value and is not known to other parties is a
   a. *caveat emptor.*
   b. material fact.
   c. misrepresentation.
   d. seller agency.

7. A judicial procedure and sheriff sale are part of what type of foreclosure?
   a. deed of trust
   b. charge-off
   c. agreement for sale
   d. mortgage

8. Landlocked land that needs a way of access would be called a(n)
   a. fee simple.
   b. separate but equal.
   c. ingress and egress.
   d. subrogation.

9. In the theory of distribution, there are four factors of production, which includes
   a. building.
   b. socialization.
   c. redistribution.
   d. labor.

10. Under Arizona Water Law, what are sparsely populated areas that are mostly farm and rural called?
    a. active management areas
    b. irrigation non-expansive areas
    c. both **a** and **b**
    d. none of the above

11. A licensee meets a potential buyer who also has interest in another neighborhood. To influence the buyer, the licensee stated that he knows for a fact that a sex offender lives in the competing neighborhood, and, in fact, the information is true. Is this legitimate?

    a. Yes, the information helped the buyer make a knowledgeable decision.

    b. No, statute imposes criminal penalties for misuse of information provided to an inquirer.

    c. Yes, as long as the information is honest and accurate.

    d. No, the licensee does not represent the buyer.

12. A certificate of purchase would be awarded for which of the following?

    a. tax lien sale

    b. trust deed sale

    c. land lease sale

    d. a homestead exemption

13. The commissioner of real estate oversees how many recovery funds?

    a. nine

    b. seven

    c. one

    d. none

14. A real estate license is valid for how many years?

    a. three

    b. two

    c. one

    d. five

15. Escrows are prorated on how many days in a year?

    a. 365

    b. 360

    c. 12 months

    d. seven days in a week

16. What is the starting rate charged on past due property taxes?

    a. 7%

    b. 10%

    c. 9.75%

    d. 16%

17. *Laches* means

    a. protection.

    b. notice.

    c. waited too long to file a mechanic's lien.

    d. residential mechanic's lien.

18. The owner of real property who rents to another is a

    a. tenant.

    b. landlord.

    c. mortgagee.

    d. none of the above

19. Which of the following does NOT apply for a deed to be valid?

    a. consideration

    b. granting clause

    c. only in writing

    d. no notary

20. A buyer makes an offer to buy a building for $500,000 with a $50,000 deposit and a closing in 30 days. The seller accepts the offer. The last week before the closing, the buyer changes his mind and defaults on the purchase. The seller at this point can do all of the following EXCEPT

    a. keep the deposit as liquidated damages.

    b. sue for nonperformance.

    c. sue the lender for the buyer's nonperformance.

    d. declare forfeiture.

21. What type of property can be depreciated?
a. primary residence
b. vacant land
c. income producing
d. second home

22. What is an encumbrance made against real property for purposes of securing debt called?
a. lien
b. loan
c. will
d. lease

23. Tempe is doing a special assessment for a property improvement. They will assess based on
a. zoning ordinances.
b. *ad valorem*.
c. building codes.
d. deed restrictions.

24. A seller entered into an agreement to sell his property but six days before closing notified the buyer he was no longer willing to go through with the contract. The buyer sued the seller to compel him to do what he agreed to do in the contract. What type of suit is this?
a. suit for compliance
b. suit for deed
c. suit for specific performance
d. subrogation

25. If an investment property has a net operating income of $135,678 and the investor's capitalization rate is 8.55%, then what is the potential value of the property?
a. $1,160,047
b. $1,586,877
c. $1,443,277
d. $1,045,998

26. A licensee receives two offers on his listing. One offer states that *time is of the essence*, while the other offer does not include this provision. Is there a difference?
a. There is no difference, as all offers are time is of the essence.
b. Yes, time is of the essence means all parties must meet the performance deadlines.
c. Time is of the essence means move quickly.
d. The offer without the language is a stronger offer.

27. If the recovery fund is less than $600,000 on June 30, the state will
a. assess the state.
b. raise taxes.
c. close down.
d. charge renewing licensees.

28. Robyn Lawrence has been parking her car on her neighbor's land for years. One day, Robyn filed a claim for title of ownership due to adverse possession. How long would she have had to be continuously using the neighbor's land?
a. 15 years
b. 20 years
c. 21 years
d. ten years

29. When a tenant is physically evicted from a rental property the legal action is called
a. actual eviction.
b. actual notice.
c. corporeal.
d. codicil.

30. The obligation a licensee has to a principal is
a. accountability.
b. obedience.
c. loyalty.
d. all of the above

31. When a buyer and a seller have agreed and signed a contract, there is
   a. time is of the essence.
   b. an expressed contract.
   c. a closed deal.
   d. a commission earned.

32. When a lender allows a borrower to control and use pledged real estate, this action is known as
   a. mortgaging.
   b. titling.
   c. hypothecation.
   d. retention.

33. The Federal Reserve Bank administers the Federal Truth-in-Lending Law, which is also known as
   a. Title V.
   b. Regulation Z.
   c. MGL Ch. 140C.
   d. Freddie Mac.

34. A licensee, representing the seller, is contacted by a licensee, representing a buyer, wanting detailed information about the building for sale. The seller's representative does not want to share that information and states that she will not "co-broke" the fees. The other licensee argues that a listing broker must cooperate. Which is true?
   a. There is no requirement to offer information by state regulation unless the licensee advertised differently.
   b. The other licensee has a claim. The licensee must give information so the buyer can make a decision.
   c. The other licensee should call the homeowner himself and get the information.
   d. A licensee must split his or her fees by law.

35. RESPA was passed in what year?
   a. 1980
   b. 1988
   c. 1974
   d. 1965

36. Net operating income divided by the capitalization rate equals
   a. the debt service.
   b. the property value.
   c. the annual interest rate.
   d. the annual percentage rate.

37. A listing agreement is an example of a(n)
   a. bilateral contract.
   b. unilateral contract.
   c. voidable contract.
   d. descriptive contract.

38. A person who receives title to real estate is known as the
   a. grantor.
   b. grantee.
   c. titletor.
   d. recipient.

39. The two types of property are
   a. commercial and residential.
   b. vacant and improved.
   c. real and personal.
   d. primary and investment.

40. How many months does it take for a mechanic's lien to become a judgment?
   a. six months
   b. 12 months
   c. none
   d. one month

41. When a borrower fails to make payments agreed to in the note, this is known as
  a. foreclosure.
  b. notice.
  c. default.
  d. violation.

42. Paul Pacific has a home equity line of credit. This is also known as a(n)
  a. second mortgage.
  b. junior lien.
  c. encumbrance.
  d. all of the above

43. The clause in a deed that would show the interest being transferred is the
  a. *redindum* clause.
  b. *habindum* clause.
  c. seizen clause.
  d. granting clause.

44. A(n)_____ is one who is legally entitled to receive property when the owner dies intestate.
  a. heir
  b. dower
  c. inchoate
  d. none of the above

45. A listing agreement is a(n)
  a. employment and service contract.
  b. employment and goods contract.
  c. contract with no time frame.
  d. contract for a list.

46. Community property is a special form of ownership available only to
  a. sole owners.
  b. corporations.
  c. married couples.
  d. limited partners.

47. The holder of a life estate may do all of the following EXCEPT
  a. pay the property taxes and special assessments.
  b. maintain the property.
  c. mortgage the life interest.
  d. direct the disposition of the property at the end of the measuring life.

48. In the market or sales data approach to appraisal, the sales prices of similar, recently sold properties are
  a. assessed.
  b. analyzed.
  c. adjusted.
  d. added.

49. Which of the following is the simplest form of ownership?
  a. severalty
  b. joint tenancy
  c. community property
  d. tenants in common

50. The formula for determining value of investment property is
  a. net operating income ÷ capitalization rate = value.
  b. potential gross income ÷ capitalization rate = value.
  c. effective gross income × capitalization rate = value.
  d. cost of replacing the property × capitalization rate = value.

51. The cost approach is best suited for estimating the value of
  a. a large tract of land.
  b. the income generated by a commercial property.
  c. a historic building.
  d. a condominium apartment.

52. How many townships are in 36 square miles?
  a. 12
  b. six
  c. one
  d. 42,560

53. Mary intended to defraud someone using a real estate contract. The status is
  a. voidable.
  b. void.
  c. valid until proven fraudulent.
  d. valid.

54. What is the only legal life estate created by statute?
  a. Torrens law
  b. homestead
  c. testate
  d. trustor

55. Which mortgage is insured by a division of the Department of Housing and Urban Development (HUD)?
  a. VA
  b. FHA
  c. FNMA
  d. all of the above

56. A junior mortgage can be obtained from all of the following EXCEPT
  a. the seller.
  b. the buyer's aunt.
  c. another bank.
  d. Fannie Mae.

57. Which would be true in a foreclosure sale?
  a. The owner would retain title to the property.
  b. The mortgagor has a six-month right of redemption.
  c. If there is a balance of sale proceeds after the debts have been paid, the mortgagor is entitled to them.
  d. The owner can pay points to avoid the foreclosure sale.

58. The earnest money deposit in the settlement statement is
  a. not shown.
  b. debited to the buyer.
  c. credited to the seller.
  d. credited to the buyer.

59. A broker charged $500 for a CMA, but nothing was signed. This is
  a. not allowed.
  b. allowable, as long as a receipt was given.
  c. fine, as long as it was disclosed.
  d. a violation of RESPA.

60. What must happen at the closing of a real estate transaction?
  a. The buyer and seller must sign the deed.
  b. The deed must be executed and delivered by the grantor.
  c. The deed must be recorded.
  d. The broker must be present.

61. If Mr. and Mrs. Braun, the sellers, signed a purchase and sales agreement with Mr. and Mrs. Wilton, and then for no apparent reason refused to go through with the sale, the buyer(s) could sue for
a. adverse possession.
b. specific performance.
c. adverse easement.
d. dower and courtesy.

62. When a principal gives a licensee the right to act on the principal's behalf, this creates
a. an agency.
b. a fiduciary.
c. an obligation of good faith and loyalty.
d. all of the above

63. The effort that brings about the producing of a buyer for a listed property is
a. the procuring cause.
b. a market analysis.
c. hypothecation.
d. cooperation.

64. Seller Dave tells the broker that he wants a net price of $225,000 and the broker can retain any amount over that as his commission. In Arizona, that would be
a. an exclusive listing.
b. not illegal.
c. advantageous to the seller.
d. advantageous to the agent.

65. The commissioner has the right to inspect the broker's records
a. at any reasonable time.
b. from 9:00 A.M.–12:00 P.M. only.
c. Fridays only.
d. none of the above

66. A broker can have a designated person assigned for a temporary leave of absence for _____ days.
a. seven
b. zero
c. 30
d. as long as he or she wants

67. How many hours are required every two years to renew your real estate license?
a. 90
b. 36
c. 24
d. 12

68. What gives municipal government the right to regulate and control the use of land for the protection of public health, safety, and the general welfare of its citizens?
a. environmental protection laws
b. a master plan
c. police power
d. Board of Registration

69. A gas station owner owns a station in an area that had no zoning, but now has been zoned as residential. The gas station owner can continue to operate his business because of
a. non-conforming use.
b. variance.
c. cluster zoning.
d. urban development.

70. A woman willed her estate as follows: 63% to her husband, 10% to her son, 12% to her daughter, and the remainder, to her college. If the college received $30,000, how much did her daughter receive?
a. $10,000
b. $15,000
c. $20,000
d. $24,000

71. Which of the following conditions is NOT required for a real estate agent to be considered an independent contractor by the Internal Revenue Service?
a. The agent must have a valid real estate license.
b. All compensation is based on commission fees, not on hours worked.
c. The agent must have a workspace or office in the broker's place of business.
d. The agent's services are performed under a written contract between the broker and the agent.

72. Jonathan paid an upfront mortgage insurance premium (MIP) of $2,566.50, which was financed with the loan, and will also pay a monthly MIP premium to be included in his payment. What type of loan did Jonathan get?
a. FHA
b. VA
c. conventional conforming
d. interest-only term loan

73. A person buys a property for $500,000 with a 10% down payment, and pays two points for a better rate. What would the amount of the points be?
a. $10,000
b. $9,000
c. $5,000
d. $4,500

74. To obtain a broker's license in Arizona, you must do all of the following EXCEPT
a. work three of the last five years as a real estate salesperson.
b. get fingerprinted.
c. speak directly to the commissioner.
d. complete 90 classroom hours.

75. A veteran would like to buy several investment properties using his VA loan. The benefit of that would be
a. zero down.
b. no credit score requirement.
c. excellent rates.
d. It would not be allowed.

76. For how long after the sale of the real estate does an owner's title policy cover the owner?
a. ten years
b. five years
c. never
d. forever

77. What is the term used when real property is taken for the good of the public at fair market value?
a. adverse possession
b. eminent domain
c. involuntary alienation
d. hostile possession

78. To comply with the TCPA, a firm that solicits cold calls must
   a. adhere to the do-not-call list.
   b. call anybody at any time.
   c. not have an office policy in writing.
   d. just use a fax machine.

79. In Arizona, what is the maximum amount the recovery fund will pay per transaction on behalf of a licensee?
   a. $5,000
   b. $10,000
   c. $15,000
   d. $30,000

80. Owner-occupied real estate is taxed at what rate on the assessed value?
   a. 10%
   b. 15%
   c. 16%
   d. negotiable

81. Heather rented a building for the purpose of operating a health club and installed a running track for members of the club. This track would be considered a(n)
   a. fixture.
   b. real property.
   c. easement.
   d. trade fixture.

82. Rob and Kristen Kershner inherited their home from his parents by a will. This would be an example of
   a. escheat.
   b. devise.
   c. demise.
   d. life estate.

83. Tyler, Rick's tenant, was arrested. Rick wants to end the tenancy. What can Rick do?
   a. He can immediately remove Tyler's personal belongings.
   b. He can change the locks.
   c. He can stop providing services.
   d. He can serve Tyler with a 30-Day Notice to Quit.

84. You wish to fill in your swimming pool with concrete. The pool size is 50 feet long, 25 feet wide, and 8 feet deep. You get an estimate of $45 per cubic yard. What would be the cost to fill in the pool?
   a. $45,000
   b. $27,195.13
   c. $20,000
   d. $16,667.67

85. If a married man willed all of his real estate to his sister and nothing to his wife, what rights would his wife have upon his death?
   a. none
   b. courtesy
   c. dower
   d. license

86. A great benefit of owning real estate is the fact that you can deduct what on your primary residence for income taxes?
   a. services
   b. loan interest and property taxes
   c. principal reductions
   d. all of the above

87. Which one of the following is NOT considered a recorded encumbrance?
   a. quitclaim deed
   b. piggyback mortgage
   c. seller carry-back
   d. deed of trust

88. Kathryn just paid off her deed of trust. She is entitled to receive a(n)
   a. deed of reconveyance.
   b. title report.
   c. ALTA policy.
   d. HUD statement.

89. A broker deposits the earnest money from a buyer into the office business account so that the rent can be paid. This would be considered
   a. a business expense.
   b. commingling of funds.
   c. legal.
   d. a personal expense.

90. To obtain a license in Arizona, a person can be
   a. a resident of the state.
   b. a nonresident of the state.
   c. both **a** and **b**
   d. neither **a** nor **b**

91. In Arizona, in order for a licensee to become a real estate broker, the person must
   a. pay the commissioner a $350 fee.
   b. obtain a license by applying for it.
   c. become a REALTOR®.
   d. be actively associated with a broker for a minimum of 25 hours per week for one year.

92. A minor signed a two-year lease for an apartment. This would be an example of
   a. a valid contract.
   b. a voided contract.
   c. a voidable contract.
   d. consummation.

93. The owner of a health-food store in a mall wants you to sell his business. What type of license would you need?
   a. none
   b. a real estate salesperson's license
   c. a real estate broker's license
   d. a commercial real estate license

94. What provides the basis for an accurate appraisal?
   a. assessment value
   b. the appraiser's knowledge
   c. the listing information
   d. the cooperation of the home inspector

95. A buyer of investment property would be most interested in what appraisal method?
   a. cost
   b. comparison
   c. income
   d. accelerated

96. Most appraisals will require the use of
   a. one approach.
   b. more than one approach.
   c. the plat.
   d. city planning.

97. Lauren just won a certificate of purchase at a property tax foreclosure sale. How long must she wait before she can enforce foreclosure and get a treasurer's deed?
a. 180 days
b. one year
c. three years
d. five years

98. A licensee sent a postcard soliciting an active listing to list with him. This is
a. allowed.
b. not allowed and a disclosure must be attached.
c. allowed as long as the seller agrees.
d. subject to a $10,000 fine.

99. The role of the appraiser is to
a. analyze the value of the property.
b. qualify the buyer for the loan.
c. both **a** and **b**
d. neither **a** nor **b**

100. A real estate investor asks your advice about the best way to take title to an investment property. What would you advise?
a. single proprietorship
b. corporation
c. a real estate trust
d. you would refer the investor to an attorney.

101. You are associated with ABC Realty and are terminating the association in order to become associated with XYZ Realty. What actions have to be taken?
a. You must notify the Department of Real Estate of your new obligation.
b. ABC Realty must notify the Department of Real Estate.
c. XYZ Realty must notify the Department of Real Estate.
d. all of the above

102. If a tenant moves into an apartment and replaces an old light with a new ceiling fan, the ceiling fan would be considered
a. real property.
b. personal property.
c. a trade fixture.
d. littoral property.

103. If a licensee were using factors of annual gross income and average selling prices of properties in a community, this would be an example of
a. capitalization.
b. gross rent multiplier.
c. comparison.
d. substitution.

104. If an investor does not comply with the CC&Rs, then the HOA can enforce with
a. specific performance.
b. judicial proceedings.
c. fines.
d. all of the above

105. One of the disadvantages of buying an investment property is
a. lack of liquidity.
b. appreciation.
c. revocation.
d. blockbusting.

106. Two real estate firms agreed not to cross over into each other's marked territory. This is a violation of
a. anti-trust.
b. HUD.
c. blockbusting.
d. steering.

107. The purpose of a mechanic's lien is
a. to collect funds when work or materials have been performed and no payment has been made.
b. to create an account with interest bearing.
c. to allow owners a way of collecting from bad general contractors.
d. to make a free loan for 120 days.

108. A person wants homestead protection against his mechanic's lien. He can
a. do it as long as it is below $150,000.
b. do it no matter how much it is.
c. not do it.
d. file a counter mechanic's lien.

109. The phrase "All transactions must be in writing to be enforceable by a court of law" pertains to which of the following?
a. Statute of Frauds
b. tenancy of sufferance
c. security agreement
d. revocation

110. What is the name of the notice that the beneficiary begins on a deed of trust to start foreclosure?
a. power of sale
b. reinstatement period
c. actual notice
d. constructive notice

111. Single-family residential appraisals are reported on
a. a USPAP form.
b. a URAR form.
c. a Banking and Capital form.
d. a truth-in-lending form.

112. If a tenant agrees with a property manager to lease an apartment on a 30-day basis, then this type of lease is known as
a. tenant in common.
b. tenant at will.
c. tenant in sufferance.
d. leased fee interest.

113. A seller discloses to a licensee that he has an old oil tank under his house unused since he converted to gas 20 years ago. The seller asks that the tank's existence not be discussed with buyers. What should the licensee do?
a. The licensee must comply under agency law and fiduciary duties.
b. The licensee upon being made privy of the tank's existence, must disclose the information to prospective buyers.
c. The licensee should ask for indemnification in his listing agreement so that he can maintain the information as confidential.
d. The licensee should obtain the state's mandatory confidentiality form on hazardous material and have the seller give the broker permission to maintain the information as confidential.

114. A person who is licensed, but not with a broker, is

a. active.

b. fraudulent.

c. inactive.

d. able to deal with the public and collect a commission.

115. Which of the following characteristics must a property have to be of value to a person for some purpose?

a. improvements, accessibility, and demand

b. scarcity, utility, and proper zoning

c. transferability, utility, scarcity, and demand

d. transferability, accessibility, and improvements

116. In Arizona, if you are convicted of a felony, you must notify the real estate commissioner within how many days?

a. ten

b. 120

c. seven

d. 30

117. A blind ad would NOT disclose which of the following?

a. if it's a condo

b. if it's in Arizona

c. if it's an agent

d. the sales price

118. The contract states that the buyer should do what before determining title and vesting?

a. Obtain legal and tax advice.

b. Talk to his or her REALTOR®.

c. Talk to the designated broker.

d. Allow the title company to recommend how to proceed.

119. Who holds bare-naked legal title?

a. trustor

b. trustee

c. buyer

d. beneficiary

120. The term *leveraging* would most likely refer to which one of the following?

a. selling real estate

b. buying real estate

c. financing real estate

d. brokering real estate

121. For how many years must rejected offers be kept?

a. five

b. three

c. two

d. one

122. When someone is renewing a judgment, he or she must do so

a. within the last 90 days of the five years.

b. within the last year of the five years.

c. at anytime during the five years.

d. there is a one-year grace period after expiration for renewal.

123. Discrimination of race was first prohibited by law by what act?

a. Civil Rights Act of 1843

b. Civil Rights Act of 1866

c. Civil Rights Act of 1960

d. Civil Rights Act of 1964

124. ADA Title I requires companies with
   a. ten or more people to accommodate people with disabilities to perform a job.
   b. 15 or more people to accommodate people with disabilities to perform a job.
   c. 15 or less people to accommodate customers.
   d. 15 or more people to accommodate customers.

125. For how long must you first prove an assured water supply to obtain a public report in an AMA?
   a. 100 years
   b. 180 days
   c. 120 days
   d. 21 days

126. How much is the transfer tax on real estate in Arizona?
   a. 3% of the sales price
   b. $5,000
   c. $495
   d. There is no transfer tax in Arizona.

127. Which of the following acronyms is consistent with real estate disclosure?
   a. SPDS
   b. FNMA
   c. COE
   d. HOA

128. What does CC&Rs stand for?
   a. contracts, codes, and restrictions
   b. covenants, codes, and rights
   c. contracts, codes, and rights
   d. covenants, codes, and restrictions

129. Which of the following is NOT required on a purchase contract to be valid?
   a. buyer and seller signature
   b. sales price
   c. notary
   d. legal description

130. Todd got three computers from his uncle through a will. This is called a
   a. chattel.
   b. bequest.
   c. corporal.
   d. dower.

131. Josie did not get a public report when she signed her contract. This was a mistake made by the builder. How long does she have to rescind the deal?
   a. 180 days
   b. one year
   c. three years
   d. five years

132. Real estate taxes are called what type of lien?
   a. positive
   b. negative
   c. state
   d. specific

133. The theme for Arizona water law is
   a. don't waste it.
   b. keep the desert.
   c. first in time, first in right.
   d. if you can float it, boat on it.

134. The governor appoints
   a. the Real Estate Advisory Board.
   b. designated brokers.
   c. the president of AAR.
   d. the county treasurer.

135. Some contracts may require performance by one party and are known as
a. unilateral.
b. bilateral.
c. monolateral.
d. sololateral.

136. A common requirement by a lender on a purchase of a house would include
a. an appraisal.
b. a title report.
c. evidence of insurance.
d. all of the above

137. A licensee is driving around a neighborhood and sees a sign in the front yard of a house that says FSBO and lists a telephone number. What does FSBO mean?
a. Real estate brokers are not allowed to call the number.
b. The house is for sale, but only to buyers directly.
c. for sale by owner
d. for sale by offers

138. One of the key components to a monthly report is
a. gross receipts.
b. real estate tax collections.
c. net operating income.
d. total operating expenses.

139. Joanna Murphy has a lease and pays rent of $1,000 monthly, which includes her utilities, water, insurance, taxes, and repairs. This type of lease is known as a
a. net lease.
b. percent lease.
c. ground lease.
d. gross lease.

140. What is the status of a licensee when a payment has been made from the recovery fund?
a. The license is suspended.
b. The license is terminated.
c. The license is active.
d. The license is inactive.

▶ Answers

1. **c.** A parcel has definite boundaries and is a specific tract of land.

2. **b.** A broker is required by law to keep records for five years.

3. **b.** Chattel is an item of tangible personal property and is most appropriately transferred by a bill of sale. A chattel mortgage is a mortgage secured by personal property.

4. **a.** The designated broker is responsible for supervising and approving all advertising.

5. **d.** The Arizona homestead exemption protects against a judgment because it is involuntary.

6. **b.** A material fact must be disclosed by the agent and the principal.

7. **d.** A mortgage foreclosure is a judicial procedure that can take up to two years.

8. **c.** Ingress and egress are part of an easement that would be recorded to allow access to a property.

9. **d.** The four factors include land, labor, capital, and management. Property value is at the highest if these factors are balanced.

10. **b.** Irrigation non-expansive areas (INAs) are sparsely populated areas.

11. **b.** Statute prohibits misuse of information provided to an inquirer. The buyer never inquired and the use of the information was to hurt the value of competition.

12. **a.** At a tax lien sale, the winner receives a certificate of purchase against a property. The homeowner has three years to redeem or he or she could lose property.

13. **c.** The real estate commissioner manages only one recovery fund.

14. **b.** A real estate license is valid for two years before renewal.

15. **b.** Escrows are prorated on 360 days in a year or 30 days in a month.

16. **d.** Tax liens are charged at 16% at the sale before the auction.

17. **c.** The term *laches* typically refers to a person who waited too long to file a mechanic's lien.

18. **b.** A landlord is a person who owns real property and rents to another.

19. **d.** Signatures of the grantor(s) must be notarized

20. **c.** The lender had nothing to do with the buyer's decision to default and is not liable.

21. **c.** Only income-producing property can be depreciated for tax purposes.

22. **a.** A lien is an encumbrance recorded on real property to secure debt.

23. **b.** *Ad valorem* is a Latin word meaning "according to value" or "your portion."

24. **c.** A court action brought against a party to a contract to force compliance with a legally binding contract is a suit for specific performance.

25. **b.** $135,678 ÷ 0.0855 = $1,586,877

26. **b.** *Time is of the essence* means all parties must abide by any deadlines or be liable for non-performance.

27. **d.** The state will charge renewing brokers and salespersons a fee.

28. **d.** For someone who had possession and use only, it would be ten years.

29. **a.** Actual eviction is when a defaulted tenant is physically removed through legal action.

30. **d.** A licensee has all of these responsibilities to the principal of a transaction.

31. **b.** When a buyer and seller have agreed and signed to the terms in a contract, they have made an expressed contract.

32. **c.** Hypothecation is when a lender allows a borrower to possess pledged real estate for use.

33. b. The Federal Reserve Bank set up Regulation Z to implement the law on Truth-in-Lending.

34. a. Licensees continually confuse the term of cooperate. To cooperate is to offer information as requested by another agent. However, an agent may decide to offer a property to buyers directly and not include outside agents.

35. c. The Real Estate Settlement and Procedures Act (RESPA) requires all settlement charges be itemized to buyers and sellers of one- to four-unit family residences and was passed in 1974.

36. b. This formula provides investors a tool in determining the value of an income-producing property.

37. a. A listing agreement does not commit a broker to find a buyer, but it does commit a seller to pay a commission fee if a buyer is found. It is a bilateral contract.

38. b. The person receiving the title, typically the buyer, is known as the grantee, while the person giving the title, typically the seller, is known as the grantor.

39. c. The two types of property are real and personal.

40. a. It takes six months for a mechanic's lien to become a judgment for five years.

41. c. Default is the term used when a borrower fails to comply with the note.

42. d. A home equity line of credit is also known as a second mortgage, a junior lien, or an encumbrance.

43. b. The habendum clause shows the interest being transferred.

44. a. An heir is the person to whom the property would go from an intestate estate.

45. a. A listing agreement is an employment and service contract with a specific starting date and ending date and a compensation.

46. c. Community property is automatically assumed when a married couple purchases real estate together, unless they specify some other form of ownership in writing.

47. d. Within the terms of the life estate, the holder's interest ends at the death of the person (typically the holder) against whose life the life estate is measured.

48. c. Sales prices of comparable properties are adjusted to match the specifications of the subject property.

49. a. Severalty is the simplest form of ownership because there is only one person involved. All other forms involve multiple owners.

50. a. Net operating income is divided by the appropriate capitalization rate to arrive at the value of the property.

51. c. The cost approach is preferable when appraising unique properties.

52. c. A township is six miles by six miles square.

53. b. A contract of fraud is void.

54. b. Homestead exemption protects against judgments up to $150,000 in Arizona.

55. b. HUD has FHA, which insures loans.

56. d. Fannie Mae does not lend money. It is part of the secondary mortgage market.

57. c. The mortgagor would be entitled to any equity.

58. d. An earnest money deposit would be a credit to the buyer.

59. a. A licensee may not charge for a CMA. Only when a buyer has been brought forth and all disclosures have been made may he or she receive compensation.

60. b. The deed must be signed and delivered by the grantor. Recording is not mandatory.

61. b. If the sellers refuse to sell, the buyer(s) can sue for specific performance.

62. d. An agency relationship occurs when the principal hires the licensee and the licensee must perform with good faith and loyalty.

63. a. Procuring cause is the effort in which the licensee produce the buyer for the listed property.

64. b. This would be a net listing, which is not illegal in Arizona, just highly unadvisable.

65. a. The commissioner or any representative from the commissioner's office may inspect the broker's records at any reasonable time.

66. c. A designated person may be assigned for 30 days. It must be in writing in the broker's office for one year from the effective date.

67. c. To keep your real estate license active, you must take 24 hours of continuing education every two years.

68. c. Police power gives the municipality the power to regulate.

69. a. A new zoning law will not affect the use of any building that was being used before the adoption of the new law.

70. d. The church received 15% of the total. 63 + 10 + 12 donated to the family equals 85%. 100% − 85% = 15% to the college. College contribution of $30,000 ÷ 15% = a total value of $200,000. The daughter received 12% of that, or $24,000.

71. c. There is no requirement for the broker to provide any office or workspace for the independent contractor.

72. a. The mortgage insurance premium (MIP) is the term used by FHA. Private mortgage insurance (PMI) is the term used in relationship to conventional loans.

73. b. Points are based on the mortgage amount. $500,000 − $50,000 (10% down payment) gives a mortgage amount of $450,000 × 2% = $9,000.

74. c. It is not necessary to speak to the commissioner; however, you must apply in writing.

75. d. The VA loan is only for primary residences and for one-time usage.

76. d. An owner's title policy covers any defects forever.

77. b. Eminent domain is when property is taken for the good of the public at fair market value. It is a type of involuntary alienation.

78. a. A firm that solicits cold calls must not call anyone on the do-not-call list.

79. d. The maximum amount the recovery fund will pay per transaction is $30,000 and up to $90,000 per licensee for if multiple transactions.

80. a. Owner-occupied real estate is taxed at 10% of the assessed value.

81. d. It is a trade fixture because it is used in the business and can be removed.

82. b. Devise is a transfer of real property by means of a will.

83. d. The landlord must serve the tenant with a Notice to Quit. The other actions are illegal.

84. d. 50 × 25 × 8 = 10,000 cubic feet ÷ 27 cubic feet = 370.37 cubic yards × $45 per cubic yard = $16,667.67.

85. c. Dower is the widow's interest in the husband's property.

86. b. Interest and taxes are deductible on your primary residence.

87. a. A quitclaim is not an encumbrance; it is a type of conveyance and is recorded.

88. a. A deed of reconveyance is recorded when it is satisfied from payments.

89. b. A broker cannot commingle funds.

90. **c.** A person can be either a resident or a non-resident.

91. **b.** You must apply and qualify for a broker's license.

92. **c.** This is a voidable contract. A minor could cancel the contract.

93. **a.** A license is not required, only when selling a business.

94. **b.** The appraiser's knowledge provides the basis of an accurate appraisal.

95. **c.** The income approach would be of most interest to an investment property buyer.

96. **b.** Appraisals will require the use of more than one approach.

97. **c.** It takes three years before you can foreclose on a certificate of purchase on a tax lien sale.

98. **b.** Licensees can only send solicitations to the public with a disclaimer stating that if the seller is currently listed with another broker he or she should disregard this as an attempt to obtain the listing.

99. **a.** The role of the appraiser is to analyze the value of the property.

100. **d.** Real estate agents cannot give legal advice.

101. **d.** Sales agents and brokers must notify the Department of Real Estate.

102. **a.** When the ceiling fan becomes affixed, it becomes real property.

103. **a.** The gross rent multiplier would be the method utilizing these factors.

104. **d.** Anyone who violates the CC&Rs shall be punishable as described in the declaration.

105. **a.** Lack of liquidity means having to sell the property in order to obtain cash.

106. **a.** This is a violation of the Sherman Anti-Trust Act.

107. **a.** A mechanic's lien is for people who have performed work or provided materials as a way to collect funds from nonpaying owners. Only six people can file a mechanic's lien: general and subcontractors, architects, engineers, material suppliers, and equipment suppliers.

108. **c.** Homestead exemption does not cover consensual liens like mechanic's liens.

109. **a.** The Statute of Frauds states that all transactions must be in writing to be enforceable by a court of law. The only exemption in real estate is leases for less than one year.

110. **a.** The power of sale is when the beneficiary starts foreclosure on a deed of trust. The beneficiary must then give constructive and actual notice before the 90-day reinstatement period.

111. **b.** A Uniform Residential Appraisal Report (URAR) is required by various agencies and organizations.

112. **b.** A 30-day tenant is a tenant at will. The landlord or tenant can provide 30-day notice at any time to vacate.

113. **b.** Despite the seller's wishes to keep the information confidential, the licensee must disclose the information to all prospective buyers that he is privy that an underground tank may exist.

114. **c.** A person who is licensed, but not with a broker, is inactive.

115. **c.** Real estate must have four characteristics to be valuable: utility, transferability, scarcity, and demand.

116. **a.** You must notify the commissioner of any conviction, name change, or address change within ten days.

117. c. A blind ad is an ad that does not indicate that it is from a real estate agent.

118. a. The contract states that the buyer should obtain legal and tax advice before determining title and vesting.

119. d. The trustee holds bare-naked legal title and acts for the beneficiary and trustor.

120. c. The term *leveraging* would pertain to financing real estate in which you can leverage another entity's larger sum of money over your own.

121. d. Rejected offers must be kept for one year and must be available for the commissioner or anyone acting on his or her behalf to review at a reasonable time.

122. b. A person must renew a judgment within the last 90 days of the five years or it will expire.

123. b. The Civil Rights Act of 1866 was the first of several pieces of legislation called the Civil Rights Act.

124. b. ADA Title I requires companies with 15 or more people to accommodate people with disabilities to perform a job.

125. a. You must submit proof of 100 years of reliable supply of water.

126. d. There is no transfer tax in Arizona.

127. a. The SPDS is the Seller's Property Disclosure Statement.

128. d. CC&Rs stands for covenants, codes, and restrictions, typically from a homeowners association.

129. c. Notary signature is not required on a purchase contract to be valid.

130. b. Personal property that is specified and transferred from a will is called a bequest.

131. c. If a public report was to be signed by a purchase and was not, then she would have three years to rescind the agreement.

132. d. An Arizona tax lien would be called specific.

133. c. The basis behind Arizona water law is "first in time, first in right," pertaining to prior appropriation. The first person to appropriate water and apply that water to use has the first right to use that water within a particular water system.

134. a. The governor appoints the nine-member Real Estate Advisory Board.

135. a. A contract requiring the act of one person is known as a unilateral contract.

136. d. A lender would want an appraisal, title report, and evidence of insurance before funding a home loan on a property.

137. c. FSBO means for sale by owner. A broker may still call the number for information, but the seller is not required to pay a commission fee.

138. c. The net operating income is gross receipts minus total operating expenses and provides an owner with the true cash flow before mortgage and taxes.

139. d. Gross lease is a lease in which the rent includes all the operating expenses to a tenant.

140. b. When payment has been made from the recovery fund, the agent's license is terminated.

▶ Scoring

Again, evaluate how you did on this practice exam by finding the number of questions you got right, disregarding, for the moment, the ones you got wrong or skipped. If you achieved a score of at least 105 questions correct, you will most likely pass the Arizona real estate sales exam.

If you did not score as well as you would like, ask yourself the following: Did I run out of time before I could answer all of the questions? Did I go back and change my answers from right to wrong? Did I get flustered and sit staring at a difficult question for what seemed like hours? If you had any of these problems, be sure to go over the LearningExpress Test Preparation System in Chapter 2 to review how best to avoid them.

You probably have seen improvement from your first two practice exam scores and this one; but if you didn't improve as much as you would like, following are some options.

If you scored below the passing score on each section, you should seriously consider whether you are ready for the exam at this time. A good idea would be to take some brush-up courses in the areas you feel less sure of. If you don't have time for a course, you might try private tutoring.

If you scored close to the minimum passing score, you need to work as hard as you can to improve your skills. Go back to your real estate license course textbooks to review the knowledge you need to do well and use the LearningExpress book, *Practical Math Success in 20 Minutes a Day*. Also, reread and pay close attention to the information in Chapter 4, "Real Estate Refresher Course"; Chapter 5, "Real Estate Math Review"; and Chapter 6, "Real Estate Glossary." It might be helpful, as well, to ask friends and family to make up mock test questions and quiz you on them.

Now, revise your study schedule according to the time you have left, emphasizing those parts that gave you the most trouble this time. Use the table on the next page to see where you need more work, so that you can concentrate your preparation efforts. After working more on the subject areas that give you problems, take the third practice exam in Chapter 8 to see how much you have improved.

EXAM 2 FOR REVIEW

Exam 2 Subject Area	Question Numbers (Questions 1–140)
Business Practice and Ethics	4, 26, 30, 31, 35, 64, 72, 78, 89, 100, 106, 113, 117, 123, 124, 137
Agency and Listing	11, 37, 45, 50, 51, 62, 63, 95, 98, 103
Property Characteristics, Descriptions, and Ownership Interests and Restrictions	1, 8, 19, 21, 39, 52, 68, 69, 77, 81, 86, 130
Property Valuation and the Appraisal Process	9, 36, 48, 94, 96, 99, 111
Real Estate Sales Contracts	20, 23, 24, 53, 58, 61, 92, 104, 109, 115, 129, 135, 136
Financing Sources	3, 22, 32, 33, 42, 55, 56, 75, 105, 120
Closing/Settlement and Transferring Title	15, 38, 43, 44, 47, 76, 82, 85
Property Management	29, 71, 102, 112
Real Estate Math	25, 70, 73, 84
Arizona Ownership Transfer	5, 10, 17, 28, 40, 46, 49, 54, 60, 87, 97, 107, 108, 119, 122, 125, 128, 131
Arizona Licensing	13, 27, 67, 74, 79, 90, 93
Arizona Activities of Licensees	2, 6, 14, 34, 65, 66, 91, 101, 114, 116, 118, 121, 134, 140
Arizona Finance Settlement	7, 12, 16, 41, 57, 59, 80, 88, 110, 126, 127, 132, 133
Arizona Leasing and Property Management	18, 83, 138, 139

8 ▶ Arizona Real Estate Sales Exam 3

CHAPTER SUMMARY

This is the third of the four practice tests in this book. Use this test to identify which types of questions are still giving you problems.

YOU ARE NOW more familiar with the content and format of the Arizona real estate sales exam, and most likely, you feel more confident than you did at first. However, your practice test-taking experience will help you most if you create a situation as close as possible to the real one. For this exam, try to simulate real testing conditions. Find a quiet place where you will not be disturbed. Make sure you have two sharpened pencils and a good eraser. You should have plenty of time to answer all of the questions when you take the real exam, but you will want to practice working quickly without rushing. Be sure to leave enough time to complete the test in one sitting. Remember, you will have three-and-a-half hours for the actual exam. Use a timer or a stopwatch and see if you can work through all the test questions in the allotted time.

As before, the answer sheet is on the next page. Following the exam, you will find the answer key and explanations. These explanations, along with the table at the end of this chapter, will help you see where you need further study.

► Arizona Real Estate Sales Exam 3 Answer Sheet

1.	ⓐ	ⓑ	ⓒ	ⓓ	48.	ⓐ	ⓑ	ⓒ	ⓓ	95.	ⓐ	ⓑ	ⓒ	ⓓ
2.	ⓐ	ⓑ	ⓒ	ⓓ	49.	ⓐ	ⓑ	ⓒ	ⓓ	96.	ⓐ	ⓑ	ⓒ	ⓓ
3.	ⓐ	ⓑ	ⓒ	ⓓ	50.	ⓐ	ⓑ	ⓒ	ⓓ	97.	ⓐ	ⓑ	ⓒ	ⓓ
4.	ⓐ	ⓑ	ⓒ	ⓓ	51.	ⓐ	ⓑ	ⓒ	ⓓ	98.	ⓐ	ⓑ	ⓒ	ⓓ
5.	ⓐ	ⓑ	ⓒ	ⓓ	52.	ⓐ	ⓑ	ⓒ	ⓓ	99.	ⓐ	ⓑ	ⓒ	ⓓ
6.	ⓐ	ⓑ	ⓒ	ⓓ	53.	ⓐ	ⓑ	ⓒ	ⓓ	100.	ⓐ	ⓑ	ⓒ	ⓓ
7.	ⓐ	ⓑ	ⓒ	ⓓ	54.	ⓐ	ⓑ	ⓒ	ⓓ	101.	ⓐ	ⓑ	ⓒ	ⓓ
8.	ⓐ	ⓑ	ⓒ	ⓓ	55.	ⓐ	ⓑ	ⓒ	ⓓ	102.	ⓐ	ⓑ	ⓒ	ⓓ
9.	ⓐ	ⓑ	ⓒ	ⓓ	56.	ⓐ	ⓑ	ⓒ	ⓓ	103.	ⓐ	ⓑ	ⓒ	ⓓ
10.	ⓐ	ⓑ	ⓒ	ⓓ	57.	ⓐ	ⓑ	ⓒ	ⓓ	104.	ⓐ	ⓑ	ⓒ	ⓓ
11.	ⓐ	ⓑ	ⓒ	ⓓ	58.	ⓐ	ⓑ	ⓒ	ⓓ	105.	ⓐ	ⓑ	ⓒ	ⓓ
12.	ⓐ	ⓑ	ⓒ	ⓓ	59.	ⓐ	ⓑ	ⓒ	ⓓ	106.	ⓐ	ⓑ	ⓒ	ⓓ
13.	ⓐ	ⓑ	ⓒ	ⓓ	60.	ⓐ	ⓑ	ⓒ	ⓓ	107.	ⓐ	ⓑ	ⓒ	ⓓ
14.	ⓐ	ⓑ	ⓒ	ⓓ	61.	ⓐ	ⓑ	ⓒ	ⓓ	108.	ⓐ	ⓑ	ⓒ	ⓓ
15.	ⓐ	ⓑ	ⓒ	ⓓ	62.	ⓐ	ⓑ	ⓒ	ⓓ	109.	ⓐ	ⓑ	ⓒ	ⓓ
16.	ⓐ	ⓑ	ⓒ	ⓓ	63.	ⓐ	ⓑ	ⓒ	ⓓ	110.	ⓐ	ⓑ	ⓒ	ⓓ
17.	ⓐ	ⓑ	ⓒ	ⓓ	64.	ⓐ	ⓑ	ⓒ	ⓓ	111.	ⓐ	ⓑ	ⓒ	ⓓ
18.	ⓐ	ⓑ	ⓒ	ⓓ	65.	ⓐ	ⓑ	ⓒ	ⓓ	112.	ⓐ	ⓑ	ⓒ	ⓓ
19.	ⓐ	ⓑ	ⓒ	ⓓ	66.	ⓐ	ⓑ	ⓒ	ⓓ	113.	ⓐ	ⓑ	ⓒ	ⓓ
20.	ⓐ	ⓑ	ⓒ	ⓓ	67.	ⓐ	ⓑ	ⓒ	ⓓ	114.	ⓐ	ⓑ	ⓒ	ⓓ
21.	ⓐ	ⓑ	ⓒ	ⓓ	68.	ⓐ	ⓑ	ⓒ	ⓓ	115.	ⓐ	ⓑ	ⓒ	ⓓ
22.	ⓐ	ⓑ	ⓒ	ⓓ	69.	ⓐ	ⓑ	ⓒ	ⓓ	116.	ⓐ	ⓑ	ⓒ	ⓓ
23.	ⓐ	ⓑ	ⓒ	ⓓ	70.	ⓐ	ⓑ	ⓒ	ⓓ	117.	ⓐ	ⓑ	ⓒ	ⓓ
24.	ⓐ	ⓑ	ⓒ	ⓓ	71.	ⓐ	ⓑ	ⓒ	ⓓ	118.	ⓐ	ⓑ	ⓒ	ⓓ
25.	ⓐ	ⓑ	ⓒ	ⓓ	72.	ⓐ	ⓑ	ⓒ	ⓓ	119.	ⓐ	ⓑ	ⓒ	ⓓ
26.	ⓐ	ⓑ	ⓒ	ⓓ	73.	ⓐ	ⓑ	ⓒ	ⓓ	120.	ⓐ	ⓑ	ⓒ	ⓓ
27.	ⓐ	ⓑ	ⓒ	ⓓ	74.	ⓐ	ⓑ	ⓒ	ⓓ	121.	ⓐ	ⓑ	ⓒ	ⓓ
28.	ⓐ	ⓑ	ⓒ	ⓓ	75.	ⓐ	ⓑ	ⓒ	ⓓ	122.	ⓐ	ⓑ	ⓒ	ⓓ
29.	ⓐ	ⓑ	ⓒ	ⓓ	76.	ⓐ	ⓑ	ⓒ	ⓓ	123.	ⓐ	ⓑ	ⓒ	ⓓ
30.	ⓐ	ⓑ	ⓒ	ⓓ	77.	ⓐ	ⓑ	ⓒ	ⓓ	124.	ⓐ	ⓑ	ⓒ	ⓓ
31.	ⓐ	ⓑ	ⓒ	ⓓ	78.	ⓐ	ⓑ	ⓒ	ⓓ	125.	ⓐ	ⓑ	ⓒ	ⓓ
32.	ⓐ	ⓑ	ⓒ	ⓓ	79.	ⓐ	ⓑ	ⓒ	ⓓ	126.	ⓐ	ⓑ	ⓒ	ⓓ
33.	ⓐ	ⓑ	ⓒ	ⓓ	80.	ⓐ	ⓑ	ⓒ	ⓓ	127.	ⓐ	ⓑ	ⓒ	ⓓ
34.	ⓐ	ⓑ	ⓒ	ⓓ	81.	ⓐ	ⓑ	ⓒ	ⓓ	128.	ⓐ	ⓑ	ⓒ	ⓓ
35.	ⓐ	ⓑ	ⓒ	ⓓ	82.	ⓐ	ⓑ	ⓒ	ⓓ	129.	ⓐ	ⓑ	ⓒ	ⓓ
36.	ⓐ	ⓑ	ⓒ	ⓓ	83.	ⓐ	ⓑ	ⓒ	ⓓ	130.	ⓐ	ⓑ	ⓒ	ⓓ
37.	ⓐ	ⓑ	ⓒ	ⓓ	84.	ⓐ	ⓑ	ⓒ	ⓓ	131.	ⓐ	ⓑ	ⓒ	ⓓ
38.	ⓐ	ⓑ	ⓒ	ⓓ	85.	ⓐ	ⓑ	ⓒ	ⓓ	132.	ⓐ	ⓑ	ⓒ	ⓓ
39.	ⓐ	ⓑ	ⓒ	ⓓ	86.	ⓐ	ⓑ	ⓒ	ⓓ	133.	ⓐ	ⓑ	ⓒ	ⓓ
40.	ⓐ	ⓑ	ⓒ	ⓓ	87.	ⓐ	ⓑ	ⓒ	ⓓ	134.	ⓐ	ⓑ	ⓒ	ⓓ
41.	ⓐ	ⓑ	ⓒ	ⓓ	88.	ⓐ	ⓑ	ⓒ	ⓓ	135.	ⓐ	ⓑ	ⓒ	ⓓ
42.	ⓐ	ⓑ	ⓒ	ⓓ	89.	ⓐ	ⓑ	ⓒ	ⓓ	136.	ⓐ	ⓑ	ⓒ	ⓓ
43.	ⓐ	ⓑ	ⓒ	ⓓ	90.	ⓐ	ⓑ	ⓒ	ⓓ	137.	ⓐ	ⓑ	ⓒ	ⓓ
44.	ⓐ	ⓑ	ⓒ	ⓓ	91.	ⓐ	ⓑ	ⓒ	ⓓ	138.	ⓐ	ⓑ	ⓒ	ⓓ
45.	ⓐ	ⓑ	ⓒ	ⓓ	92.	ⓐ	ⓑ	ⓒ	ⓓ	139.	ⓐ	ⓑ	ⓒ	ⓓ
46.	ⓐ	ⓑ	ⓒ	ⓓ	93.	ⓐ	ⓑ	ⓒ	ⓓ	140.	ⓐ	ⓑ	ⓒ	ⓓ
47.	ⓐ	ⓑ	ⓒ	ⓓ	94.	ⓐ	ⓑ	ⓒ	ⓓ					

► Arizona Real Estate Sales Exam 3

1. If people obtain new financing on a property they already own and pay off the existing loan to buy another property, they are
   a. financing.
   b. purchasing.
   c. selling.
   d. refinancing.

2. A grantee is also the
   a. seller.
   b. buyer.
   c. agent.
   d. title company.

3. On what date do unpaid property taxes become a lien in Arizona?
   a. December 31
   b. October 1
   c. February 21
   d. January 1

4. Leading prospective homebuyers to or away from certain areas would be
   a. redlining.
   b. steering.
   c. legal.
   d. in violation of RESPA.

5. If you lived in a common law state and you married a person who owned his or her property in severalty, you would
   a. not have any ownership rights.
   b. become a 50% co-owner automatically.
   c. become a grantor.
   d. be entitled to one-third of the ownership.

6. A buyer and a seller have a purchase and sales agreement to close on the sale by the fifteenth day of the next month. Which of the following would be the most important factor?
   a. the earnest money
   b. the assessed value of the property
   c. notarizing the purchase and sales agreement
   d. time is of the essence

7. Wear and tear on a property would be an example of what type of obsolescence?
   a. economic
   b. function
   c. physical
   d. scarcity

8. Effective gross income would be
   a. annual gross rents less an amount for vacancy and collection costs.
   b. gross income less the debt service.
   c. gross income less the operating expenses.
   d. the building's cash flow.

9. A runner ran the Flagstaff Marathon, which is 26.2 miles, in four hours. What was the length of the course in feet?
   a. 138,336
   b. 43,560
   c. 137,800
   d. 3,800,400

10. A mechanic's lien must be filed by the general contractor within how many days after completion of the work?
   a. 20
   b. 90
   c. 120
   d. 180

11. When a purchaser has approved a public report, this is evidenced by
 a. taking a picture.
 b. signing the public report.
 c. signing a public report receipt.
 d. going to the public report website and clicking approved.

12. When would an owner disclose that he or she is an owner-agent?
 a. when he or she holds a real estate license and is selling his or her own real estate
 b. when he or she holds a real estate license and is selling, leasing, or exchanging his or her own real estate
 c. when he or she holds a real estate license and is listing another's real estate
 d. when he or she holds an insurance license and his or her own real estate

13. How long shall real estate schools maintain all records for each student attending?
 a. one year
 b. three years
 c. five years
 d. forever

14. With interest in the state of Arizona, what does the acronym ADEQ stand for?
 a. American Division of Economic Quality
 b. Arizona Division of Economic Quality
 c. American Department of Environmental Quality
 d. Arizona Department of Environmental Quality

15. A person who advertises that he or she has a license, and does not, or a licensee who practices while incarcerated, shall be subject to a
 a. class 5 felony.
 b. class 6 felony.
 c. $10,000 fine.
 d. $5,000 fine.

16. While showing houses, Libby purposefully kept taking the same protected class to a certain area of the city. She is
 a. redlining.
 b. steering.
 c. blockbusting.
 d. co-operating.

17. A tenant makes a verbal agreement to rent space from a landlord on a 30-day basis and pay separately for trash removal. After the first month, the tenant stops paying trash removal and the landlord argues that they have an agreement. Is the agreement enforceable?
 a. Yes, but he will have to get it in writing first.
 b. Yes, and the landlord has grounds to evict.
 c. No, because verbal agreements are not enforceable.
 d. No, because it is in violation of the landlord tenant act.

18. A due-on-sale clause most likely means that you
 a. can wrap the loan.
 b. can assume the loan.
 c. can sell to anyone who wants your loan.
 d. have to pay the loan off when exchanging the title.

19. The difference between what is owed and the value of a piece of property is the
   a. equity.
   b. mortgage balance.
   c. combined loan-to-value (CLTV).
   d. loan-to-value (LTV).

20. The first half of taxes due are paid in arrears using the prorated portion of
   a. a system of a 12-month average.
   b. a special assessment.
   c. the current year's assessed taxes.
   d. the previous year's assessed taxes.

21. If a buyer backs out of an agreement to buy because he or she changes his or her mind,
   a. the seller keeps the deposit.
   b. the buyer will lose his or her deposit.
   c. the earnest money is subject to loss.
   d. all of the above

22. Economic life in reference to appraising is
   a. how long the rate will go.
   b. the amount of market share one has.
   c. the time a building is profitable.
   d. the time it takes to sell a building.

23. Homestead protects
   a. mortgages.
   b. equity.
   c. liens.
   d. cash.

24. Places where a judgment would show up are
   a. public records, credit reports, and title reports.
   b. magazines, newspapers, and radio.
   c. credit reports and SPDS.
   d. title reports and the IRS.

25. A mechanic's lien takes lien priority on what day?
   a. 21 days after work began
   b. the day it was recorded
   c. the day work began
   d. the day work was completed

26. Ed's tenant is late on rent by more than 25 days. The first step Ed should take is to
   a. send a ten-day notice to quit.
   b. serve notice.
   c. send a five-day notice to pay.
   d. give 48 hours' notice.

27. A public report receipt is signed
   a. while signing the contract to buy.
   b. before signing the contract to buy.
   c. ten days after receipt.
   d. once ground has broke on construction.

28. Kim, the licensee, did not disclose that there was a murder on the property 25 years ago. What can happen to her and her license?
   a. She can be sued.
   b. She will lose her license.
   c. nothing
   d. She can be sued and lose her license.

29. Kelly operates as a real estate TEAM. What must she do?
   a. Send the list to the department.
   b. Hire anyone who has a license with the same broker she has.
   c. both **a** and **b**
   d. neither **a** nor **b**

30. A variance in zoning would best be described
as a(n)
a. exception.
b. rule.
c. objection.
d. evaluation.

31. An apartment building has ten units. It would
be exempt from
a. an appraiser.
b. a mortgage broker.
c. a good faith estimate.
d. RESPA.

32. Karen made five offers that were all rejected on
the same day. How long must her broker keep
copies of the rejected offers?
a. five years
b. not necessary
c. one year
d. 180 days from the rejection date

33. TCPA stands for what regulation issued
October 16, 1992?
a. Telephone Client Privilege Association
b. Telephone Consumer Protection Act
c. Telephone Consumer Phoning Act
d. Tele-Communications Protection Act

34. On a 1031 exchange, the definition of *boot*
would be closest to
a. the part that is not taxable.
b. the part that is taxable.
c. non–like-kind property transferring.
d. like-kind property exchanging.

35. A document signed by the seller and buyer
stating the sales price for the assessor's office
is called an
a. affirm affidavit.
b. affidavit of mortgage.
c. affidavit of contract.
d. affidavit of property value.

36. Brad just sold his home and paid for the
owner's title insurance policy. What does his
insurance NOT cover?
a. Brad, the seller
b. the buyer of Brad's home
c. the mortgage company
d. the title company

37. What must a client be given with respect to a
material fact?
a. full disclosure
b. non-disclosure
c. limited disclosure
d. agency disclosure

38. Which of the following items is true about dual
agency?
a. They are legal in Arizona.
b. It is when the same broker represents the
buyer and seller in the same transaction.
c. They must be in writing.
d. all of the above

39. A listing agreement entitles brokers to which
one of the following?
a. chattel
b. commission
c. homestead
d. laches

40. When a person says that he or she wants to leave a legacy behind, which of the following would be the most correct answer?
   a. He or she wants to leave a lot of money to family members.
   b. He or she wants to leave a lot of money to charity.
   c. He or she wants to gift a lot of personal property by will.
   d. He or she wants to gift a lot of money.

41. How did Hank benefit from the term *contingent* in his contract that was accepted by the seller?
   a. when he qualified for the loan at a below market rate
   b. when his home sold for full price on time
   c. when his new loan did not go through
   d. when his appraisal came in over the sales price

42. Purchasing property by reinvesting proceeds from refinancing already owned properties is called
   a. appreciation.
   b. steering.
   c. pyramiding.
   d. riparian.

43. Qualifying the buyer for a mortgage is the function of the
   a. broker.
   b. principal.
   c. mortgagor.
   d. mortgagee.

44. A statement that is made with the intent to deceive, with the knowledge that it is untrue, is considered to be
   a. misrepresentation.
   b. *caveat emptor.*
   c. execution.
   d. ethical.

45. Broker James received an offer of $195,000 on a property listed at $200,000. Before he presents the offer to the seller, he receives another offer from a different buyer for $202,000. What must Broker James do?
   a. Call the first buyer and reject the offer of $195,000.
   b. Present only the highest offer.
   c. Present both offers.
   d. Decide which is the best offer for the sale.

46. Mike had it with the horrible living conditions his landlord allowed. The landlord neglected all upkeep, and Mike moved out. This would be an example of
   a. five-day notice.
   b. actual eviction.
   c. constructive eviction.
   d. notice to quit.

47. If two licensees have an issue with their commission, what must they do?
   a. Allow the deal to close.
   b. Put a lien on the property.
   c. Sue each other.
   d. Send a complaint to the Department of Real Estate.

48. What is a conditional commitment a part of?
   a. a LSR
   b. FHA appraisal
   c. preapproval letter
   d. VA loan appraisal

49. Property that has been accumulated by a married person without the other is called
   a. joint property.
   b. community property.
   c. unenforceable.
   d. stepped-up property.

50. In a condo complex with 40 units, the seller is responsible for what?
   a. giving the buyer all HOA papers
   b. collecting the prorated HOA fee
   c. signing an HOA affidavit
   d. disclosing to the president of the HOA

51. A master planned community is
   a. a platted subdivision with a community center and an elementary school.
   b. two-platted subdivisions with a community center.
   c. two or more separate platted subdivisions with CC&Rs.
   d. 5,000 or more dwellings sharing the same CC&Rs.

52. How often is the least the state Real Estate Advisory Board can meet?
   a. once a week
   b. once a quarter
   c. twice a year
   d. once a year

53. Where do applicants' fingerprint cards go first after submission to the state real estate department?
   a. county sheriff for criminal background check
   b. Department of Public Safety
   c. city police department
   d. FBI

54. Up to $10,000 can be the fine for first offense and violation of the
   a. ADA.
   b. recovery fund.
   c. Fair Housing Act.
   d. AMA.

55. Rocco went on a listing appointment to discover from the owner of the property that the house is in full violation of the existing zoning law because of an add-on that the owner did earlier this year. Rocco should
   a. not take the listing.
   b. disclose only when asked.
   c. file an exemption waiver with the state.
   d. take the listing.

56. A person just received a settlement from an insurance company from a dispute. What will the insurance company make the person sign?
   a. disclaimer
   b. quitclaim
   c. subordination
   d. subrogation

57. An executed contract would best be described as
   a. signed by the buyer.
   b. closed.
   c. open.
   d. non-voidable.

58. When a disabled person with a seeing eye dog rents a property, what is true about the deposit?

a. A landlord can charge extra.

b. A landlord cannot charge extra.

c. A landlord can charge based on the size of the animal the disabled person must use for assistance.

d. none of the above

59. What term do lenders use when transferring the servicing or selling the loan to another lender?

a. assumption

b. transfer

c. assignment

d. mortgagee

60. A REIT needs a minimum of how many members?

a. one

b. 25

c. 50

d. 100

61. An acre contains approximately how many square feet?

a. 5,270

b. 40,000

c. 43,560

d. 42,560

62. Which of the following is true about real estate property taxes?

a. Commercial rate is 10%.

b. Land rate is 25%.

c. Residential and land is 10%.

d. Residential is 10%.

63. An employee of a general contractor wants to file a mechanic's lien against an owner because his employer did not pay him. Which of the following is true?

a. He can file as long as he does a 20-day notice.

b. He cannot file because he lacks a relationship.

c. He can file and claim 1.5 times the amount due.

d. none of the above

64. For how many months are cash proceeds from the homestead law protected?

a. 12

b. six

c. 18

d. 24

65. A lawyer without a real estate license was practicing real estate while settling an estate. He can

a. file with the commissioner for an exemption.

b. do it because it's part of an estate settlement.

c. not do it.

d. do as many as he likes.

66. A way of holding title in real estate by two or more people with undivided interest and no right of survivorship or equal parts is called

a. community property.

b. tenants in common.

c. joint tenants.

d. all of the above

67. In real estate agency relationships, the agreement between a seller and the licensee is known as a
   a. listing agreement.
   b. sales agreement.
   c. binder.
   d. purchase offer.

68. Janet Jones, a licensee, placed an advertisement in the newspaper. She advertised her name, her office address, her telephone number, and her educational background. What was one important item she was missing?
   a. the area she services
   b. her areas of specialty
   c. her experience
   d. her broker's and agency's name

69. Regardless of who sells the house, the broker will collect a commission. This type of listing offers the most protection, therefore, to the broker. This is called a(n)
   a. open listing.
   b. net listing.
   c. exclusive right to sell listing.
   d. exclusive agency listing.

70. The remaining balance on Shari Larson's mortgage is $185,500. The interest rate is 8.5% and the monthly payment is $1,425.50. How much of her next monthly payment will be applied to the principal?
   a. $1,426.50
   b. $112.54
   c. $113.96
   d. $43.79

71. The trustee just gave you constructive notice and actual notice. How many days do you have to reinstate your loan in good standing?
   a. 180
   b. 30
   c. none
   d. 90

72. Which of the following sales is exempt from a public report?
   a. the sale of 160 acres or more
   b. the sale of six lots or more to the same buyer
   c. the sale of commercially zoned parcels
   d. all of the above

73. What is the correct order of the two largest landowners in Arizona?
   a. Native Americans, U.S. government
   b. U.S. government, Native Americans
   c. state of Arizona, U.S. government
   d. Native Americans, state of Arizona

74. In Arizona, what government body controls ground and surface water?
   a. Department of Real Estate
   b. real estate commissioner
   c. Department of Water Resources
   d. Arizona legislature

75. In Arizona, if you die without a will or heirs (escheat), the state will sell your property and keep the money for how many years in case an heir materializes?
   a. one
   b. three
   c. seven
   d. 30

76. Before a property owner can have a septic tank installed, he or she must have the soil tested to determine how much wastewater the soil can absorb by ordering a
   a. percolation test.
   b. pest inspection.
   c. field investigation.
   d. home inspection.

77. Remediation and testing for asbestos can only be done by contractors who have been specifically trained and are approved by either the
   a. local municipality or Maricopa County.
   b. federal or state government.
   c. Department of Health or the EPA.
   d. EPA or the state of Arizona.

78. Kalid changed real estate brokers seven times in one year. What was the charge for each broker change?
   a. $20
   b. $90
   c. no fee
   d. $120

79. The economic characteristics of land that affect the value would include
   a. construction and labor costs.
   b. proximity to landfills.
   c. relative scarcity, improvements, and area preference.
   d. eminent domain.

80. A salesperson may be hired by his or her broker as a(n)
   a. part-time employee.
   b. independent contractor.
   c. full-time employee.
   d. all of the above

81. A subagency relationship cannot be created without
   a. the principal's consent.
   b. a written contract.
   c. the buyer's permission.
   d. approval of the licensee's broker.

82. Expense adjustments that are prorated on the closing statement appear as
   a. debits only.
   b. debits and credits.
   c. abstract of title.
   d. encroachments.

83. Which of the following would NOT be considered a freehold estate?
   a. fee simple estate
   b. life estate
   c. estate for the years
   d. defeasance fee estate

84. The formal judicial proceedings to prove the validity of a deed is called
   a. courtesy.
   b. probate.
   c. life tenant.
   d. chattel.

85. An owner of real estate has which of the following ownership rights?
   a. air rights
   b. surface rights
   c. subsurface rights
   d. all of the above

86. A real estate gift by a will would be called a(n)
   a. devise.
   b. acquisition.
   c. prescription.
   d. succession.

87. The process of applying all three appraisal approaches on the same property to determine value is called
  a. summary.
  b. comparison.
  c. reconciliation.
  d. assessment.

88. If a house had no closets or windows in the bedrooms, this would be an example of what type of depreciation?
  a. physical
  b. functional
  c. economic
  d. obsolescence

89. What would most affect the value of real estate?
  a. the appraisal
  b. the location
  c. the book value
  d. the age of the building

90. If you owned unit number nine in a condominium complex, what would you own?
  a. the tennis courts and health club
  b. the hallways in the building
  c. an equal share of each unit in the complex
  d. the air space within unit number nine

91. A husband and wife jointly own a rental property in Scottsdale in which they do not live. If they sell the house, what would their capital gain exclusion be?
  a. zero
  b. $250,000
  c. $500,000
  d. $100,000

92. An addition to a will that could transfer real property and personal property would be called a(n)
  a. bequest.
  b. gift.
  c. codicil.
  d. agreement of sale.

93. The purpose of metes and bounds boundaries is
  a. meridians.
  b. to allow a surveyor to walk the boundaries.
  c. ranges.
  d. a bearing system.

94. In an FHA mortgage, if the appraised value is less than the selling price, and the borrower wants the house, then he or she can
  a. pay the difference in cash.
  b. cancel the loan.
  c. apply for another loan.
  d. obtain a second loan.

95. What is the rescission period on a time-share?
  a. none
  b. three days
  c. seven days
  d. ten days

96. Which type of corporation must have one class of stock, no corporation shareholders, and fewer than 75 shareholders?
  a. LLC
  b. Subchapter S
  c. 1120
  d. limited partnership

97. How long must a landlord wait before he or she can access a unit after notice?

a. 24 hours

b. two days

c. three days

d. five days

98. Which of the following laws does NOT affect Arizona real estate?

a. ARS

b. MVD

c. Statute of Frauds

d. federal

99. When are the first half of property taxes due?

a. February 1

b. March 1

c. April 15

d. October 1

100. The Arizona real estate sales exam consists of how many questions?

a. 75 federal and 75 state

b. 60 federal and 80 state

c. 30 state and 70 federal

d. 80 federal and 60 state

101. In Arizona, if you have an impounded PITI account for your mortgage, who pays the property taxes?

a. the broker

b. the buyer

c. the seller

d. the lender

102. If your neighbor has agreed to allow your orange tree to hang over his lot line, he has agreed to a(n)

a. easement.

b. party.

c. ingress.

d. encroachment.

103. FHA loan payoffs prorate

a. for the entire month's interest.

b. for each day used.

c. *per diem*.

d. as any loan would when paying off.

104. A licensee who assists a buyer and a seller in completing an agreement but does not represent either party is known as a(n)

a. subagent.

b. facilitator.

c. open agent.

d. dual agent.

105. A lease, as a contract, is an example of a

a. duocontract.

b. bilateral contract.

c. systematic contract.

d. regulatory contract.

106. The Subdivided Land Questionnaire is consistent with what item first?

a. public report

b. subdividing land

c. selling lots

d. Notice of Intention

107. Rich Lowry met a real estate broker for dinner to discuss making an offer on a building. During dinner, Rich had too many glasses of wine. Before Rich went home, he drafted an offer to purchase the building for the real estate broker to present to the seller. If the seller accepts the offer, is the offer invalid?
   a. No, because Rich is an adult over the age of 18 years.
   b. No, because Rich is not mentally ill.
   c. No, but it is voidable by Rich because he was incompetent.
   d. Yes, because Rich was clearly intoxicated.

108. When a mortgage is involved, who would order the appraisal?
   a. a lender
   b. the broker
   c. the seller
   d. FHA

109. A licensee is required by Arizona law to notify all prospective buyers about
   a. the dangers of lead paint to buildings built prior to 1978.
   b. freeway access.
   c. the requirement of radon testing.
   d. a seller with credit problems.

110. A property manager would carry casualty insurance for
   a. loss of rent due.
   b. increase in any construction costs.
   c. plate glass breakage.
   d. injury to workers.

111. Which one of the following would NOT be a characteristic of an exempt domestic well?
   a. fewer than two acres of land
   b. used for bottling water for people
   c. 35 gallons a minute or fewer
   d. beneficial domestic use to land

112. The commissioner may waive a portion of the national pre-licensing classes if a person has a
   a. license in good standing in another state.
   b. nice car.
   c. good business plan.
   d. lot of leads.

113. The word *reinstatement* goes with what type of foreclosure?
   a. judicial
   b. nonjudicial
   c. deed of trust
   d. both **b** and **c**

114. The only navigable river in Arizona is the
   a. Gila.
   b. Salt.
   c. Colorado.
   d. Riparian.

115. Britt wants to open a branch of her real estate office. How many people must work there?
   a. two
   b. one
   c. three
   d. at least five full time

116. The formulation of rules with respect to the legal practice of real estate are created by the
   a. voting public.
   b. National Association of REALTORS®.
   c. commissioner of real estate.
   d. Arizona Real Estate Advisory Board.

117. The client would also be known as the
a. consumer.
b. friend.
c. principal.
d. beneficiary.

118. Self-help for minor defects is
a. one-half of one month's rent or $300, whichever is greater.
b. one month's rent or $300, whichever is greater.
c. up to $500 per occurrence.
d. the amount of the cleaning deposit.

119. Arizona superfund sites are
a. tax free.
b. city bond grants.
c. WQARF.
d. AHERA.

120. Tyler got permission to hunt on Robbie's land. Tyler probably has a
a. license.
b. certificate of approval.
c. will.
d. deer.

121. What is NOT included in a promissory note?
a. interest rate charged
b. loan amount
c. appraisal fee
d. legal description

122. Which of the following transfers the deed upon final payment of the loan?
a. agreement for sale
b. land contract
c. deed of trust
d. both **a** and **b**

123. The name of the requirement to disclose the APR on a loan is
a. Regulation Z.
b. Regulation B.
c. three-day right of rescission.
d. none of the above

124. A real estate office got together and decided to get a certain group of minorities into their area so they can get prices down for listings. They are
a. redlining.
b. steering.
c. blockbusting.
d. all of the above

125. What is a tax-deferred exchange on an investment property known as?
a. 1031
b. 1003
c. 1008
d. 203-b

126. Who would be the person that signs a deed of reconveyance?
a. buyer
b. trustee
c. trustor
d. beneficiary

127. Dawn just got a listing in Casa Grande through a friend. She should
a. get signed permission for a sign.
b. put a sign near the freeway.
c. have an open listing.
d. charge an upfront advertising fee.

128. Which one of the following applies to joint tenancy?
- **a.** interest
- **b.** one person
- **c.** no right of survivorship
- **d.** none of the above

129. Sherman Anti-Trust is when agents
- **a.** get together and try to set a commission rate for an area.
- **b.** do not want to sell to a certain minority group.
- **c.** only sell to people age 55 and above.
- **d.** want to get sellers to sell fast over newcomers.

130. Rina signed a counteroffer; at this point, she would be the
- **a.** offeree.
- **b.** offeror.
- **c.** counteror.
- **d.** counteree.

131. Laws that are based on court decisions and tradition are known as
- **a.** general.
- **b.** state.
- **c.** common.
- **d.** federal.

132. The accrued, prorated property taxes are shown on a closing statement as
- **a.** debit to seller and credit to buyer.
- **b.** a debit to seller only.
- **c.** credit to seller and debit to buyer.
- **d.** debit to seller and credit to tax district.

133. The purchase contract states that real property taxes shall be prorated as of
- **a.** October 1.
- **b.** March 1.
- **c.** the date of the contract.
- **d.** close of escrow.

134. When a tenant has an option to buy a building, this type of property rights is referred to as
- **a.** an option.
- **b.** real property.
- **c.** real estate.
- **d.** benefits.

135. In the sale of real estate, a seller is obligated to convey
- **a.** an environmentally clean site.
- **b.** a title that is good and marketable.
- **c.** personal property.
- **d.** leased fee title.

136. Independent contractors, prior to being hired for services by property management, require
- **a.** proof that they have separate worker's compensation.
- **b.** proof that they are insured and bonded.
- **c.** proof that they have a real estate license in case of leasing situations.
- **d.** a completion of a W-2 form.

137. Mortgage brokers are helpful to borrowers as they
- **a.** originate and issue loans for homebuyers.
- **b.** locate borrowers and find lenders and process applications.
- **c.** review credit reports and issue mortgages.
- **d.** are nonprofit organizations that exist as a service for first-time homebuyers.

138. Once a real estate firm has a designated broker, do all the licensees in the firm with a broker's license have the same authority as the designated broker?

a. yes, once a written disclosure has been signed

b. no, only the principal owner can be the designated broker

c. no, only the original licensees for the buyer and seller are the designated brokers

d. no, there can be only one designated broker

139. Heather took her time to get her real estate license renewed. What happened?

a. nothing within the 120-day grace period

b. Her license was terminated.

c. Her license was expelled.

d. Her license was suspended.

140. An attorney in Arizona would be required to have a real estate license when

a. doing practice outside his or her scope of work.

b. holding an open house.

c. showing homes to multiple groups of first-time homebuyers.

d. all of the above

► Answers

1. d. If people pay off an existing loan with a new loan on a property they already own, then they are refinancing.

2. b. The grantee is the buyer and the seller is the grantor.

3. d. Unpaid property taxes will become a lien on January 1.

4. b. You cannot steer a person into or away from specific neighborhoods.

5. b. You would automatically become a 50% co-owner.

6. d. Time is of the essence; if the property is to close by the fifteenth of the month, then it must be accomplished by this date.

7. b. Wear and tear would be physical obsolescence.

8. a. Effective gross income is gross rents less an amount for vacancy and collection expenses.

9. a. There are 5,280 feet in a mile × 26.2 miles = 138,336 feet.

10. c. A general contractor must file within 120 days after completion of the work.

11. c. A purchaser should sign the receipt only after he or she has read and accepted the public report.

12. b. It is mandatory to disclose owner-agent when you hold a real estate license and are selling, leasing, or exchanging your own real estate.

13. c. Real estate schools shall maintain all records for each student attending the school for five years.

14. d. ADEQ stands for Arizona Department of Environmental Quality, and it protects public health and the environment.

15. b. Any person who advertises that he or she has a license and he or she does not, or a licensee who practices while incarcerated, shall be subject to a class 6 felony.

16. b. Steering is taking the same protected class to a certain area of the city or neighborhood.

17. b. Verbal lease agreements with terms are enforceable in Arizona.

18. d. A due-on-sale is when you have to pay the loan off when exchanging or selling the property.

19. a. The difference between what is owed and the value of real estate is the equity. What is owed would include all mortgages, liens, and any judgments, if applicable.

20. d. The previous year's assessed taxes are what are used for assessing the first half of taxes due March 1.

21. d. If the buyer changes his or her mind then he or she is subject to losing the deposit or earnest money to the seller.

22. c. Economic life is how long an investment building is profitable.

23. b. Homestead protects a person's equity up to $150,000.

24. a. Public records, credit reports, and title reports are the most common places that a judgment would show up.

25. c. Mechanics' liens take lien priority on the day that work began. If another lien was recorded before the mechanic lien, then the mechanic lien will not loose its lien position.

26. c. The first step a landlord takes when a tenant is late on rent is to send a five-day notice to pay.

27. b. A buyer signs a public report before signing the contract to buy.

28. c. The agent cannot lose her license or have any criminal or civil action brought against her in this case.

29. c. Any agent who works and advertises as a TEAM must send the name list to the department and must have a real estate license with the same broker that agent has.

30. a. A variance is an exception to the existing zoning law.

31. d. RESPA only covers residential real estate up to four units.

32. c. Rejected offers, no matter how many you have with the same buyer, must be kept for a minimum of one year.

33. b. TCPA is an acronym for the Telephone Consumer Protection Act, which was issued October 16, 1992, to protect consumers from unsolicited phone calls.

34. b. *Boot* is the term that the IRS recognizes as the part of a 1031 exchange that is taxable.

35. d. The document the county uses for the assessor's office to determine the sales price on each transaction is an affidavit of property value.

36. b. The owner's title insurance protects the buyer if a problem started with the title that was not discovered during the title search.

37. a. All material facts must be given full disclosure because they affect a buyer's decision to buy.

38. d. Dual agency is legal in Arizona, it must be in writing, and it is when the same broker represents the buyer and seller in the same transaction.

39. b. The listing agreement is the instrument that establishes the contractual arrangement the seller will pay in the form of a commission.

40. c. Legacy is when a person gifts either personal property or money as specified in a will.

41. c. The term *contingent* benefited him because when he did not qualify for his new loan, unless otherwise stated, he would be able to get a full return of his earnest deposit without loss.

42. c. Pyramiding is the process of reinvesting proceeds from refinanced properties, which are already owned, into additional properties.

43. d. The mortgagee lends the money, and it is the mortgagee's responsibility to qualify the buyer.

44. a. Misrepresentation is a statement that is known to be untrue and is made with the intent to deceive.

45. c. All offers must be presented to the seller.

46. c. Constructive eviction is when a tenant can no longer inhabit a domain because it is no longer livable or the seller is no longer providing an agreed-upon service, such as water or air conditioning.

47. a. When a disagreement arises between licensees and brokers, they must first allow the contract to close then seek remedy.

48. b. The conditional commitment is the FHA's statement of appraised value.

49. c. Property that has been accumulated by a married person without his or her spouse is called unenforceable, due to the fact that Arizona requires both spouses to sign or have one disclaim.

50. a. In all complexes with fewer than 50 units the seller is responsible, not the homeowners association (HOA), for providing all information regarding the HOA.

51. c. A master planned community has two or more separate platted subdivisions with a master declaration of CC&Rs.

52. b. The Arizona Real Estate Advisory Board meets at least once a quarter at a designated place within the state.

53. b. The Department of Public Safety will conduct a criminal history records check and can exchange with the FBI for national criminal history records.

54. c. The first fine or penalty for a violation of the Fair Housing Act is up to $10,000.

55. a. He should not take a listing that is in violation of a zoning law.

56. d. Subrogation is when a person acknowledges that he or she is substituting payment for any future rights of claim.

57. b. An executed contract is one that has been fully fulfilled and delivered as agreed upon by the parties, or *closed*, in real estate terminology.

58. b. A landlord may not charge for a pet deposit because a person has animal assistance.

59. c. Assignment is the term when a lender sells, transfers, or assigns a new lender to do the servicing.

60. d. A real estate investment trust (REIT) must have at least 100 members. One of the main benefits are no corporate income tax.

61. c. An acre contains 43,560 square feet.

62. d. Residential is taxed at 10% of the assessed value; land is taxed at 15%.

63. b. He cannot file because he lacks a relationship. Employees and foremen cannot file mechanics' liens.

64. c. Proceeds from the homestead law are protected for 18 months or until a new homestead is acquired, whichever one is sooner.

65. b. He can do it because it's part of an estate settlement. He cannot practice like a REALTOR® without a license.

66. b. Tenants in common is a way for unmarried people to hold title to real estate with unequal or undivided interest and no right of survivorship.

67. a. The agreement that a licensee has with his or her seller is called a listing agreement.

68. d. All agent advertising must include the name of the broker and the agency, which must be prominently displayed.

69. c. An exclusive right to sell listing agreement is the listing that is encouraged by most brokers. It should also provide the homeowner with the most extensive advertising, as the broker will be entitled to the commission regardless of how someone hears about the house.

70. b. ($185,500 × 0.085) ÷ 12 = $1,313.96 interest for one month; $1,426.50 − $1,313.96 = $112.54.

71. d. You have 90 days after the trustee started the power of sale to reinstate your loan or you will lose in a foreclosure at the trustee's sale.

72. d. All of these sales would be exempt from a public report.

73. b. The U.S. government owns approximately 50% of Arizona, and Native Americans own approximately 25%.

74. c. The Department of Water Resources (DWR) controls all water usage and permits on the state's behalf.

75. c. If a person dies escheat, then the state will sell the property and hold the funds for seven years in case an heir materializes.

76. a. A percolation test is required prior to installing a septic tank; the septic tank must also be large enough to accommodate the number of occupants that will be residing in the home.

77. d. Because asbestos, if disturbed, has the potential to pose severe health risks, great care must be taken to protect individuals at or nearby the affected area. The Environmental Protection Agency (EPA) or the state of Arizona both provide an intensive training program for individuals whose job it is to remove the asbestos.

78. a. The charge to change brokers is $20.

79. c. In addition to relative scarcity, improvements, and area preference, the economic characteristics of land include permanence of investment.

80. d. A licensee is required by law to be supervised by his or her broker, and may be hired as an employee, full time or part time, or as an independent contractor.

81. a. Subagents are those upon whom the power of a licensee has been conferred by the listing agent, but can be created only with the principal's consent.

82. b. Entries for expenses are shown as debits and credits to the appropriate parties.

83. c. This is a non-freehold. The others are all freehold estates.

84. b. Probate is the judicial procedure to prove the validity of a deed.

85. d. Air rights, surface rights, and subsurface rights are all rights of ownership.

86. a. Devise is when ownership is transferred by means of a will.

87. c. Reconciliation is the process of applying all three appraisal methods.

88. b. This is functional loss of value, as most homes would have closets and windows in the bedrooms.

89. b. Location of the property is the most important feature of real estate.

90. d. Air space is the only area of ownership. All of the other choices are common areas.

91. a. There are no exclusions for capital gains in non–owner-occupied buildings.

92. c. The codicil is the addition to the will that could transfer real and personal property.

93. b. This allows the surveyor to identify the length and boundaries of the property.

94. a. The buyer must pay the difference in cash and may utilize secondary financing to accomplish this.

95. c. The rescission period on a time-share is seven days.

96. b. A Subchapter S Corporation has one class of stock, no corporation shareholders, no nonresident alien, and fewer than 75 shareholders.

97. b. A landlord must wait two days after notice to access a tenant's dwelling.

98. b. The Motor Vehicle Division (MVD) does not have any laws related to real estate.

99. d. The first half of property taxes is due in arrears on October 1. The second half would be due March 1 the following year in arrears always.

100. d. The Arizona real estate sales exam consists of 80 federal and 60 state multiple-choice questions.

101. d. If you have a PITI impound account, the borrower will pay the lender one-twelfth of the property taxes each month and the lender will pay the taxes every March and October.

102. a. An allowance over one party's property to another is an easement.

103. a. An FHA loan is charged the entire month's worth of interest regardless if it is paid off on the first or thirtieth of the month.

104. b. A facilitator works with buyers and sellers in reaching an agreement, but has no fiduciary responsibility to either party.

105. b. A lease is an example of a bilateral contract in which the contract binds two parties equally.

106. d. The subdivider will fill out a Subdivided Land Questionnaire first for Notice of Intention, so a public report can be obtained from the commissioner of real estate.

107. c. A person who is intoxicated does not have legal competency. The offer is voidable, but only by Rich, because only the person with the disability can void a contract.

108. a. The lender orders the appraisal regardless of who pays for it.

109. a. Licensees are required to notify all prospective purchasers and tenants about the dangers of lead paint in buildings constructed prior to 1978.

110. c. Casualty insurance can cover many issues, such as plate glass breakage, theft, broken furnace, etc.

111. b. Bottling water would not be a characteristic of an exempt domestic well; it would be considered an Active Management Area (AMA).

112. a. The commissioner may waive a portion or all of the national pre-license requirement if a person has a license in good standing in another state.

113. c. Reinstatement would be a deed of trust foreclosure, which is a nonjudicial foreclosure. A mortgage foreclosure would be a judicial foreclosure.

114. c. The Colorado is the only navigable river in Arizona. Landowners only own land to the high-water mark, but none below the water.

115. b. A branch of a real estate office can operate legally with only one licensed individual.

116. c. The commissioner of real estate creates, enforces, and restricts the rules of real estate practice for its licensees.

117. c. The client is the principal in the transaction.

118. a. The self-help for minor defects allows a tenant one-half of one month's rent or $300, whichever is greater.

119. c. The superfund or mini-superfund is Arizona's state legislation for the Water Quality Assurance Revolving Fund (WQARF) that includes retroactive liability for past releases that affect the environment or water.

120. a. A license is the most likely, as Tyler got permission to hunt on Robbie's land.

121. c. The appraisal fee would not be on a promissory note.

122. d. An agreement for sale and a land contract are the same, in each case, the deed is transferred when the debt is paid entirely.

123. a. Regulation Z is the federal requirement for all lenders to disclose the interest rate in the form of an APR, which considers the upfront costs of the loan in conjunction with the interest rate.

124. c. Blockbusting occurs when agents agree to create alarm by alerting homeowners to sell fast because of minorities moving in.

125. a. A 1031 tax-deferred exchange can occur only on investment property.

126. b. The trustee would sign the deed of reconveyance when the debt has been paid.

127. a. All signs on anyone's property require written permission.

128. a. Joint tenancy would be defined as the interest being held by two or more persons with right of survivorship.

129. a. Sherman Anti-Trust is when agents get together and try to set a commission rate for an area or in general.

130. b. When she signed the counteroffer, she became the offeror because she is the one offering an agreement.

131. c. Common law is established by court decisions and tradition. Agency law is mostly a form of common law.

132. a. Unpaid, year-to-date property taxes are owed by the seller and are credited to the buyer, who will be responsible for payment when taxes are due.

133. d. The purchase contract states that real property taxes shall be prorated as of the close of escrow (COE).

134. b. Real property includes rights, interests, and benefits that are inherent with real estate.

135. b. A seller is conveying title that is good and marketable. However, a buyer should determine if the seller has clear title prior to the purchase of the property.

136. a. Independent contractors are not employees of property management. They may be specialists, such as a plumbers or manual laborers. In all cases, however, employers must provide worker's compensation insurance for employees unless they are independent contractors.

137. b. Mortgage brokers do not issue loans, but do locate borrowers and lenders as an intermediary. They are not a direct lender.

138. d. There can only be one designated broker; people with brokers' licenses have the same authority as those with salespersons' licenses.

139. b. Failure to renew your license will result in termination.

140. d. Attorneys are required to have a license anytime they are doing real estate outside of the normal practice of their job. In certain cases, a license is not required, such as when settling an estate.

▶ Scoring

Again, evaluate how you did on this practice exam by finding the number of questions you got right, disregarding, for the moment, the ones you got wrong or skipped. If you achieved a score of at least 105 questions correct, you will most likely pass the Arizona real estate sales exam.

If you did not score as well as you would like, ask yourself the following: Did I run out of time before I could answer all the questions? Did I go back and change my answers from right to wrong? Did I get flustered and sit staring at a difficult question for what seemed like hours? If you had any of these problems, be sure to go over the LearningExpress Test Preparation System in Chapter 2 to review how best to avoid them.

You probably have seen improvement from your first two practice exam scores and this one; but if you didn't improve as much as you would like, following are some options.

If you scored below the passing scored on each section, you should seriously consider whether you are ready for the exam at this time. A good idea would be to take some brush-up courses in the areas you feel less sure of. If you don't have time for a course, you might try private tutoring.

If you scored close to the minimum passing score, you need to work as hard as you can to improve your skills. Go back to your real estate license course textbooks to review the knowledge you need to do well and use the LearningExpress book, *Practical Math Success in 20 Minutes a Day*. Also, reread and pay close attention to the information in Chapter 4, "Real Estate Refresher Course"; Chapter 5, "Real Estate Math Review"; and Chapter 6, "Real Estate Glossary." It might be helpful, as well, to ask friends and family to make up mock test questions and quiz you on them.

Now, revise your study schedule according to the time you have left, emphasizing those parts that gave you the most trouble this time. Use the table on the next page to see where you need more work, so that you can concentrate your preparation efforts. After working more on the subject areas that give you problems, take the fourth practice exam in Chapter 9 to see how much you have improved.

EXAM 3 FOR REVIEW

Exam 3 Subject Area	Question Numbers (Questions 1–140)
Business Practice and Ethics	4, 16, 28, 31, 33, 37, 44, 54, 58, 68, 107, 124, 129
Agency and Listing	38, 39, 45, 55, 67, 69, 81, 88, 89, 104, 117, 120, 135
Property Characteristics, Descriptions, and Ownership Interests and Restrictions	19, 30, 60, 61, 76, 77, 85, 90, 93, 96, 102, 131
Property Valuation and the Appraisal Process	7, 22, 48, 79, 87
Real Estate Sales Contracts	2, 6, 17, 21, 41, 56, 57, 95, 105, 125, 130
Financing Sources	1, 18, 42, 43, 59, 94, 103, 121, 123, 137
Closing/Settlement and Transferring Title	5, 40, 66, 82, 84, 86, 122, 128
Property Management	8, 46, 101, 110, 134
Real Estate Math	9, 70, 132
Arizona Ownership Transfer	10, 11, 14, 23, 24, 25, 27, 51, 63, 64, 72, 73, 74, 106, 111, 114, 119
Arizona Licensing	13, 52, 53, 78, 100, 112
Arizona Activities of Licensees	12, 15, 29, 32, 47, 49, 65, 75, 80, 83, 98, 108, 109, 115, 116, 127, 133, 136, 138, 139, 140
Arizona Finance Settlement	3, 20, 35, 36, 50, 62, 71, 91, 92, 99, 113, 126
Arizona Leasing and Property Management	26, 34, 97, 118

$$^3 8\,8$$
$$1400$$
$$352\ ^{00}$$
$$88$$
$$123\ ^{200}$$

$$^{3}900$$
$$1232 \text{ correct}$$
$$168 \text{ missed}$$

CHAPTER

9 ▶ Arizona Real Estate Sales Exam 4

CHAPTER SUMMARY

This is the last of the four practice tests in this book based on the Arizona real estate sales exam. Using all of the experience and strategies that you gained from the other three exams, take this exam to see how far you have come.

THIS IS THE last practice exam in this book, but it is not designed to be any harder than the other three. It is simply another representation of what you might expect on the real test. Just as when you take the real test, there should not be anything here that surprises you. In fact, you probably already know what is in a lot of it! That will be the case with the real test, too.

For this exam, pull together all the tips you have been practicing since the first practice exam. Give yourself the time and the space to work. Because you won't be taking the real test in your living room, you might take this one in an unfamiliar location, such as a library. Make sure you have plenty of time to complete the exam in one sitting. In addition, use what you have learned from reading the answer explanations on previous practice tests. Remember the types of questions that caused problems for you in the past, and when you are unsure, try to consider how those answers were explained.

After you have taken this written exam, you should try the computer-based test using the CD-ROM found at the back of this book. That way you will be familiar with taking exams on computer.

Once again, use the answer explanations at the end of the exam to understand questions you may have missed.

► Arizona Real Estate Sales Exam 4 Answer Sheet

1.	(a)	(b)	(c)	(d)
2.	(a)	(b)	(c)	(d)
3.	(a)	(b)	(c)	(d)
4.	(a)	(b)	(c)	(d)
5.	(a)	(b)	(c)	(d)
6.	(a)	(b)	(c)	(d)
7.	(a)	(b)	(c)	(d)
8.	(a)	(b)	(c)	(d)
9.	(a)	(b)	(c)	(d)
10.	(a)	(b)	(c)	(d)
11.	(a)	(b)	(c)	(d)
12.	(a)	(b)	(c)	(d)
13.	(a)	(b)	(c)	(d)
14.	(a)	(b)	(c)	(d)
15.	(a)	(b)	(c)	(d)
16.	(a)	(b)	(c)	(d)
17.	(a)	(b)	(c)	(d)
18.	(a)	(b)	(c)	(d)
19.	(a)	(b)	(c)	(d)
20.	(a)	(b)	(c)	(d)
21.	(a)	(b)	(c)	(d)
22.	(a)	(b)	(c)	(d)
23.	(a)	(b)	(c)	(d)
24.	(a)	(b)	(c)	(d)
25.	(a)	(b)	(c)	(d)
26.	(a)	(b)	(c)	(d)
27.	(a)	(b)	(c)	(d)
28.	(a)	(b)	(c)	(d)
29.	(a)	(b)	(c)	(d)
30.	(a)	(b)	(c)	(d)
31.	(a)	(b)	(c)	(d)
32.	(a)	(b)	(c)	(d)
33.	(a)	(b)	(c)	(d)
34.	(a)	(b)	(c)	(d)
35.	(a)	(b)	(c)	(d)
36.	(a)	(b)	(c)	(d)
37.	(a)	(b)	(c)	(d)
38.	(a)	(b)	(c)	(d)
39.	(a)	(b)	(c)	(d)
40.	(a)	(b)	(c)	(d)
41.	(a)	(b)	(c)	(d)
42.	(a)	(b)	(c)	(d)
43.	(a)	(b)	(c)	(d)
44.	(a)	(b)	(c)	(d)
45.	(a)	(b)	(c)	(d)
46.	(a)	(b)	(c)	(d)
47.	(a)	(b)	(c)	(d)

48.	(a)	(b)	(c)	(d)
49.	(a)	(b)	(c)	(d)
50.	(a)	(b)	(c)	(d)
51.	(a)	(b)	(c)	(d)
52.	(a)	(b)	(c)	(d)
53.	(a)	(b)	(c)	(d)
54.	(a)	(b)	(c)	(d)
55.	(a)	(b)	(c)	(d)
56.	(a)	(b)	(c)	(d)
57.	(a)	(b)	(c)	(d)
58.	(a)	(b)	(c)	(d)
59.	(a)	(b)	(c)	(d)
60.	(a)	(b)	(c)	(d)
61.	(a)	(b)	(c)	(d)
62.	(a)	(b)	(c)	(d)
63.	(a)	(b)	(c)	(d)
64.	(a)	(b)	(c)	(d)
65.	(a)	(b)	(c)	(d)
66.	(a)	(b)	(c)	(d)
67.	(a)	(b)	(c)	(d)
68.	(a)	(b)	(c)	(d)
69.	(a)	(b)	(c)	(d)
70.	(a)	(b)	(c)	(d)
71.	(a)	(b)	(c)	(d)
72.	(a)	(b)	(c)	(d)
73.	(a)	(b)	(c)	(d)
74.	(a)	(b)	(c)	(d)
75.	(a)	(b)	(c)	(d)
76.	(a)	(b)	(c)	(d)
77.	(a)	(b)	(c)	(d)
78.	(a)	(b)	(c)	(d)
79.	(a)	(b)	(c)	(d)
80.	(a)	(b)	(c)	(d)
81.	(a)	(b)	(c)	(d)
82.	(a)	(b)	(c)	(d)
83.	(a)	(b)	(c)	(d)
84.	(a)	(b)	(c)	(d)
85.	(a)	(b)	(c)	(d)
86.	(a)	(b)	(c)	(d)
87.	(a)	(b)	(c)	(d)
88.	(a)	(b)	(c)	(d)
89.	(a)	(b)	(c)	(d)
90.	(a)	(b)	(c)	(d)
91.	(a)	(b)	(c)	(d)
92.	(a)	(b)	(c)	(d)
93.	(a)	(b)	(c)	(d)
94.	(a)	(b)	(c)	(d)

95.	(a)	(b)	(c)	(d)
96.	(a)	(b)	(c)	(d)
97.	(a)	(b)	(c)	(d)
98.	(a)	(b)	(c)	(d)
99.	(a)	(b)	(c)	(d)
100.	(a)	(b)	(c)	(d)
101.	(a)	(b)	(c)	(d)
102.	(a)	(b)	(c)	(d)
103.	(a)	(b)	(c)	(d)
104.	(a)	(b)	(c)	(d)
105.	(a)	(b)	(c)	(d)
106.	(a)	(b)	(c)	(d)
107.	(a)	(b)	(c)	(d)
108.	(a)	(b)	(c)	(d)
109.	(a)	(b)	(c)	(d)
110.	(a)	(b)	(c)	(d)
111.	(a)	(b)	(c)	(d)
112.	(a)	(b)	(c)	(d)
113.	(a)	(b)	(c)	(d)
114.	(a)	(b)	(c)	(d)
115.	(a)	(b)	(c)	(d)
116.	(a)	(b)	(c)	(d)
117.	(a)	(b)	(c)	(d)
118.	(a)	(b)	(c)	(d)
119.	(a)	(b)	(c)	(d)
120.	(a)	(b)	(c)	(d)
121.	(a)	(b)	(c)	(d)
122.	(a)	(b)	(c)	(d)
123.	(a)	(b)	(c)	(d)
124.	(a)	(b)	(c)	(d)
125.	(a)	(b)	(c)	(d)
126.	(a)	(b)	(c)	(d)
127.	(a)	(b)	(c)	(d)
128.	(a)	(b)	(c)	(d)
129.	(a)	(b)	(c)	(d)
130.	(a)	(b)	(c)	(d)
131.	(a)	(b)	(c)	(d)
132.	(a)	(b)	(c)	(d)
133.	(a)	(b)	(c)	(d)
134.	(a)	(b)	(c)	(d)
135.	(a)	(b)	(c)	(d)
136.	(a)	(b)	(c)	(d)
137.	(a)	(b)	(c)	(d)
138.	(a)	(b)	(c)	(d)
139.	(a)	(b)	(c)	(d)
140.	(a)	(b)	(c)	(d)

▶ Arizona Real Estate Sales Exam 4

1. An escrow or impound account would include which of the following?
   a. principal and interest
   b. tax and insurance
   c. homeowners association
   d. all of the above

2. Which of the following need NOT be in writing to be valid?
   a. a sale with a five-day closing period
   b. a listing for 60 days or fewer
   c. an option to buy for fewer than 24 months
   d. a lease for under a 12-month duration

3. A clause in which the lender relieves the borrower of personal liability to pay the deficiency judgment is called a(n)
   a. acceleration clause.
   b. due-on-sale clause.
   c. prepayment penalty.
   d. exculpatory clause.

4. Owner's title insurance protects the _____, is written for the _____, and is _____.
   a. new owner; sales price; not transferable
   b. new owner; sales price; fully transferable
   c. previous owner; loan amount; not transferable
   d. lender; mortgage; transferable

5. The buyer in a cooperative apartment received shares of stock in the cooperative and a
   a. proprietary lease.
   b. bargain and sale deed.
   c. joint tenancy.
   d. limited partnership.

6. How many class hours must a person complete before being eligible to take the real estate exam?
   a. three one-hour classes
   b. 90 hours
   c. six-hour boot camp class
   d. 24 hours every two years

7. Property taxes are levied _____ and paid _____.
   a. annually; semiannually
   b. semiannually; annually
   c. in arrears; monthly
   d. assessed; annually

8. Which of the following is associated with $150,000?
   a. ALTA insurance
   b. RESPA fine
   c. homestead exemption
   d. recovery fund

9. Lance just signed a buyer-broker agreement with a new licensee. What is he owed from the licensee now?
   a. lowest price homes available
   b. discounts on home warranties
   c. fiduciary responsibility
   d. unilateral contracts

10. The licensee just remembered that the swing set does not convey with the sale, which everyone has already signed. To make sure the buyer knows, she can modify by
   a. having the buyer sign an addendum acknowledging it.
   b. having the buyer and seller sign the modification.
   c. having the seller sign the modification.
   d. writing in the existing sales contract on page seven additional terms and conditions.

11. If Shelly just won a certificate of purchase, she just came from what type of sale?
   a. deed of trust
   b. trustee's sale
   c. sheriff's sale
   d. tax lien sale

12. Which of the following people is allowed to file a residential mechanic's lien?
   a. engineer
   b. real estate agent
   c. general contractor
   d. equipment supplier

13. Which of the following is true about the homestead exemption?
   a. It allows you to leave the state and never pay taxes.
   b. It is a tax-free shelter up to $500,000.
   c. It protects your equity up to $150,000 against involuntary creditors.
   d. It protects your equity up to $150,000 against voluntary creditors.

14. If a branch of your neighbor's olive tree extends over your property, this would be called a(n)
   a. testator.
   b. encroachment.
   c. riparian.
   d. littoral.

15. Property owner Davis inherited property from his mother in a life estate and then immediately sold the property to buyer Ryder. If property owner Davis dies, who owns the property?
   a. grantee
   b. executor
   c. remainder person
   d. no one

16. If Ryan owned a commercial investment property and then sold it, how could he defer the capital gain taxes?
   a. By completing a 1031 exchange.
   b. The taxes cannot be deferred.
   c. The person must wait until reaching age 55 before selling.
   d. A licensee must be hired.

17. To comply with and keep active your Arizona real estate licensee status, you should
   a. take continuing education classes.
   b. become an attorney.
   c. develop an office policy for the associates to follow.
   d. become a general contractor.

18. A buyer enters into an exclusive buyer agency contract with Broker Borden and then buys a property with Broker Carl without Broker Borden being involved in the sale. Who owes Broker Borden a commission?
    a. Broker Carl
    b. the buyer
    c. the seller
    d. Broker Borden is not entitled to a commission.

19. A title company is responsible for
    a. establishing the commissions for the licensees.
    b. providing the transportation.
    c. preparing the purchase and sales agreement.
    d. preparing the HUD Uniform Settlement Form.

20. A variety of land uses will add to property value as long as the uses are in
    a. conformity.
    b. balance.
    c. progression.
    d. regression.

21. The buyer of a condo with more than 100 units receives
    a. the CC&Rs from the HOA.
    b. the CC&Rs from the seller.
    c. the CC&Rs from the buyer's agent.
    d. the CC&Rs from the listing agent.

22. An owner may sell his or her home and not pay a commission, even though it is exclusively listed with an agency, when he or she has a(n)
    a. exclusive right to sell listing agreement.
    b. exclusive agency listing.
    c. net listing.
    d. open listing.

23. A purchase and sales agreement would be an example of what type of contract?
    a. unconscionable
    b. executory
    c. executed
    d. all of the above

24. If a tenant entered into a lease and gave the seller a deposit and then backed out, the seller can
    a. keep the deposit.
    b. call the sale incomplete.
    c. return the deposit.
    d. split the deposit.

25. If an agent received a $40 fee every time a termite report was done and never disclosed properly, this would be a violation of
    a. RESPA.
    b. HUD.
    c. Arizona IRS codes.
    d. FHA.

26. Ten days would be the time period in which a licensee shall inform
    a. the commissioner of a new car.
    b. the commissioner of a new address.
    c. the broker of a new address.
    d. the broker of a new car.

27. The amortization of a mortgage means
    a. the amount of each monthly payment applied to interest remains the same.
    b. the mortgagor can prepay the loan without a penalty.
    c. payments will be constant and will pay off the principal and interest.
    d. only interest will be paid off.

28. A mortgage in which the seller will deliver a deed upon receipt of the final mortgage payment is a(n)
a. purchase money mortgage.
b. secondary mortgage.
c. land sales contract.
d. equity mortgage.

29. Insurance in which the insuring company is obligated to take action to defend the title, take action to perfect it, or to compensate the insured for loss is
a. mandatory.
b. called title insurance.
c. escheat.
d. provided by the seller.

30. Under a seller carry-back, the seller is also the
a. title company.
b. appraiser.
c. mortgagor.
d. mortgagee.

31. How long is the redemption period on a deed of trust after the trustee sale?
a. one year
b. 180 days
c. 120 days
d. There is none.

32. A landlord who owns a two-family house collects $1,200 in rent from each tenant on the first day of the month. On the twelfth of the month, the landlord sells the property. The adjustment would be an amount of
a. $960 due to the buyer.
b. $1,400 due to the seller.
c. $1,440 due to the buyer.
d. $1,520 due to the seller.

33. What is a factor on a foreclosure using a mortgage over a deed of trust?
a. It takes longer.
b. It is a shorter period.
c. It is less money.
d. It is more popular in Arizona.

34. A buyer makes an offer to the seller to buy his building. The seller likes the entire offer but makes some very minor changes, signs it, and delivers the offer to the buyer. The seller has just
a. signed a binding contract.
b. made a counteroffer.
c. signed a novation contract.
d. accepted the buyer's offer.

35. Real property is defined as
a. land, structures, and appurtenances.
b. rights, interests, and benefits.
c. being tangible, but immobile.
d. equipment, personal property, and real estate.

36. If a piece of real property is assessed at a 25% rate, then it is
a. land.
b. commercial.
c. residential.
d. a vacant lot.

37. Arizona administers the Truth-in-Lending Law, which is also known as
a. ARS 17-43.
b. FHA 203-b.
c. VA 2-1 360.
d. Regulation Z.

38. The Real Estate Advisory Board must have nine members who are actively or passively engaged in real estate and a term lasting
a. five years.
b. six years.
c. three years.
d. seven years.

39. The three types of conveying deeds in Arizona are
a. bargain and sale deeds, special warranty deeds, and general warranty deeds.
b. deeds of trust, quitclaim deeds, and general warranty deeds.
c. trustee deeds, disclaimer deeds, and special warranty deeds.
d. granting deeds, bargain and sale deeds, and general warranty deeds.

40. The following classified ad was printed in the Sunday newspaper by a listing broker: For sale, Sante Fe Style House, approx. 4,000 sf, asking $450,000, located in Tucson, Arizona. Call Rob at 555-123-4567. What is legally missing from this ad?
a. the age of the house
b. Rob's full name
c. identifying that Rob is a broker
d. identifying that Rob is a broker and the firm's name

41. Government has four powers that can affect ownership, which includes
a. enforcement.
b. escheat.
c. sales tax.
d. emblements.

42. A major purchaser of home loans would be the
a. Federal National Mortgage Association.
b. Federal Reserve Bank.
c. Federal Deposit Insurance Corporation.
d. National Association of REALTORS®.

43. The U.S. government authorized a survey system to develop a legal description of real estate known as
a. metes and bounds.
b. perimeter survey.
c. rectangular survey.
d. congressional survey.

44. A U.S. rectangular survey consists of how many acres?
a. 640
b. 520
c. 1,150
d. 2,355

45. There are three types of depreciation, including
a. proximate deterioration.
b. economic deterioration.
c. absolute deterioration.
d. inverted deterioration.

46. As part of the original purchase, a new owner agrees to a required number of monthly payments to the former owner. All the payments have now been made and the former owner is conveying title to the new owner. This transaction is known as a(n)
a. lease with an option to purchase.
b. installment agreement.
c. sales agreement with a delayed settlement.
d. wraparound contract.

47. A person may void a contract, EXCEPT due to which of the following reasons?
   a. The person is intoxicated.
   b. The person is a minor.
   c. The person is illiterate.
   d. The person is not an attorney.

48. When an insurance company or a lender limits certain groups in a certain geographical area, they are
   a. redlining.
   b. steering.
   c. blockbusting.
   d. assessing.

49. HUD administers which law?
   a. common
   b. general
   c. fair housing
   d. homesteads

50. Angelo, a property manager, failed to give a full account and return of the security deposit within the 14-day statutory requirement. He could be liable for how much?
   a. $1,000
   b. $5,000
   c. one and one-half times the original amount
   d. twice the amount or twice the amount wrongfully held if an inaccurate return was made

51. A foreign judgment means that the
   a. judgment probably came from Europe.
   b. judgment came from another state outside of Arizona.
   c. judgment probably was owed in pesos.
   d. person was Canadian, and therefore, it is foreign.

52. What would be something you would find on a credit report when screening a prospective tenant?
   a. his or her previous rental history payment
   b. name of nearest relative
   c. names of the bank account holder he or she deals with
   d. none of the above

53. The role of the designated broker at the closing is to
   a. prepare the deed.
   b. prepare the mortgage.
   c. prepare the closing statement.
   d. The designated broker has no official role at closing.

54. The body of laws that control listings is
   a. facilitator law.
   b. dual agency law.
   c. law of agency.
   d. buyer agency.

55. The three types of agency contracts the public uses when working with an agent for the broker in Arizona are
   a. listing, purchase agreement, and property management.
   b. listing, buyer broker, and property management.
   c. listing, ER, and property management.
   d. all of the above

56. A buyer-broker agreement must be presented to the buyer and signed
a. at the time of closing.
b. by the buyer's lender.
c. at the first personal meeting with a buyer to discuss property.
d. at the time of the offer.

57. In Arizona, a licensee who has an inactive license must do which of the following to activate the license?
a. Retake the licensing test.
b. Complete 12 hours of continuing education.
c. Complete 24 hours of continuing education.
d. Activate with an employing designated broker.

58. In order to be a qualified real estate instructor in Arizona, the person is required to
a. be a college graduate.
b. have a broker's license for five years.
c. be approved and authorized by the Board of REALTORS®.
d. be approved and authorized by the Department of Real Estate.

59. At a meeting, a group of brokers agrees that they will not charge less than a 5% commission on their listings. This would be an example of
a. price fixing.
b. adverse negotiation.
c. a commission split.
d. a bilateral contract.

60. In arriving at the final opinion of value, the appraiser
a. averages the methods.
b. analyzes the approaches and bases the value on the most appropriate approach.
c. will always use the market approach.
d. will use the assessed value of the property.

61. The Federal Fair Housing Act of 1866 prohibits
a. blockbusting.
b. steering.
c. redlining.
d. discrimination based on race.

62. When dealing with zoning laws, the licensee
a. needs to join the Advisory Board.
b. does not need to be familiar with them.
c. needs a thorough knowledge of the bylaws of the local communities.
d. should give gifts to the inspectors and become friendly with them.

63. An insurance claims representative would use what appraisal method to determine the amount of damage to an insured's home?
a. market data
b. cost approach
c. income approach
d. all of the above

64. A seller wishes to net $285,000 from the sale of his property. He agrees to a 5% commission plus $500 for advertising. What would the selling price be?
 a. $300,526
 b. $299,250
 c. $299,775
 d. $315,810

65. Which of the following applies to a security deposit in Arizona?
 a. It cannot exceed one month's rent.
 b. It must be deposited in an interest-bearing escrow account.
 c. It cannot exceed one and one-half times of one month's rent.
 d. It needs to be registered with the ADRE.

66. Kasper has found that his tenant left a bunch of stuff in his rental unit. How long does he have to store if before he can disperse?
 a. 14 days
 b. 21 days
 c. 50 days
 d. He can sell it immediately.

67. It is required that the licensee does what on the contract if the house was built prior to 1978?
 a. give a lead-based paint disclosure
 b. provide a full inspection
 c. nothing
 d. cancels

68. A listing in which an owner instructs a licensee NOT to put a termination date would be
 a. void.
 b. restrictive.
 c. avulsion.
 d. demise.

69. The sales contract refers to close of escrow (COE) as when the
 a. deed is recorded in the appropriate county recorder's office.
 b. loan has funded and dispersed.
 c. closing documents have been signed by all parties.
 d. keys have been delivered to the new buyer.

70. The sales contract states that, "at a minimum, the buyer's loan information section completed, describing the current status of the buyer's proposed loan, is attached hereto." This form is the
 a. HUD.
 b. LSR.
 c. LSU.
 d. preapproval letter.

71. Intentional misrepresentation would be best described as
 a. false statement to induce.
 b. false statement by mistake.
 c. no buyer-broker agreement signed.
 d. implied agency.

72. Tim was upset with the way his contract was going. He now wants to seek legal action so as to enforce the agreement. This is called
 a. general performance.
 b. specific performance.
 c. liquid performance.
 d. enforceable retainer.

73. Which of the following words would be associated with a deed of trust?
 a. sheriff sale, judicial
 b. abandonment, redemption
 c. nonjudicial, reinstatement
 d. certificate of sale

74. To be paid a commission from a real estate transaction, you must
  a. be paid by your broker.
  b. be paid by the buyer directly.
  c. be paid by the title company.
  d. do a really good job.

75. One attraction to financing a home using a VA loan would be
  a. zero down investor.
  b. zero down primary.
  c. low MI.
  d. no income verification.

76. To get your real estate broker's license, you must
  a. have two of the last three years' experience as a real estate salesperson.
  b. have three of the last four years' experience as a real estate salesperson.
  c. have three of the last five years' experience as a real estate salesperson.
  d. have had all your experience in Arizona.

77. If you inherited seven acres of land and sold three-fourths of the land at $2.50 a square foot and one-half of the remaining land for $3.50 a square foot, how much money did you make?
  a. $133,402
  b. $303,920
  c. $705,127.50
  d. $571,725

78. A mortgage that incorporates existing mortgages and is subordinate to them is known as a
  a. take-over mortgage.
  b. secondary mortgage market.
  c. wraparound mortgage.
  d. primary mortgage.

79. The role of a property manager is to
  a. collect your rent.
  b. pay your bills.
  c. furnish your units.
  d. all of the above

80. HUD requires that a real estate office display
  a. all listings.
  b. fingerprints.
  c. the Fair Housing poster.
  d. agent pictures.

81. The appraisal on a VA loan is referred to as
  a. URAR.
  b. CMA.
  c. conditional commitment.
  d. certificate of reasonable value.

82. Which of the following ads are not consistent with Truth-in-Lending advertising guidelines?
  a. negative-am loans available
  b. interest only
  c. just $1 down
  d. 5.233% APR

83. A certificate of sale is from a
  a. mortgage foreclosure sale.
  b. deed of trust sale.
  c. tax lien sale.
  d. HUD auction.

84. Tina had a claim for $40,000 against the recovery fund on one deal. How much may she be able to get?
  a. all $40,000
  b. up to $90,000
  c. $30,000
  d. 1.5 times the claim

85. A listing belongs to
  a. the listing agent.
  b. associate brokers only.
  c. the licensee who signed the ER.
  d. the designated broker.

86. Money that is presented with an offer that must indicate where it exists and how much is referred to as
  a. earnest.
  b. good faith.
  c. deposit.
  d. all of the above

87. A tax parcel number is
  a. not a legal description.
  b. irrelevant to the assessor.
  c. not public knowledge.
  d. based on the age of the home.

88. A benchmark would most likely be used by which profession?
  a. lender
  b. contractor
  c. surveyor
  d. lawyer

89. Footings are made from which material?
  a. wood
  b. metal
  c. gypsum
  d. concrete

90. Kristie is planning to purchase a house for $500,000 with a 20% down payment. The lender will give a loan for the balance at 6% interest-only during the first ten years. What is the monthly interest-only payment without taxes and insurance?
  a. $2,000
  b. $24,000
  c. $1,722
  d. $1,422

91. A property lot's dimensions are 200' frontage, 150' sidelines, and 200' rear lot line. How many square feet is the property?
  a. 700
  b. 30,000
  c. 60,000
  d. 120,000

92. The three parts of the Code of Ethics are relative to
  a. public, client, and fellow professionals.
  b. public, government, and radio stations.
  c. Internet, clients, and realtors.
  d. books, magazines, and tapes.

93. What is the name of the regulation to assist consumers so that they can readily compare the various credit terms available to them?
  a. Regulation Z
  b. Regulation 21E
  c. Regulation 1031
  d. none of the above

94. An asphalt company gives a property owner an estimated cost of $15 per cubic foot to install a driveway that is 40 feet long by 20 feet wide with a height of 3 inches of asphalt over the driveway. What would be the cost to install the driveway?
   a. $1,200
   b. $1,500
   c. $3,000
   d. $18,000

95. In order to practice real estate in Arizona, a salesperson must
   a. be affiliated with a broker.
   b. join the multiple-listing service.
   c. become a REALTOR®.
   d. obtain an appraiser's license.

96. The commissioner of real estate must have at least five years' experience in which of the following fields?
   a. title insurance
   b. banking
   c. real estate
   d. all of the above

97. If a licensee receives a verbal offer, he or she must
   a. present it.
   b. verbally counteroffer.
   c. have it put it in writing.
   d. not necessarily present it.

98. Who is the first to know when a loan is in default under a deed of trust?
   a. trustee
   b. beneficiary
   c. listing agent
   d. sheriff

99. A buyer-broker agreement must have
   a. a property address.
   b. a starting and ending date.
   c. a sales price.
   d. the name of the licensees.

100. Prepossession would be best described as
   a. the seller remains in the property after closing.
   b. the buyer moves in the property before closing.
   c. the house is vacant and the tenant is prorated.
   d. closing in the middle of the month.

101. What federal law prohibits kickbacks from title companies to licensees?
   a. HUD
   b. FNMA
   c. FHA
   d. RESPA

102. Of all the deeds, which one has the greatest protection?
   a. deed of trust
   b. bargain and sale deed
   c. general warranty deed
   d. special warranty deed

103. The correct paperwork that allows one person to legally sign for another is called
   a. tenant in common.
   b. power of attorney.
   c. exclusive right.
   d. easement.

104. When the government takes over a neighbor-hood to build freeways for public use, it is called
  a. constructive eviction.
  b. sheriff sale.
  c. taxation.
  d. eminent domain.

105. Which of the following is NOT a voluntary lien?
  a. mortgage
  b. home equity line of credit
  c. real estate tax
  d. pool loan

106. Chattel is
  a. personal property.
  b. movable property.
  c. neither **a** nor **b**
  d. both **a** and **b**

107. The evidence that a person owns real property is called
  a. title.
  b. trust deed.
  c. note.
  d. zoning.

108. What is the area of a section?
  a. 43,560 square feet
  b. 640 acres
  c. a square mile
  d. none of the above

109. Steve and Matt bought an office complex together as tenants in common. Steve has a will in place, so if he dies, it will be testate. If this happened, then
  a. Matt gets the property on a stepped-up basis.
  b. Steve's heirs will receive Steve's portion.
  c. it will go into probate first.
  d. Matt will have first right of refusal.

110. You must notify the commissioner within ten days with which of the following?
  a. name change
  b. address change
  c. conviction
  d. all of the above

111. Benji wants to put a sign on the corner near his listing to help his listing get more exposure. He must
  a. tell his broker.
  b. have the owner of all properties he wants to put a sign on sign a paper giving permission.
  c. give public notice by placing an ad in the paper and putting a note on the owner's door.
  d. do nothing—he can put a sign anywhere.

112. How long is the redemption period on a mort-gage foreclosure?
  a. six months
  b. 120 days
  c. 270 days
  d. There is no redemption period on a mort-gage foreclosure.

113. Who issues the public report?
  a. builder
  b. subdivider
  c. commissioner of real estate
  d. all of the above

114. Each new licensee shall complete a six-hour contract writing class, which includes
  a. three hours of real estate legal issues and three hours of contract law.
  b. three hours of commissioner rules and three hours of contract law.
  c. three hours of real estate math and three hours of contract law.
  d. six hours of contract writing.

115. Arizona has approximately how many square miles, and what is our rank in size for states in the United States of America?
  a. 114,000 square miles and sixth in size
  b. 211,000 square miles and fourth in size
  c. 98,000 square miles and eighth in size
  d. 112,000 square miles and third in size

116. The entity responsible for collecting taxes in each county is the
  a. county assessor.
  b. county treasurer.
  c. clerk of the county.
  d. Maricopa County.

117. In Arizona, the two classifications of water are
  a. ground and surface.
  b. well and surface.
  c. river and lake.
  d. riparian and grandfathered.

118. The word *corporeal* could be simply defined as
  a. tangible.
  b. intangible.
  c. inheritable.
  d. movable.

119. A lease would be an estate that
  a. expires on a certain date.
  b. has the landlord's consent.
  c. has novation.
  d. is intestate.

120. Leading prospective homebuyers to or away from certain areas would be
  a. redlining.
  b. steering.
  c. legal.
  d. in violation of RESPA.

121. A deposit is given with an offer because
  a. it is the only means to possibly bind an offer.
  b. the seller cannot accept offers without consideration.
  c. it indicates to a seller that the buyer is serious.
  d. it takes the property off the market.

122. At the closing, if the broker held the escrow funds, then he or she should
  a. write a check from the general funds and bring it to the closing.
  b. keep any amount that is due to the broker's commission invoice and bring the difference.
  c. have a check written from a separate escrow account.
  d. place a lien on the property until his or her fee is paid.

123. A residential buyer, after the acceptance of an offer, can have a property professionally inspected for the presence of lead paint within
  a. five days of the offer acceptance.
  b. ten days of the offer acceptance.
  c. 15 days of the offer acceptance.
  d. 30 days of the offer acceptance.

124. A listing agent is another name for a licensee
  a. representing a buyer interested in houses.
  b. representing a seller with property to sell.
  c. representing a seller who may someday own property to sell.
  d. who works for a broker.

125. A real estate listing is a(n)
  a. list of properties.
  b. employment contract or agreement with a real estate broker and seller.
  c. employment contract with a principal broker and a new salesperson.
  d. license issued by the Arizona Registration Board of Real Estate.

126. Arizona property taxes would be in second position to a(n)
  a. mortgage.
  b. IRS tax lien.
  c. deed of trust.
  d. none of the above

127. One of the main purposes of the closing statement is to
  a. make the agreement.
  b. disclose all costs involved to the buyer and seller.
  c. let the licensees know how much their commission is.
  d. see the amount of the annual property taxes.

128. Unless renewed, a judgment, as it stands, is valid for how long?
  a. 180 days
  b. three years
  c. five years
  d. seven years

129. Appraiser Ryan appraised a property at $350,000, which reflected a 30% drop in value. What was the original purchase price of this property?
  a. $269,231
  b. $245,000
  c. $455,000
  d. $500,000

130. Each renewal class is equivalent to how many hours?
  a. six
  b. 12
  c. 24
  d. none of the above

131. If a landlord failed to provide water and the tenants moved out for their own protection, this would be considered
  a. actual eviction.
  b. constructive eviction.
  c. eminent domain.
  d. subleasing.

132. The City of Scottsdale leased a three-acre parcel of real estate to Jennifer Jones for 99 years. This is what type of lease?
  a. net lease
  b. escalation lease
  c. ground lease
  d. sale and leaseback

133. You are appraising a mobile home park, which is on a major highway that has been developing into a commercial area. Which concept would you have to apply?
a. highest and best use
b. insurable value
c. salvage value
d. replacement cost

134. If a large manufacturing plant was allowed to construct a new plant near a new subdivision, the depreciation for the subdivision would be considered
a. substitution.
b. physical.
c. functional.
d. economic.

135. Most states exempt properties owned by which of the following from real estate taxes?
a. veterans
b. elderly
c. farmers
d. nonprofit churches

136. In Arizona, when there is a change of home address for a licensee, who must notify the commissioner?
a. the licensee
b. the broker principal
c. both a and b
d. neither a nor b

137. A nonresident of Arizona must do which of the following to obtain an Arizona real estate license?
a. He or she must move into the state.
b. He or she must conform to the same examination requirements as an Arizona resident.
c. He or she must be employed by an out-of-state broker.
d. He or she must be employed by an Arizona broker.

138. What type of mortgage is most beneficial to a buyer?
a. zero down
b. adjustable mortgage
c. interest-only mortgage
d. Every mortgage should be the client's decision.

139. For how long must Subdivider Sam keep the receipt for giving the public report?
a. five years
b. 180 days
c. one year from the date of move-in
d. three years

140. When selling personal property, it is customary to use a
a. settlement statement.
b. bill of sale.
c. closing statement.
d. title company.

► Answers

1. **b.** Impound or escrow accounts are for taxes and insurance and are typically held by the lender or servicer and paid for on the borrower's behalf.

2. **d.** A verbal lease in Arizona is valid for terms fewer than 12 months.

3. **d.** In the exculpatory clause, the lender waives the right to a deficiency judgment and relieves the borrower of personal liability.

4. **a.** An owner's title insurance policy protects the new owner, is written for the sales price, and is not transferable.

5. **a.** A co-op apartment is personal property, not real estate, and no deed is involved. The owners become shareholders in the overall organization and have a proprietary lease to their apartments.

6. **b.** A person must complete 90 hours of class time before being eligible to take the real estate exam.

7. **a.** Property taxes are levied annually and paid semiannually.

8. **c.** The Arizona homestead exemption is up to $150,000 protection of equity against involuntary liens.

9. **c.** Fiduciary responsibility includes confidentiality, obedience, loyalty, and accountability.

10. **b.** Any modifications to the contract must be signed by the buyer and seller.

11. **d.** At a tax lien sale, you win a certificate of purchase.

12. **c.** On residential real estate, a general contractor is allowed to file a mechanic's lien with a 20-day notice.

13. **c.** The homestead exemption is up to $150,000 equity protection against involuntary creditors, such as judgments and nonconsensual liens.

14. **b.** Encroachment is when the property of one party intrudes onto another's property.

15. **c.** The remainder person would own it, not the buyer.

16. **a.** This person can do a 1031 tax-deferred exchange by buying a like-kind property.

17. **a.** Licensees must take 24 hours of continuing education every two years to keep their license active.

18. **b.** The buyer would owe Broker Borden the commission because the buyer had signed an exclusive buyer agency contract.

19. **d.** The title company is responsible for preparing the HUD Uniform Settlement Form.

20. **b.** A range of land uses will contribute to value as long as they are in balance.

21. **a.** The buyer of a condo with more than 100 units receives the CC&Rs from the HOA.

22. **b.** An exclusive agency listing is one in which the owner retains the right to sell the property on his or her own without owing a commission.

23. **b.** A purchase and sales agreement would be an example of an executory contract.

24. **a.** The seller would be fully entitled to the deposit because the tenant and seller had a binding agreement.

25. **a.** Any form of kickback or referral fee that is not disclosed properly is a violation of RESPA.

26. **b.** You must notify the commissioner within ten days of an address change, conviction, or name change.

27. **c.** Amortization means making constant payments to pay off the principal and interest.

28. **c.** In a land sales contract, the deed is not executed until the final loan payment is made.

29. **b.** Title insurance is purchased by the borrower.

30. **d.** In a seller carry-back, the seller is also the lender, so he or she would be the mortgagee.

31. d. There is not a redemption period on a deed of trust, only on a mortgage foreclosure. On a deed of trust, it is a 90-day reinstatement period.

32. c. Rent collected in advance: $1,200 × 2 = $2,400; $2,400 ÷ 30 days = $80 per day. If the closing is on the twelfth, the seller is entitled to 12 days worth of rent and the buyer is entitled to 18 days. The adjustment of 18 days × $80 = $1,440 due to the buyer.

33. a. The foreclosure period on a mortgage over a deed of trust is much longer. It involves a judicial process.

34. b. Any changes made to any offer of any kind represent a new offer or a counteroffer, no matter how minor the changes may be.

35. a. Real property is that which is permanently attached, such as land, structures, and appurtenances.

36. b. Commercial property is taxed at a 25% rate in Arizona.

37. d. Arizona adheres to the federal Truth-in-Lending Law, also known as Regulation Z.

38. b. All nine members of the Real Estate Advisory Board will have a six-year term with the Department of Real Estate as appointed by the governor.

39. a. Bargain and sale deeds, special warranty deeds, and general warranty deeds are the three types of conveying deeds used, the difference being the warranty.

40. d. All advertisements of properties available must disclose that the ad is from a broker with the name of the broker, the brokerage firm name, and telephone number.

41. b. Escheat is titular power of the government that when a person dies and leaves no will or ascertainable heirs, the government can claim ownership to that person's real estate.

42. a. The Federal National Mortgage Association is also known as Fannie Mae. Other purchasers include Freddie Mac and Ginnie Mae.

43. c. The U.S. government developed the U.S. rectangular survey, also known as U.S. Public Lands Survey System, for properties west of the Ohio River during the 1800s.

44. a. Each survey divides land into townships. Each township is six square miles, or 640 acres.

45. b. The three types of deterioration include physical, functional, and economic deterioration.

46. b. When the new owner has paid all of the contracted periodic installments, the former owner conveys title.

47. d. The first three items are grounds for a voided contract, but anyone can enter into a contract. A person does not need to be an attorney to enter into a contract. Every day, people enter some type of legal contract arrangements to conduct business.

48. a. Redlining is the practice of denying or raising the cost of service to certain groups going into certain areas.

49. c. HUD administers all issues related to fair housing.

50. d. A landlord would have to pay twice the amount of the deposit or twice the amount wrongfully held if an inaccurate return was made.

51. b. A foreign judgment is any judgment that was awarded in another state and can be recorded in Arizona.

52. d. A credit report will not disclose previous rental history unless reported by the prior landlords. It will not state nearest relative or banking institutions unless a credit line has been granted.

53. d. The broker does not prepare any of the closing documents.

54. c. The law of agency is the body that controls and regulates real estate agency and, therefore, listings.

55. b. Listing, buyer broker, and property management are the three types of agency contracts used in Arizona.

56. c. The buyer-broker agreement must be given at the first meeting to discuss property.

57. d. To activate a license, the licensee would have to be hired with an employing designated broker.

58. d. To be a real estate instructor in Arizona, the person must be approved and authorized by the Department of Real Estate.

59. a. This is an example of price fixing, which is illegal.

60. b. The appraiser does not average. He or she will analyze and place the weight on the most appropriate approach.

61. d. The Federal Fair Housing Act of 1866 prohibits discrimination based on race only.

62. c. The licensee must have a thorough knowledge of the local bylaws in order to assist all parties with confidence.

63. b. The cost approach is used because damage would be determined by the replacement cost.

64. a. $285,000 plus the advertising fee of $500 equals $285,500, which equals 100%. Subtract the 5% commission and you have 95%. Divide $285,500 by 95% and the resulting figure is $300,526.

65. c. In Arizona, the security deposit cannot exceed one and one-half of one month's rent and must be held separately.

66. b. The landlord must store the possessions for 21 days.

67. a. It is required that the licensee give a lead-based paint disclosure.

68. a. For a listing to be valid, it must have a beginning date and ending date.

69. a. The sales contract refers to close of escrow (COE) as when the deed is recorded in the appropriate county recorder's office.

70. b. The LSR is the loan status report. The LSU is the loan status update. The latter form is designed to update the agents and parties while in process.

71. a. Intentional misrepresentation is a false statement to induce another for your benefit.

72. b. Specific performance is when a person seeks legal action to enforce an agreement or contract.

73. c. Of the words described, the deed of trust is a nonjudicial process, unlike a mortgage foreclosure that is judicial. The reinstatement period is for 90 days after the trustee begins the power of sale.

74. a. In all transactions, you can only receive compensation from your commission by your designated broker.

75. b. An advantage of a VA loan would be the zero down feature for primary residences only.

76. c. To obtain your broker's license, you must have three of the last five years' experience as a real estate salesperson from Arizona or any other state.

77. c. 7 acres × 43,760 sq. ft. = 304,920 sq. ft. total; three-fourths of 304,920 is 228,690 sq. ft. (75%). 228,690 at $2.50 a foot = $571,725. Half of the remaining would be 304,920 − 228,690 = 76,230 divided by 2 = 38,115 × $3.50 a sq. ft. is $133,402.50 + $571,725 = $705,127.50 proceeds.

78. c. A wraparound mortgage incorporates existing mortgages and becomes subordinate to them.

79. d. A property manager can do all of these things. Owners should not rely on a property manager to pay their bills or furnish their units.

80. c. HUD requires that all offices display the Fair Housing poster.

81. d. The VA refers to the appraisal as the certificate of reasonable value.

82. c. Just $1 down would require additional disclosure describing the remaining factors of the loan, such as loan amount, APR, terms, conditions, and fees.

83. a. You can obtain a certificate of sale from a mortgage foreclosure sale, which is a nonjudicial auction sale of real property.

84. c. The recovery fund will award up to $30,000 per incident on a single transaction and up to $90,000 from one salesperson from three or more transactions.

85. d. All listings belong to the designated broker at all times and may not be taken with that person if terminated.

86. d. Money that is presented with an offer that must indicate where it exists and how much is referred to as earnest, good faith, and initial deposit.

87. a. A tax parcel number is not a legal description. It is not based on age, rather on location. It is public record and used by the county assessor's office.

88. c. Surveyors use benchmarks to facilitate survey requests.

89. d. Footings are made from concrete.

90. a. First calculate the loan balance by multiplying $500,000 \times .20 = $400,000$. The loan is $400,000 \times 0.06 = $24,000$ per annum divide by 12 months = $2,000.

91. b. Square feet is measured by length $\times$ width. The lot is a rectangle of 150×200. Therefore, $150 \times 200 = 30,000$ square feet.

92. a. The three parts of the Code of Ethics are relations to the public, client, and fellow professionals.

93. a. Regulation Z of the Truth-in-Lending Law requires a meaningful disclosure must be given to the borrower regarding the cost of obtaining credit.

94. c. $40' \times 80' \times .25 \left(\frac{3}{12}\right)'' = 200$ cubic feet $\times$ $15 per cubic foot = $3,000.

95. a. To practice real estate, a salesperson must be affiliated with a broker.

96. d. The commissioner of real estate must have at least five years' experience in any of the following fields: real estate, banking, or title insurance.

97. d. A verbal offer is an offer that is not in writing, and it is not required for an agent to present to the seller.

98. b. The beneficiary would be the first to know, then the trustee would start the power of sale to begin the reinstatement period for 90 days.

99. b. For a buyer-broker agreement to be valid, it must have a starting date and ending date.

100. b. Prepossession is when the buyer moves into the property before it actually closes. This is taking possession prior to owning.

101. d. The Real Estate Settlement and Procedures Act (RESPA) prohibits any type of kickback to real estate agents for any type of referral.

102. c. General warranty deed has the most strength, protection, and warranties.

103. b. A power of attorney is a legal binding document that allows one person to sign for another.

104. d. Eminent domain is when the government takes over anything for the benefit of the public.

105. c. Real estate tax would not be a voluntary lien because if it turned into a lien, it would be recorded involuntary.

106. d. Chattel is personal and movable property. Real property cannot be moved and comes with rights, interests, and benefits.

107. a. When a person owns real property, it will be evidenced by holding title that is recorded in the county where the property is located.

108. c. A section is a square mile; it is a mile long on each side.

109. b. Unless otherwise noted in the will, Steve's heirs will receive Steve's portion of the property.

110. d. You must notify the real estate commissioner of any name change, address change, or conviction within ten days.

111. b. All signs must have written permission from the owners.

112. a. On a mortgage foreclosure, the redemption period is for six months.

113. c. The commissioner of real estate will issue the public report after the subdivider files a Notice of Intention.

114. a. It is required that each new licensee complete a six-hour contract writing class that includes three hours of real estate legal issues and three hours of contract law.

115. a. Arizona has approximately 114,000 square miles and is sixth in size in the United States.

116. b. The county treasurer is the entity responsible for collecting taxes in each county.

117. a. The two classifications or designations for water in Arizona are ground and surface.

118. a. Corporeal would be best described as tangible. In real estate, it would be the attached building, surface, subsurface, and rights that go with these items.

119. a. A lease has a specific ending date.

120. b. You cannot steer a person into or away from specific neighborhoods.

121. a. The deposit is also known as earnest money to bind an offer to purchase if both parties execute the offer.

122. c. All escrow funds must be held in a separate escrow accounting checkbook. Commingling of funds is not allowed, except for monies to pay local bank fees or to maintain a minimum balance for the escrow account.

123. b. The buyer has ten days from the acceptance of an offer to inspect for lead paint at the buyer's expense and to have a professional inspection for the presence of lead paint.

124. b. A listing agent is a licensee representing actual property for sale and the seller is the actual client.

125. b. It is an agreement or contract detailing the description of the property, terms and conditions of commission payment, and length of the marketing. It is a marketing agreement between a real estate agent and seller.

126. d. Arizona property taxes are always in first position to any encumbrance or lien.

127. b. The main purpose of the closing or settlement statement is to disclose all costs involved to the buyer and seller.

128. c. A judgment is valid for five years and must be renewed in the last 90 days before the end of the five years.

129. d. $100\% - 30\% = 70\%$; $\$350,000 \div .70 = \$500,000$

130. d. A renewal class is credit for three hours toward the 24 hours required by the commissioner every two years.

131. b. If a landlord fails to provide services and the premises became uninhabitable, constructive eviction occurs when the tenant vacates.

132. c. A ground lease is a lease that is for more than 50 years.

133. a. Utilization of this concept would likely produce the highest net return over a period of years.

134. d. Economic obsolescence relates to loss of value from causes outside the property.

135. d. Nonprofit organizations do not have to pay real estate taxes.

136. c. Both the licensee and the broker principal must notify the commissioner of a change of home address.

137. b. Nonresidents do not have to move into the state, nor be employed by an Arizona broker, but they must meet the same examination requirements.

138. d. Buyers purchasing property should pick the type of mortgage that makes them most comfortable.

139. a. Anyone who is required to have a receipt for the public report to be signed must keep the receipt for giving a public report for five years.

140. b. A bill of sale would be the proper contract and receipt for a personal property transaction.

▶ Scoring

Once again, in order to evaluate how you did on this last exam, find the number of questions you answered correctly. The passing score for this practice exam is 105 correct answers (75%), but just as on the real test, you should be aiming for something higher than that on these practice exams. If you haven't reached a passing score on both sections, look at the suggestions for improvement at the end of Chapter 8. Take a look at the table on the following page to see what problem areas remain.

The key to success in almost any pursuit is complete preparation. By taking the practice exams in this book, you have prepared more than many other people who may be taking the exam with you. You have diagnosed where your strengths and weaknesses lie and learned how to deal with the various kinds of questions that will appear on the test. So, go into the exam with confidence, knowing that you are ready and equipped to do your best.

EXAM 4 FOR REVIEW

Exam 4 Subject Area	Question Numbers (Questions 1–140)
Business Practice and Ethics	10, 25, 40, 48, 49, 59, 61, 71, 72, 80, 82, 92, 101, 120, 138
Agency and Listing	9, 18, 20, 22, 54, 62, 97, 124, 125, 133
Property Characteristics, Descriptions, and Ownership Interests and Restrictions	5, 14, 41, 43, 44, 87, 88, 89, 98, 104, 106, 108, 135
Property Valuation and the Appraisal Process	45, 60, 63, 81, 134
Real Estate Sales Contracts	23, 46, 47, 69, 70, 100, 103, 121, 140
Financing Sources	1, 3, 27, 30, 37, 42, 75, 78, 93
Closing/Settlement and Transferring Title	4, 15, 19, 29, 102, 105 109 127
Property Management	52, 79, 119, 131
Real Estate Math	64, 77, 90, 91, 94, 129
Arizona Ownership Transfer	8, 11, 12, 13, 31, 38, 51, 73, 84, 86, 107, 113, 115, 116, 117, 126, 128, 132, 139
Arizona Licensing	26, 57, 58, 76, 96, 130
Arizona Activities of Licensees	6, 17, 34, 36, 50, 53, 55, 56, 67, 68, 74, 85, 95, 99, 110, 111, 114, 122, 123, 136, 137
Arizona Finance Settlement	7, 16, 21, 28, 32, 33, 35, 39, 83, 112, 118
Arizona Leasing and Property Management	2, 24, 65, 66

How to Use ▶
the CD-ROM

SO YOU THINK you are ready for your exam? Here's a great way to build confidence and *know* you are ready: Use LearningExpress's Real Estate Licensing Tester AutoExam CD-ROM software developed by PEARSoft Corporation of Wellesley, Massachusetts. The CD, included inside the back cover of this book, can be used with any PC running Windows 95/98/ME/NT/2000/XP. (Sorry, it doesn't work with Macintosh.) The following description represents a typical "walk through" of the software.

To install the program:

1. Insert the CD-ROM into your CD-ROM drive. The CD should run automatically. If it does not, proceed to Step 2.
2. From Windows, select **Start**, then choose **Run**.
3. Type D:\Setup.
4. Click **OK**.

The screens that follow will walk you through the installation procedure.

From the Main Menu, select **Take Exams**. (After you have taken at least one exam, use **Review Exam Results** to see your scores.)

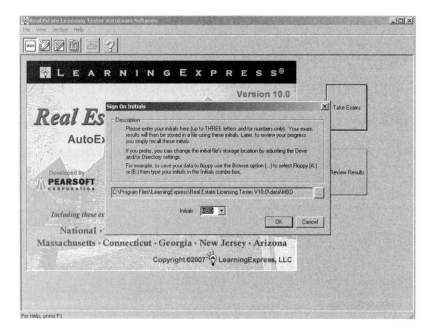

Now enter your initials. This allows you to record your progress and review your performance for as many simulated exams as you would like. Notice that you can also change the drive and/or folder where your exam results are stored. If you want to save to a floppy drive, for instance, click on the **Browse** button and then choose the letter of your floppy drive.

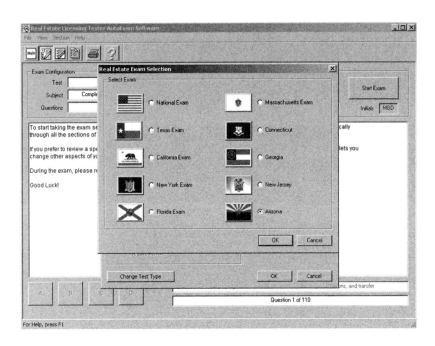

Now, because this CD-ROM supports ten different real estate exams, you need to select your exam of interest. Let's try Arizona, as shown above.

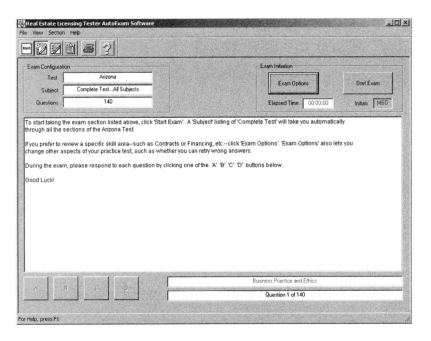

Now you are in the **Take Exams** section, as shown above. You can choose **Start Exam** to start taking your test, or **Exam Options**. The next screenshot shows you what your **Exam Options** are.

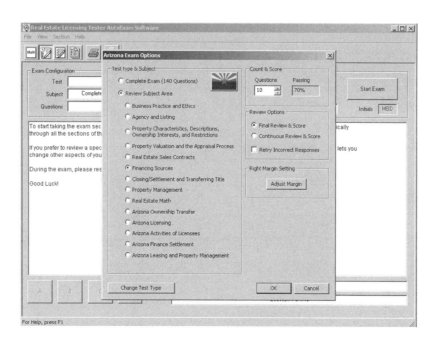

Choosing **Exam Options** gives you plenty of options to help you fine-tune rough spots. How about a little math to warm up? Click **Review Subject Area**, and then the **Real Estate Math** option. Choose the number of questions you want to review right now. On the right, you can choose whether to wait until you have finished to see how you did (**Final Review & Score**), or have the computer tell you after each question whether your answer is right (**Continuous Review & Score**). Choose **Retry Incorrect Responses** to get a second chance at questions you answered incorrectly. (This option works best with **Review Subject Area** rather than **Complete Exam**.) If you have chosen the wrong exam, you can click **Change Test Type** to go back and choose your exam. When you finish choosing your options, click **OK**. Then click the **Start Exam** button on the main exam screen. Your screen will look like the one shown next.

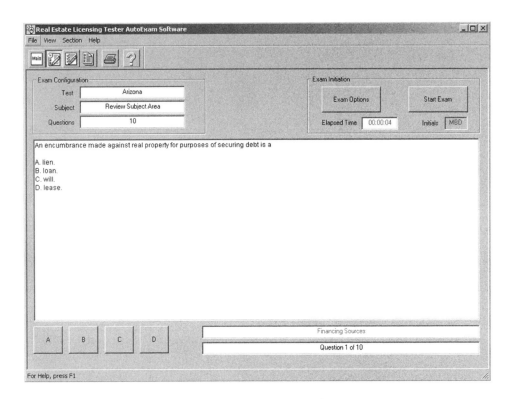

Questions come up one at a time, just as they will on the real exam. Click on A, B, C, or D to answer.

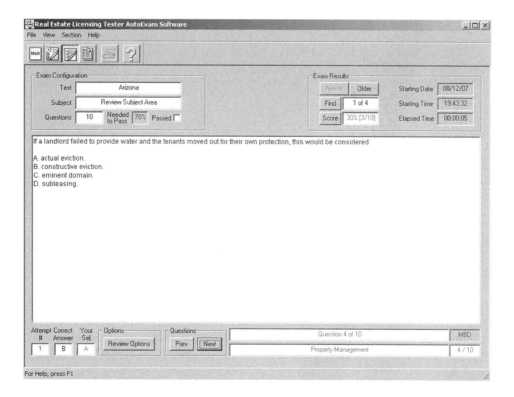

When you have finished your exam or subject area, you will have the option of switching to **Review Results.** (If you don't want to review your results now, you can always do it later by clicking on the **Review Exams Section** button on the toolbar.) When you use **Review Results**, you will see your score and whether or not you passed. The questions come up one at a time. Under **Review Options**, you can choose whether to look at all the questions or just the ones you missed. You can also choose whether you want an explanation of the correct answer displayed automatically under the question.

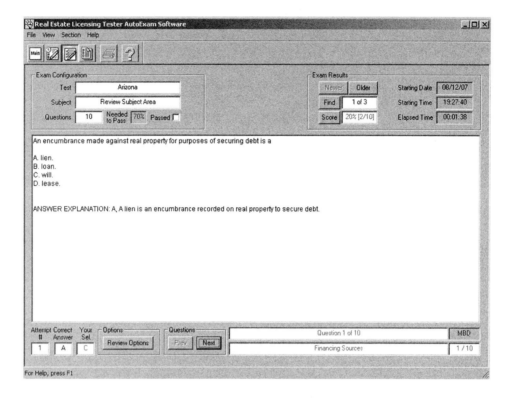

When you are in the **Review Results** section, click on the **Find** button to look at all the exams you have taken.

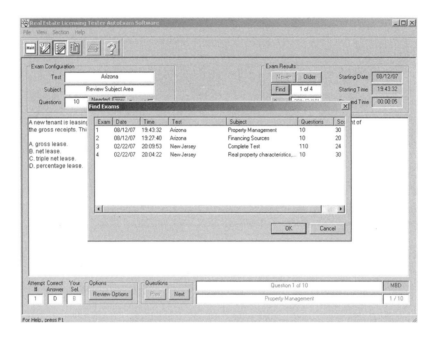

By default, your exam results are listed from newest to oldest, but you can sort them by any of the headings. For instance, if you want to see your results arranged by score, you can click on the **Score %** heading. To go to a particular exam you have taken, double-click on it.

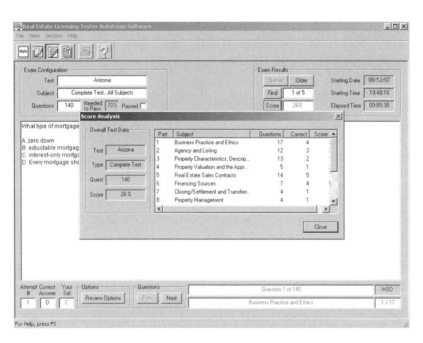

In the **Review Results** section, if you click on the **Score %** button, you will get a breakdown of your score on the exam you're currently reviewing. This section shows you how you did on each of the subject areas on the exam. Once again, you can sort the subject areas by any of the column headings. For instance, if you click on the

Score % heading, the program will order the subject areas from your highest percentage score to your lowest. You can see which areas are your strong and weak points, so you will know what to review.

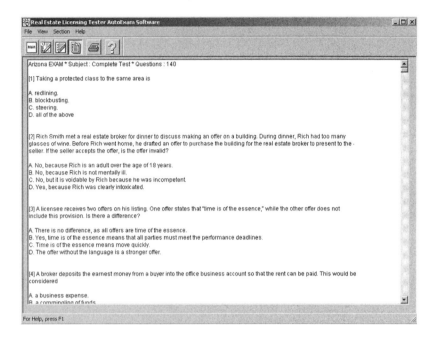

What's that? No time to work at the computer? Click the **Print Exams** menu bar button and you will have a full-screen review of an exam that you can print out, as shown above. Then, take it with you.

For technical support, call 800-295-9556.

Notes

Notes

Notes

Notes

Notes

Notes

Notes

Notes

Notes